MW01635669

THE
HERITAGE
DETECTIVE
HELEN EDWARDS

LEKWUNGEN TERRITORIES

The author acknowledges that the land on which these stories occurred is the traditional territory of the Coast Salish peoples, and specifically recognizes the Lekwungen-speaking people, known today as the Songhees and Esquimalt Nations, and that their historic connections to these lands continue to this day.

The hidden stories
of ordinary Victorians
who did extraordinary things

VOLUME ONE

Edwards Heritage Consulting
VICTORIA, BRITISH COLUMBIA, CANADA
2023

BOOKS BY HELEN EDWARDS

The Winter House: Ross Bay Villa, co-authored with Jennifer Nell Barr and Mary Doody Jones, 1998 (re-published as *Ross Bay Villa: A Colonial Cottage* in 1999).

The History of Professional Hockey in Victoria, B.C., 1911–2011, 2019.

Dutchy's Diaries, Life as a Canadian Naval Officer, In His Own Words: 1916–1929, 2020.

Dutchy's Decades: Life as a Canadian Naval Officer, 1930–1950, 2022.

This book is dedicated to Mary Elizabeth Bayer,
heritage preservationist extraordinaire, who took a young woman
under her wing and inspired me to volunteer in this field for decades.
She may be gone now, but her influence will last forever.

—H.E.

ISBN 978–1–7388726–0–2 (paperback)
ISBN 978–1–7388726–1–9 (electronic book)

FIRST PUBLISHED IN 2023 BY
Edwards Heritage Consulting
Victoria, British Columbia, Canada

For further information or more copies of *The Heritage Detective*
please write to heritagelady@gmail.com

Book design by Arifin Graham, Alaris Design
All photos from Helen Edwards' collection unless otherwise noted

PRINTED AND BOUND IN CANADA BY VICTORIA BINDERY

Contents

Foreword

The stories that we tell, the stories of others that we share, are so important. Increasingly important at a time when emailed letters, for example, will ultimately disappear into the ether, rather than being discovered, at some time in the perhaps distant future, in a trunk in the attic.

Helen Edwards is a storyteller whose passionate, and relentless research, results in the telling of stories that might otherwise be lost. She is telling those stories at a particularly important point in time, a time when there is a seemingly endless supply of information on the internet but, also a time, when we will look back and realize that many personal stories, that perhaps did not warrant internet postings, will have disappeared.

Helen recognizes the importance of the stories of ordinary people and has dedicated herself to telling their stories. The 'attic treasures' that she has discovered will enrich the understanding of our community for generations to come.

Pam Madoff
FORMER CITY COUNCILLOR
VICTORIA, BRITISH COLUMBIA

Introduction

As I said in my first "Heritage Detective" article published in September 2005: "I have always been curious. My questions and experimentation often got me into trouble when I was young, but I have learned to channel my inquisitive nature into a rewarding and sometimes-profitable vocation." Last year, when I began to put this book together, I was checking out a site where a building had been moved. I turned around and to my astonishment, discovered 1420 Fort Street – seen on the cover of this book! It has served as the inspiration for the other buildings I added to the book.

I had written short articles for years but being published spurred me to undertake research and to write countless articles about old houses, historic sites, and the people who are connected with them. Unfortunately, two neighbourhood magazines no longer exist – and even when they were published, the stories only reached a limited audience. Other articles were in local newsletters and also had few readers. However, given the diversity of buildings and sites in the Capital Regional District, there were stories to be researched everywhere, and it was up to me to document them. I have also included articles I researched and wrote but never published for various reasons. As I was taking photographs of what the buildings looked like now, I discovered some little buildings that had to be researched and their stories – and how they survived – are often fascinating tales in their own right. Their stories deserve to be told.

Many articles were written to strict word guidelines, and often there was no room for photographs, the very thing that gives interest in a story. Ironically, the articles with the most words often had the fewest images available. This issue will be rectified by including as many photos as possible in this book, as I firmly believe that "a picture is worth a thousand words." In addition, during my research, I discovered connections between different buildings and sites, so some articles contain some of the same information. In most cases, I have left the original material as written so that each piece can stand on its own. There was so much material that I have divided it into two volumes.

As I wrote many of these columns in the late years of the twentieth century or the early years of the twenty-first, I have conducted additional research to bring the stories up to date. I have added paragraphs to the end of the original material, including a current photograph wherever possible.

The stories are arranged roughly by address, with part one featuring the first published column. In addition, I have included two articles that dealt with general heritage topics to set the stage for my exploration of my region.

At the end of most of my columns, I asked readers to search their family collections for something they would like to have researched. I knew from my own experience that hundreds of exciting photos could be found in private collections, and I wanted to bring some of them to the light of day. Feedback was good, and I did use some of the ideas submitted.

What struck me was the connection between different buildings, different owners, and businesses. In addition, the same names often appear in more than one place, linking the diverse stories together.

I hope you enjoy reading about interesting buildings and sites, some of which have been demolished since I told their stories. For extant places, feel free to view them from the street where you can, but please respect the owners' privacy and do not walk on their property.

Helen Edwards, January 2023
VICTORIA, BRITISH COLUMBIA

About the author

Helen Edwards has turned a lifelong fascination with local history into a 50-year career of writing about and advocacy of heritage conservation. She got the bug early, when her father made sure to include visits to museums and historical sites in family vacations. Years later, in 1976, when she and her husband John happened across a local heritage organization booth while shopping in a mall, it only seemed natural to join the Hallmark Society (now the Hallmark Heritage Society) the very same day, and so they did.

A heritage professional for ten years, Helen was instrumental in founding the BC Association of Heritage Professionals (BCAHP), and, as a volunteer with the Hallmark Society, set up the filing system for its archival files. She has served on heritage boards at the local, provincial, and national levels, and is currently a member of Victoria's Heritage Advisory Panel. At the neighbourhood level, she was the heritage consultant for the Rockland Neighbourhood Association for several years, researching and developing four walking tours for that neighbourhood. Today, having lived among heritage buildings in Victoria all her life, Helen lives in a heritage house only a block away from where she grew up.

Researching and writing about heritage subjects came naturally as well to a Victoria native with a passionate curiosity about local history. For the last 40 years, Helen has written about heritage buildings and the people who lived and worked in them in numerous magazines, newsletters, and online posts. Her articles on heritage topics have appeared in academic journals and mainstream magazines, including Heritage Canada's magazine. She wrote a bi-monthly column for the *Moss Rock Review*, Fairfield's community magazine, until it ceased publication. This is Helen's fifth book on local history.

When not writing history, Helen is a huge sports fan. She joined the ownership group of the Victoria HarbourCats, Nanaimo NightOwls, and Victoria Golden Tide and loves to promote the teams. She will combine these two passions when she writes a book about the early years of the HarbourCats, including interviews with former players and coaches.

For more information about Helen and her work, visit https://helenedwards.ca/

Author Notes

As most of the vital events I found were housed at the BC Archives, I have not created endnotes for them. Thus, only births, marriages, and deaths from outside British Columbia will be documented. All other sources, including published material and websites, will be referenced.

Much of the information about residency at a specific address was gleaned from digitized city directories available through the Vancouver Public Library. As with vital events, these will only appear in endnotes if they are sourced elsewhere.

Researching during a pandemic with closed repositories is different from what I was used to so, I could not access land records and other items that I would usually work with. However, it is the people and their stories that are important and most personal information is accessible online.

The index in this book will contain only the names of people mentioned in the manuscript, while addresses will be listed in the table of contents.

Acknowledgments

I could not have written this book without the support of many people. Special thanks to Ken Sudhues, my editor and heritage fact-checker, and to Jennifer Nell Barr, who helped with historical details. It is so much fun to work with old friends.

Sincere thanks to the unseen persons who have digitized old newspapers. You have made my research task far less demanding than even a few years ago. Special thanks to Dave Obee of the *Times Colonist*, who added the *Victoria Daily Times* to the previously scanned *British Colonist*. You have saved me hours of research time.

I extend thanks to Chandler Bolt and the staff at selfpublishing.com who pushed me to succeed, particularly my writing coach, Scott Allan, and my colleagues, who encouraged me to write the best book I could. I must also acknowledge the support of David Petrovay, who I met at an online marketing course years ago and continue to meet with every second week for mutual support. Zoom is good for networking like this.

This book owes some of its existence to baseball. I wrote many words while on HarbourCats road trips and also on trips to Seattle to watch the Mariners play. There is nothing like a hotel room with no interruptions for getting things done. Ferry rides can be very productive as well. Thanks to my summer billets, who inspired me to get the book finished.

Special thanks to David Greer for his timely editing.

Designer extraordinaire Arifin Graham of Alaris Design takes my words and images and transforms them into a work of art. I couldn't publish without his skill and support.

To my family, who is getting used to the idea that I am, indeed, a full-time author, thanks for your support. It's nice to know you have my back.

In the Beginning …

In which the Heritage Detective moniker is born, and the writing of columns begins in earnest.

Katie McCluskey

This article was published in the September 2005 issue of *Platinum*, a magazine that focussed on the Fairfield neighbourhood.

I have always been curious. My questions and experimentation often got me into trouble when I was young, but I have learned to channel my inquisitive nature into a rewarding (and sometimes-profitable) vocation.

I enjoy wandering around Victoria, with a digital camera in hand, recording sights and events that seem interesting. With our built landscape changing, my photograph is often the only record of what was once on a site. I also spend hours looking at old photographs, wondering who the people are and why that particular shot was taken. On occasion, I am asked to help clients discover the stories behind old family photographs.

Katie McCluskey standing on Johnson Street

My career as an official "heritage detective" began when a client from Los Angeles contacted me to see if I could track down some information about her grandmother Katie McCluskey. She brought an old album of photographs obviously taken in Victoria in the early years of the twentieth century, but she didn't know anything about the buildings shown. From what she had heard from family lore, Katie had been orphaned in a Midwest American state in her teens and had made her way to Victoria – a long trip for anyone, particularly for a young woman alone. However, she quickly found work to support herself as she was a resourceful soul and a hard worker.

Family history records indicated that Katie had returned to her former home to bring her three brothers to Victoria. My client thought her grandmother had been the manager of a hotel around 1912 but had no idea of its name. Among the photographs in the old album was one of a young woman in front of a hotel and another with her standing in the street facing the hotel with the businesses across the road visible. The common element was the hotel canopy just visible in the street scene. Other photographs could give me clues, but these were the most promising. My assignment was to determine what hotel she had managed and if it was still standing.

Armed with a magnifying glass, I scrutinized the photographs. Then, taking the clue from the businesses across the street, I searched old Victoria City Directories to find the addresses of the merchants in question. One name – Watson and McGregor – was quite evident, while its neighbour to the east (which turned out to be Wriglesworth Fish and Game Merchants) was a bit fuzzy. The name of a barbershop on the main floor of the Watson & McGregor building was impossible to read. Starting with the 1909 directory, I found that the Watson and McGregor firm was a hardware store specializing in plumbing, stoves and ranges, and tinsmithing. Their address that year was 647 Johnson Street; William J. Wriglesworth was located at 575 Johnson Street. As the addresses were a block apart, I knew my search had just begun. The 1910 directory showed the same information.

Hotel guests in vintage car

By 1914, the Wriglesworth business had moved to 1421 Broad Street and changed its focus to fish and poultry. However, Watson and McGregor were still on Johnson Street, and I could now identify the barbershop's name. It was Eagle Baths and Barber Shop and had its premises on the main floor of the Watson & McGregor building at 649 Johnson Street.

When I searched the 1917 directory, I hit the jackpot. William Wriglesworth had moved his business to 651 Johnson Street, immediately next to the Watson and McGregor building, exactly as shown in the photograph of the young woman. I could now search for the hotel across the street – and I found it. At 642 Johnson Street was the St. James Hotel, with Miss Katherine

McCluskey shown as the proprietor. The St. James Billiard and Pool Parlour was clearly shown in another photograph as part of the hotel complex.

Now that I had a hotel name and address, I could search more effectively. According to City of Victoria records, the St. James Hotel was built in 1912 to a design by Bresemann and Durfee, Architects. The original owner was listed as Charles Hayward.

At some point in her early career, Katherine must have made the acquaintance of Charles Hayward. Born in 1839 at Stratford, Essex, England, he came to Victoria in 1862. This local entrepreneur was a pioneer carpenter who constructed the scaffoldings for hangings in Bastion Square. In what I can only assume was a logical step for him, he began a new career as an undertaker in 1867. Eventually, he founded the British Columbia Funeral Furnishing Company, later known as Hayward's Funeral Chapel. Hayward was also involved in the mining and manufacturing industries. He was noted for his public life as a City of Victoria Alderman in 1873, 1874, and 1899, and Mayor from 1900 to 1902. He was a founding member of the Church of Our Lord (1874) with his friend Bishop Cridge and, as a community leader, gave freely of his time to charities such as the B.C. Protestant Orphanage (now known as the Cridge Centre for the Family) built on Hayward Heights and the Children's Aid Home. He was also one of the first directors of the Royal Jubilee Hospital when it was opened in 1890. Charles Hayward was known as the "booster of tourism." He was a founding member of the Tourist Association of Victoria, whose aim was to promote Victoria's image as a "pleasure and health resort." His name is found, with that of his wife Sarah, on one of the bricks laid along Government Street, marking the outline of the original Fort Victoria.

Katherine worked as the manager of the St. James Hotel until around 1917 when she left Victoria for a new home. But Katherine's story does not end with discovering the hotel's name. I still had to determine if the hotel and the buildings across the street were still part of our urban landscape.

This part of the search was relatively easy. I took a walk down Johnson Street, stood in approximately the same position as the original photographer, and tried to duplicate the scenes. Fortunately, all three buildings are still in their original locations, although altered since their construction. The St. James Hotel, now known as the Carlton Plaza, was increased in size in 1981 by building an addition to the west. The former Watson and McGregor commercial block was built around 1910 by architect A. Maxwell Muir. The main floor has been changed substantially, but the upper storey remains true to its original design. Finally, the building at 651 Johnson has also been altered on the main floor, but its second floor is remarkably similar to the old photograph.

We know that Katie's brothers Don, Lester, and Robert lived in Victoria, as shown in several City Directories, first residing at the hotel with their sister, then, one by one, striking out on their own. One photograph, which has yet to be researched, shows the three brothers posing in front of a telephone pole on a yet-unidentified street. I will tell that story another day.

Katie's brothers on an unidentified street

The problem with being a "heritage detective" is that the search never ends. Although I had obtained the information my client had requested and written a final report, I was still curious about other photographs in the collection. One, in particular, showed a streetcar in a deep snowbank. This time, the names of businesses were quite legible under a magnifying glass, making a search easier. Clearly visible were Ivel's Soda & Drugs, Geo. Powell & Son Hardware, and the Empress Theatre. The streetcar is identified as the "Uplands Fort" car.

As Victoria residents know, we have significant snowstorms infrequently, so it is relatively easy to date photographs taken in extreme winter conditions. This photograph had to have been taken during the record-breaking snowfall of 1916. The next logical step in my quest for information would be to check the 1916 City Directory. Unfortunately, not all directories have survived – never having been printed on good quality paper – and there are significant gaps in

The Uplands Fort Streetcar, 1916

official documents. I started with the 1910 records. Here I found two pieces of the puzzle. The New Empress Theatre, which proudly announced its "showing of moving pictures," was located at 1407 Government Street and Geo. Powell & Sons, hardware merchants, at 1411 Government Street. Ivel's Soda & Drugs operated from 1045 Fort Street. Happily, as I had identified the street on which the photographs had been taken, I could narrow my search field. The 1912 Directory showed Ivel's Pharmacy at 1415 Government Street. Now I knew exactly where the photographer had stood to take a photograph, and I could reproduce it, although I declined to stand in the middle of a very busy Government Street! Amazingly, all these buildings are still in existence and can still be recognized.

1407 Government Street was built in 1889 as a new warehouse for the growing firm of Brackman and Ker Milling Company. The Jeune Brothers Sail Loft and Tent Factory also operated from this site until the firm moved to its present location on Johnson Street. Moving pictures were shown in the New Empress Theatre as early as 1903. 1411 Government Street was built in 1891 and is considered a fine example of the Italianate style. The decorative spandrels and brickwork and the tall Victorian windows are still visible. The building is part of a group of structures constructed along Government Street around the turn of the twentieth century due to the economic boom from the Klondike Gold Rush. This building was recently rehabilitated, and several missing architectural features were restored. The former Westholme Hotel at 1413–1421 Government was built for the Westholme Lumber Company by architect H.S. Griffith in 1910. It contained retail outlets on the main floor – including Ivel's Soda & Drugs, Frost & Frost Hats, Dominick Pallantier Pool Room, and the Lloydminster Townsite Co. The street front at ground level has been dramatically altered, but the distinguishing feature of glazed brick on the upper storeys remains today.

Victoria is ripe with sites that need to be investigated, and there are hundreds of photographs in municipal and provincial archives that are not identified. Watch for future editions of the Heritage Detective in which we learn about a pioneer judge and the home that Samuel Maclure designed for him in Fernwood, old advertisements painted on the sides of buildings, and the firms that lie behind the names, and what lies beneath "modernizations" done after World War II.

The Carlton Plaza Hotel today

2022 UPDATE

The Carlton Plaza has remained virtually unchanged architecturally since the article was written; it is now part of the Best Western chain. Across the street, the Watson and McGregor building is still relatively intact on the second floor, with modern interventions on the main floor to accommodate storefronts. To the east, the form of the building at 651 Johnson Street has been drastically altered, although the bones of the original are still there. However, it is on Government Street that significant changes have taken place. The former Westholme Hotel was destroyed in a spectacular fire in the early morning of May 6, 2019.[1]

Many Victorians do not know that it was one of the finest hotels in the city in its day. Visiting hockey teams would stay there and eat in the Songhees Grill. Ironically, after the destruction by fire of the Driard Hotel, the liquor licence had been transferred to the new Westholme Hotel. By 1954, it was one of the first places in Victoria to get a beer as strict liquor laws were relaxed. The hotel continued until 1965 when it was renovated, and a new addition was added to the northern side. Now called The Century Inn, the bar's décor was centred around a Persian theme, with live music added to the offerings. By the mid-1980s, the hotel was declining in importance and became known as the Victoria Plaza Hotel, primarily known for Monty's Strip Club.

645 Johnson Street, 2022

Gone were the days of luxurious dining. About 2011, the property was purchased by League Assets, who were developing land in Colwood. They revealed plans for upgrading the hotel, but, unfortunately, plans fell through when the company collapsed due to financial issues. The property was purchased in 2018 by Pacific Gate Investments. It sat vacant as proposals were made, but none were acceptable to the City. I wonder what would have happened had the vacant building not been destroyed in a fire. It continued to burn until there was nothing left except part of one wall. History was gone instantly, and, to date, the cause of the blaze has never been determined. Today, the land sits behind a barricade with its future still uncertain. One thing is for sure; with the developer released from the need to protect a building that had been listed on the National Register of Historic Places in Canada, there will be no rebuilding of The Westholme.

I have also discovered that Katherine was an aggressive businessperson. In 1913,

Site of the former Westholme Hotel, 2022

she obtained a permit to allow the St. James Hotel to "sell spiritous liquor" by having the licence transferred from the Pioneer Saloon, located at 2000 Store Street.[2] [3] On the lighter side of life, she won a gold bracelet from Shortt, Hill, and Duncan at a Fancy Masquerade held at the Drill Hall in aid of the Seamen's Institute.[4]

I have still not been able to identify the street on which the brothers posed in front of a telephone pole. The photograph is very fuzzy, but I will keep trying. Nor have I been able to trace Katherine or the brothers after 1917 in Canada or the United States.

What is Heritage, Anyway?

This article was published in the November/December 2009 issue of *Moss Rock Review*

The word "heritage" is now being bandied about as the latest buzzword to sell everything from pet food to office furniture, but what does the term really mean?

Everyone has a different idea. However, a recent survey of the internet reveals the following thoughts:

The University of Massachusetts at Amherst Center for Heritage and Society defines heritage as "the full range of our inherited traditions, monuments, objects, and culture. Most important, it is the range of contemporary activities, meanings, and behaviors that we draw from them."

South Africa History Online provides: "Heritage is a collection of practices or ways of doing things that are handed down from parents to children as traditions. Heritage is also about family and when and where people have been raised."

The City of Ballarat in the Australian State of Victoria offers: "Heritage is something that gives us a sense of place and informs us about who we are and how our society has developed over time. Heritage can be something valued by a single person, or it can be part of a wider group's sense of identity and character."

The BBC News notes: "Heritage is not just about sticks and stones. It's about people's memories, and it's about things making sense to people, part of the accumulated culture of their communities."

Closer to home, the Heritage Foundation of Newfoundland and Labrador defines heritage as "... the sum total of all the things that have shaped you and your community. You are probably familiar with the built heritage: special buildings or monuments in your town. Heritage buildings are important because they help to define a town's character and uniqueness."

Although all these definitions from all over the globe are different, there is a common thread running through them. I prefer to define heritage as the things in life that I could not live without. Heritage is an essential part of the present we live in – and of the future. As many have said in the past, "how will we know where we are going if we don't know where we come from?"

Heritage is so much more than the built environment, although most people think of that when they hear the word. And ... it means different things to different people. In the built environment, several factors determine the heritage value of a building or site: the age, the architect or builder, the original owner, subsequent owners, the uniqueness of the design, the environment in which it sits and, perhaps most important, why does the community value this site? Of course, heritage structures must also be economically viable to justify the costs of restoration and subsequent maintenance.

A community has a heritage – what happened in the past that shaped what the area has become today. Often, this is shown in built form but can also be in the form of cultural or natural landscapes. For example, think of Beacon Hill Park – what a heritage site – used over the years by First Nations, once housing a racetrack, a place for family picnics, the home of the ducks that generations of children have loved to "feed," and areas of native plants that remind us of ages past.

People have their personal heritage as well. What things would you always take with you in a move to a new home? Family photos are perhaps the most obvious reminders of who we are, who went before us, and the next generation. However, memories are also important – intangible reminders of our past. Songs remind us of special times, and smells recall "grandma's kitchen."

People, communities, and nations must preserve examples of their heritage so that future generations can understand their roots. As we baby boomers age, we begin to look back to discover what our parents and grandparents went through. By understanding their heritage items, we can understand why we value certain things.

Heritage is so much more than bricks and boards, and we should celebrate it in all its forms.

Preserving our Heritage

This article was published in the September/October 2007 issue of *Moss Rock Review* and later in the Autumn 2014 issue of the *Rockland Neighbourhood Association Newsletter*

Sometimes the heritage detective has to take the time to reflect on exactly what she does. In the last few months, I have been asked several times why is it important to save old buildings, clock towers, walls, fences, etc. The quick answer is always the same: they are links to our past, and if we don't know where we come from, how will we know where we are going? But… it goes deeper than that. All cities are alike, except to those who live in them. Victoria is unique to us, and so is its history.

For me, all the buildings represent a visual link to the time of my grandparents and previous generations. I have fond memories of the wraparound porch on their house on View Street, (where I spent the first three years of my life) just down from where Central Middle School is today. As a very young toddler, I spent hours exploring my environment – the white sidewalk outside the house, the cool basement carved out of bedrock, the quirky hallways – all were very special to me then. I wish I could go back to see what the house looks like now, but it was demolished years ago, and the site is now a parking lot for an apartment complex.

The author with her grandmother at 1172 View Street (now demolished)

I have fond memories of the two-storey houses that used to line Rockland Avenue between Cook and Linden. To a child, they were marvellous places inhabited by "little old ladies" who were very generous with treats to youngsters. No wonder we liked to pass by on our travels. One by one, they came down to be replaced by anonymous boxes; first apartment blocks, followed by condominiums. The few that remain have become more valuable as they are the exception rather than the rule. Now mostly the site of multiple units, Cook Street was also once lined by two-storey Edwardian homes. As a school-age child, I had friends who lived in many of these homes, some later demolished, and others converted for commercial use. We are told that change is inevitable, but uncontrolled change causes concern.

I firmly believe that my exposure to heritage buildings at an early age helped to shape the adult I became. For the past 30 years, I have been an active heritage preservationist, developing along the way a tough skin to ward off the inevitable slings and arrows.

I am concerned about the insensitive changes being made in the name of progress, specifically in Fairfield. Why tear down functional, liveable buildings then leave the vacant lots as eyesores? Shouldn't there be a law against that? Once structures are gone, they don't come back – and the streetscape is altered forever. How about destroying heritage mansions because "they are expensive to maintain"? Anyone who purchases such a property should be aware of the potential costs before they do so.

Attempting to hold a neighbourhood to ransom is, in my opinion, unethical. To say that zoning must be changed to allow high-rise development that is clearly contrary to an official neighbourhood plan is unacceptable. If you care about your neighbourhood, take the time to become informed on issues. Write letters, make phone calls, talk to friends and neighbours. Don't let things happen, then complain that somebody should've done something. In the words of a current radio commercial: "I am somebody and I will do something." Get involved; it's your neighbourhood!

Jeremiah Chivers and his life on Wallace Island

Research on this island was completed in 2006 and excerpts were published in the June 2006 and September/October 2006 issues of *Moss Rock Review.*

Wallace Island, located in Trincomali Channel off the northeast shore of Salt Spring Island, is perhaps best known as the home of David Conover, the Army photographer who discovered Marilyn Monroe. But it is the story

Wallace Island from above JONATHAN YARDLEY PHOTO

of Jeremiah Chivers, the first European landowner on the island, that speaks directly to the development and settlement of British Columbia. In many of the Gulf Islands, as in the rest of the province, a long period of aboriginal habitation dating back at least 5,000 years was followed by a frontier society of loggers, fishermen, farmers, and miners. Although Wallace Island never developed to the extent that the larger islands have, it is nonetheless representative of the trends. Jeremiah Chivers' extended family also represents the evolution of the province with their connections to milestones in British Columbia history.

Jeremiah Chivers was born in Glasgow, Scotland January 28, 1838[5] to Catherine (Meikle) Chivers and her husband John, a Paper Box Maker.[6] He was their third child – a daughter Elizabeth was born in 1831 and Margaret in 1834.[7] He came from a long line of Jeremiahs, named for a Huguenot ancestor[8] who had fled France following the Revocation of the Edict of Nantes in October 1685. After the Revocation, over 80,000 French manufacturers and workers fled to the British Isles, bringing industries such as papermaking, silk making, tanning, furniture making, and silversmithing. As a result, England and Scotland became an exporter, rather than an importer of items such as velvets, satins, silks, taffetas, laces, gloves, buttons, serge cloth, beaver and felt hats, linens, ironware, cutlery, feathers, fans, girdles, pins, needles, combs, footwear, and many more items manufactured by the new Huguenot citizens. It is interesting to note that Jeremiah's grandfather, also named Jeremiah, was a stocking weaver and his uncle George was a master boot and shoemaker.[9]

Leaving his home in Glasgow in 1862, he travelled to Leith with his sister Margaret where he boarded the *Cyclone*, one of many passengers bound for the promise of the goldfields of the Cariboo. His only companion was his white terrier "Foxy" – from then, Jeremiah was never without at least one dog. The voyage was completed in just over four months "partly because they had favourable weather around Cape Horn." "Uncle," as his family knew him, sent letters of his exploits to his family and maintained a diary, a portion of which is still in the family's possession.[10] Among his fellow passengers on the voyage was Dr. Jackson who was Victoria's medical officer at the time of the smallpox outbreak here[11] and noted photographer Frederick Dally[12] who recorded details of the long voyage in a diary.[13]

On his way to the Cariboo, Jeremiah travelled by boat and canoe as far as Yale, then took the Hudson's Bay Trail to Lytton. There were stations along the trail to the Cariboo approximately 120 miles apart, serving meals and providing contact points for the prospectors. Along the banks of the Thompson River, Jeremiah noted the presence of winter homes of the local first nations – made of mud or clay, conical in shape, and with no doors. The entrance was via a smoke hole in the roof, and the ladder was a young pine tree. He also prospected in Cassiar, Omineca, and Skeena country. He operated a trading business in Alaska – one of the first to do so – before returning to the south, where he settled on

Galiano Island on December 29, 1875. Despite reports to the contrary, his mining and trading ventures must have been moderately successful, as he regularly sent money to his parents and gold nuggets to his sisters. His sister Margaret, still living in Scotland, had married John Shaw on February 3, 1863. By the mid-1870s, her husband, a stonecutter, had developed silicosis, also known as stone cutter's disease, and had been advised to "go abroad." Jeremiah encouraged the family – two adults and their four children (Robert, Margaret, John, and "Uncle's" namesake Jeremiah Chivers) – to come to Galiano Island. As her parents were now deceased, Catherine having died in 1869 and John in 1874, Margaret felt she was free to leave Scotland for the sake of her husband's health.

The family left from Leith in 1877, travelling via the steamer *Ethiopia* to New York City[14] where they boarded a train for the transcontinental trip to Sacramento. On arrival at the end of the steel, they boarded a steamer for the trip down the Sacramento River to San Francisco. The *City of Panama* brought them to Victoria, and the *Emma* stopped on her trip to Nanaimo to transfer the family and their goods to Jeremiah's ample rowboat. A full description of the trip and arrival are documented in *Early Days among the Gulf Islands* by Jeremiah's niece Margaret Shaw Walter, aged 13 at the time of their arrival.[15]

On November 6, 1888, Jeremiah acquired through pre-emption 4073, 160 acres – Lot 83 – on Galiano Island fronting on what is now Shaw's Landing. On June 5, 1882, he filed a "Certificate of Improvement" noting that he had occupied the land and had made improvements "in the extent of Two Dollars and Fifty Cents an Acre," and on November 9, 1888, secured a crown grant after payment of the fee of $10.00. John Shaw had obtained 60 acres in Section 7 early in 1888 for a fee of $5.00.[16]

Jeremiah's sister Elizabeth had married butcher John Muir on December 31, 1859; their family including son William remained in Scotland. Little is known of Jeremiah's uncle Jeremiah (born August 1, 1803) or his aunt Jemima Crawford Chivers (1814–1891). However, the lineage of Uncle George Chivers (1807–1863) and Aunt Jean (born 1810 and married to John Dickson on December 31, 1816) is well documented. Therefore, it would appear that descendants of these branches of the family tree remained in Scotland.[17]

In 1889, Jeremiah purchased via Crown grant 145 acres comprising Lot 12 of Wallace Island, then called Narrow Island,[18] and moved there with his dog, transferring ownership of the Galiano property to the Shaws. In this case, he paid the crown grant fee of $5.00 and a purchase price of $145.00. He was also required to declare that "the land ... is unfit for cultivation, does not include meadow or swampland, and is valueless for lumbering purposes." He built a two-room home on his new property, furnished it with homemade furniture, and planted a small orchard, living long enough to see the trees grow into total production. He never married, but his family reports that he lived a happy life with numerous trips to Galiano Island to visit his relatives and to Salt Spring Island to sell his fruit. Eventually, Jeremiah built himself a four-roomed cottage with larger windows, a good fireplace, and many conveniences. Unfortunately, he set fire to some brush intending to clear some more land, the wind changed, and the new cottage was destroyed. He never rebuilt, living in the small cabin until he died in 1927. He is buried in the family plot at St. Mark's Anglican Church Cemetery on Salt Spring Island, on land that had been donated by his niece's husband, Arthur Walter. On his headstone is a verse taken from Isaiah XLI:6: "They helped every one his neighbour: and every one said to his brother, Be of good courage."

On Jeremiah's death, the land on Wallace Island reverted to the crown. It was eventually acquired by the Mouat Brothers, then sold in early 1936 to a California boys' school for the purpose of establishing a summer camp.[19] It was at this camp that David Conover worked as a counsellor during his college years.

Jeremiah Chivers outside his cabin with his dog, date unknown
PHOTOGRAPH PROVIDED BY HIS FAMILY

Jeremiah's nephew, Arthur Brittan Walter, took the time to write notes in the flyleaf of Conover's first book *Once Upon An Island*, correcting what he considered to be errors in the text and adding to the details of the life of this BC pioneer. Arthur Walter's granddaughters are cataloguing the family papers – an extensive collection if the excerpts they have provided are any indication.

Margaret Shaw remained at the family farm on Galiano Island after her husband's death in 1890; John Shaw became the first Postmaster on the island – a post he would hold for twenty years. Margaret married Englishman Arthur Walter in 1888 and moved to his property "Woodhill" on Salt Spring Island. Jeremiah Chivers Shaw signed up with Canadian Pacific Steamships at age 16 and was the master of several ships. He was tragically lost in October 1918[20] when the *Princess Sophia* ran aground on Vanderbilt Reef in Lynn Canal.[21]

The story of David Conover is better documented but is the connection with Hollywood glamour that led to the success of his Wallace Island Resort. On June 25, 1945, Private Conover was sent by CO Ronald Reagan to take publicity shots of women in war work at Radioplane Corp. He discovered Norma Jean Dougherty working in the production line and recognized her natural beauty.

After a two-week photo shoot, he was sent overseas to the Philippines but left her money to study modelling. Norma Jean soon became a star in the movie industry, changing her name to Marilyn Monroe.

Remembering his summer work on Wallace Island, David travelled there with his wife Jeanne on his discharge from the army in 1946. They decided to sell their Los Angeles bungalow and purchase the island. First living in Jeremiah's original home, they built a wharf, then slowly developed a resort from which three buildings remain. They scavenged building materials from the shore to make ends meet and, at one time, bought the Secretary Islands to the north, logged them, then sold them two years later to help pay the mortgage on Wallace Island. Proceeds from the sale of Conover's early Marilyn Monroe photographs helped finance the Wallace Island Resort. In 1952, the Conovers travelled to Hollywood; a 1953 publicity shot for the Wallace Island Resort includes Marilyn Monroe in the photograph. Contrary to popular belief, she never travelled to the island, although several Hollywood stars did anchor their yachts off the island. The Conovers maintained sporadic contact with the Hollywood starlet over the next decade until her death.[22]

Once the financial worries were over, the resort operated well. As David noted: "when we bought the island we didn't realize the bargain we had in mink, eagles, and deer; neither did we know that we were buying a monstrous 'status symbol.' Abroad, every American is considered wealthy, but add the opulence of island ownership and you've become a multimillionaire. Island poor- what a paradox! How fortunate we are to be blessed with so rich a poverty."[23] [24]

A good portion of the island, including the resort, was sold in 1960 to a group from Seattle, Washington, who formed the Wallace Island Holding Company while David built a new home on the unsold acreage where he lived until he died in 1983. In 1990, the Wallace Island Holding Company sold their portion of the island to the provincial government; today, it is the Wallace Island Provincial Marine Park. The two resident European families are remembered through place names on the island. Jeremiah Chivers is recalled by Chivers Point at the north end of Wallace Island, while the Conovers are remembered in Conover's Cove.

The boaters and divers who enjoy Wallace Island Marine Park most likely have no idea of the connection of this small island with a pioneer miner or his fascinating extensive family history. Yet, it's a tale that is worth telling.

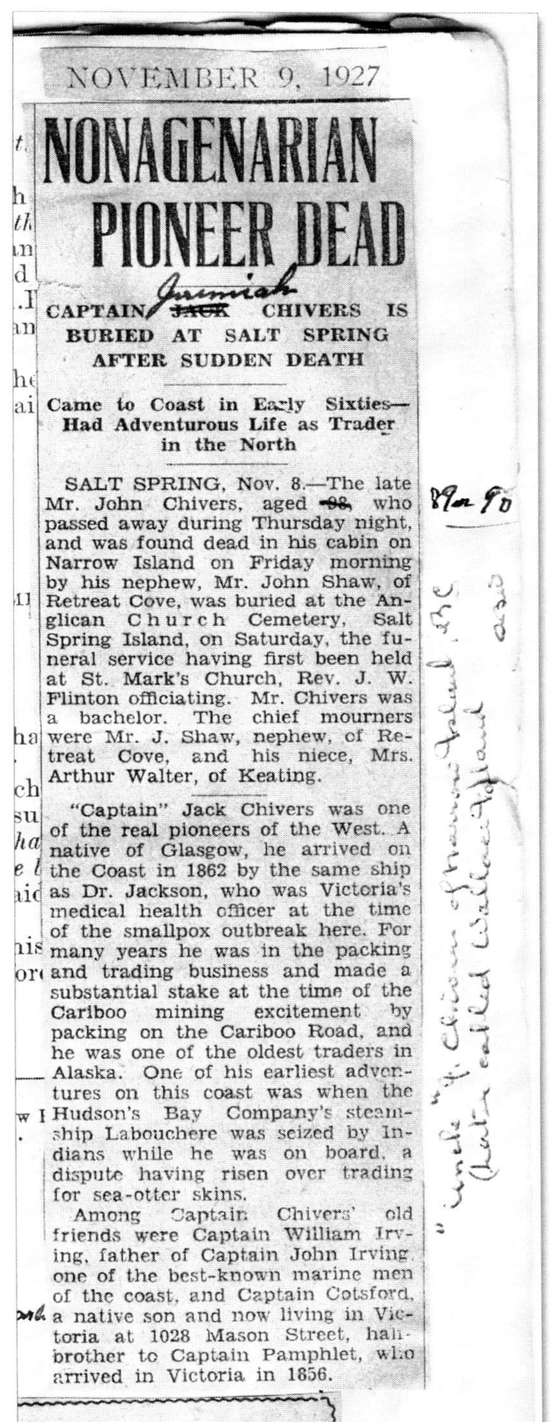

NOVEMBER 9, 1927

NONAGENARIAN PIONEER DEAD

CAPTAIN ~~JACK~~ Jeremiah CHIVERS IS BURIED AT SALT SPRING AFTER SUDDEN DEATH

Came to Coast in Early Sixties—Had Adventurous Life as Trader in the North

SALT SPRING, Nov. 8.—The late Mr. John Chivers, aged ~~98,~~ 89 or 90 who passed away during Thursday night, and was found dead in his cabin on Narrow Island on Friday morning by his nephew, Mr. John Shaw, of Retreat Cove, was buried at the Anglican Church Cemetery, Salt Spring Island, on Saturday, the funeral service having first been held at St. Mark's Church, Rev. J. W. Flinton officiating. Mr. Chivers was a bachelor. The chief mourners were Mr. J. Shaw, nephew, of Retreat Cove, and his niece, Mrs. Arthur Walter, of Keating.

"Captain" Jack Chivers was one of the real pioneers of the West. A native of Glasgow, he arrived on the Coast in 1862 by the same ship as Dr. Jackson, who was Victoria's medical health officer at the time of the smallpox outbreak here. For many years he was in the packing and trading business and made a substantial stake at the time of the Cariboo mining excitement by packing on the Cariboo Road, and he was one of the oldest traders in Alaska. One of his earliest adventures on this coast was when the Hudson's Bay Company's steamship Labouchere was seized by Indians while he was on board, a dispute having risen over trading for sea-otter skins.

Among Captain Chivers' old friends were Captain William Irving, father of Captain John Irving, one of the best-known marine men of the coast, and Captain Cotsford, a native son and now living in Victoria at 1028 Mason Street, half-brother to Captain Pamphlet, who arrived in Victoria in 1856.

"Uncle" J. Chivers of Narrow Island BC (later called Wallace Island)

Jeremiah Chivers obituary, with family notes

Streetcar on Government Street HALLMARK HERITAGE SOCIETY ARCHIVES

James Bay and Downtown Victoria Buildings

Articles about structures in the James Bay Neighbourhood and Downtown Victoria

69 Menzies Street

A heritage detective thinks about the stories that are hidden behind the doors of our buildings. Often the most interesting tales are extraordinary things that happened to "ordinary" people. And ... sometimes we come across links to events in the past, often long forgotten in today's busy, ever-changing world. How we stumble upon the mysterious past is often as convoluted a journey as the twists and turns of everyday life.

While researching the history of Wallace Island, I came across the name of Jeremiah Chivers, the first non-aboriginal landowner on the island. Curiosity got the better of me and I began to dig. A month later (aided by a chance contact on the internet through which I gained valuable information), I knew a lot about Jeremiah Chivers; most intriguing to me was his nephew and namesake, Jeremiah Chivers Shaw.

I already knew that he had been born in Scotland and had come to Canada with his parents to join "Uncle Jeremiah" on Galiano Island. From a family history written by his sister, I also knew he had signed on with Canadian Pacific Navigation Company at age 16 and stayed on when the company was bought by the CPR. I also knew he had died in 1918. Was he a casualty of World War I? A quick check of the government records confirmed that he was not one of the war dead. What I found next put his life in context with the maritime history of our coast and led me down a different research path.

Jeremiah (known as Jerry) served on many of the Canadian Pacific coastal steamers. In the early years of the twentieth century, these ships were the links between isolated ports and the more populous major cities. Goods were transported back and forth as were foodstuffs, the mail, and passengers. A great source of revenue for the company was the transportation of northerners to the south each fall. As was common in the Yukon in the early twentieth century after the boom of the Klondike was over, people tended to live there only during the good weather. Once the rivers began to ice up, there was a mass exodus to the south. The last

69 Menzies Street, 2022

trip to the south for 1918 was scheduled to leave Skagway, Alaska on October 23. Travellers made their way down river from Dawson City, from Whitehorse, and overland via the White Pass and Yukon Railway to Skagway, Alaska.

By 1918, Jerry had worked his way up the "ladder" – he had served as Captain on the *Beatrice*, the *Macquinna* and the *Tees* – and was the 1st officer of the *Princess Sophia.* After an uneventful trip north from Vancouver, the *Sophia* docked at Skagway on October 23. Once she was loaded to capacity, she departed at 10:10 pm, three hours late. Passengers made their way to their cabins and prepared for the long trip to Seattle. An hour into the voyage, a blinding snowstorm suddenly enveloped the ship, making navigation through Lynn Canal difficult. The *Princess Sophia* was steaming along just past 2:00 a.m. October 24 when she ran aground at the centre of Vanderbilt Reef. The captain alerted the Canadian Pacific office in Juneau, 20 miles to the south, requesting assistance. He prepared the lifeboats for evacuation of passengers, but the gale force winds and rough seas, made it impossible. Passengers waited patiently in the hope that other boats could eventually save them. In the early evening hours of October 25, the ship slipped off Vanderbilt Reef and sank. All aboard were lost, 278 passengers and 65 crew. All that was visible of the *Princess Sophia* was the mast; the only survivor of this tragedy was a small dog that swam to a nearby island. Jerry Shaw's widow Agnes received a pension of $20.00 per month. She continued to live in the family home at 69 Menzies Street until her remarriage and move to Sidney. Next time you are driving down Menzies Street in James Bay, think about the story behind the house.

Commemorative plaque for SS **Princess Sophia**, *Inner Harbour*

The Colonist Hotel

FORMERLY THE PARK HOTEL

I began research on this property after a colleague found a photo with a notation of the name of the building. The search proved to be intriguing.

One of the buildings in Victoria with the most interesting story has to be The Park Hotel, located directly across from Beacon Hill Park. It was built by William Lush and his new bride, Mrs. Henrietta Immel, who were married February 11, 1863. Born in Ireland, Bill came to Canada during the 1858 gold rush. He was a hard-living fellow who drank to excess and partied loud and long if newspaper reports of his behaviour are to be believed.

The Colonist Hotel, c. 1900 M07162, COURTESY CITY OF VICTORIA ARCHIVES

Before her marriage, Henrietta was a hotel operator in her own right as the proprietor of the Metropolitan Lodging House on Yates Street in downtown Victoria, opposite Wells Fargo Co. It had opened for business in February 1861 with a notice appearing in The British Colonist stating: "Mrs. H. Immel having leased the above premises and fitted them up in a first class style as a lodging-house, is now prepared to receive Lodgers."[25] The ad also noted that the four front rooms were set up for families. In fact, she had planned to increase the size of her holdings, having purchased a brick building on Langley Street. However, those plans fell through when she married Mr. Lush. So instead, she offered the Metropolitan Lodging House for sale or lease as she "wished to retire."[26] Together, they planned a new hotel on the outskirts of town across from Beacon Hill Park. They purchased an acre of land from Wharf Street merchant Richard Carr, the father of noted Canadian artist Emily Carr. Evidently, Mr. Carr needed cash at the time, so he was persuaded to sell the land. It was understood that the couple would not operate a public house, but as soon as the hotel was built, that is exactly what they did. Emily described the hotel in her *Book of Small* as "the horridest pub in town." Her father built a fence and planted a stand of trees on the east side of his property so his children would not have to witness the raucous behaviour at the hotel.

The Hotel was the site of many parties, some lasting long into the night. It opened with great fanfare in September 1864, being advertised as a "delightful retreat." The Lushes entertained their friends with lavish food and drink, after which they opened for business.[27] They held a select quadrille party every Friday evening with Allen's Quadrille Band in attendance.[28] The quadrille was a dance that was fashionable in 19th-century Europe and was brought to English society from Paris in 1815. It consisted of four or five country dances and depended more on the cooperative execution of intertwining figures or floor patterns than on intricate step work. It was similar to American square dancing and was popular in North America into the 20th century.[29] To attract more guests, the hotel made "Arrangements ... for conveyances to and from town."

Victorians, ready for any excuse for a party, celebrated July 4th in grand style. We learn that a grand ball planned at the Park Hotel for that date in 1865 was postponed as there was a huge picnic at Cadboro Bay as well as a gathering of Sunday School children and their friends in the neighbourhood of the Female Infirmary.[30] By 1866, the hotel was celebrating the Queen's birthday on May 24th with a ball starting at 2 pm with free admission to all[31] and offered the same type of celebration on July 4th that year.[32]

All was not rosy at the Park Hotel, as Mrs. Lush was sued by Mrs. Phillips, who had answered an ad in a San Francisco newspaper. The latter had been interviewed by Mrs. Lush and accepted a position as a waitress and chambermaid in what she thought would be a quiet, respectable hotel. Arriving in September on the *Del Norte*, Mrs. Phillips and Ellen Connoway, hired at the same time, had been driven to the hotel in a carriage. However, she had served only one day as "she found the employment utterly different to what she expected." She testified in court that "two respectable gentlemen ... had cautioned her in the barroom of the Park Hotel about staying there if she wished to be considered respectable." Mrs. Phillips eventually found herself a new position, but she left that after a month as she wished to return to San Francisco. At the end of the day, a jury returned a verdict of $75 and costs in favour of the plaintiff.[33]

William Lush had his share of court dates as well. He was arrested in September 1869 and charged with assault on a marine causing serious harm.[34] The result of the trial was never reported in the local press. On the business side, a petition was presented to the licensing court requesting that a liquor licence for the Park Hotel be denied as "the character of the house is most infamous." The application was refused.[35] However, subsequent applications for a liquor permit were approved, and the hotel continued to operate. Horse races were run across the street at Beacon Hill Park, so the race patrons were encouraged to visit the hotel after the day of events was concluded. By 1870, Mr. Lush was also operating a bowling alley on Government Street. As might be expected, the establishment had a bar supplied with the "best of wines, liquors, and cigars."[36] Mr. Lush was accused of using abusive and threatening language against a local citizen. As a result, the justice "addressed a severe lecture to Mr. Lush and directed him to find two securities in the sum of $150 each and ordered him to enter into his own recognizance to be of good behaviour for six months in the sum of $500."[37] This judgement does not seem to have done much good as Mr. Lush continued to have legal issues for some time.

In February 1873, Mr. Lush was one of the many signatories of a petition against a new law entitled "An Act to Extend the Rights of Property of Married Women." The men felt that the bill interfered "in the sacred relationship existing between husband and wife" and would lead to "domestic infelicity."[38]

He continued to have liquor licenses renewed despite his legal issues. His last court appearance related to a charge of "selling liquor to an Indian." He was fined $150 plus costs and was given until 3 pm to raise the funds or be imprisoned. Just before that time, he entered the Ten-Pin Alley (which had recently closed) after having what he called "the last drink I shall ever take." When he did not appear at court at the appointed hour, court officials spent time looking for him. When Mr. Lush was found, he appeared to be drunk but fell to the ground where he had several violent spasms, after which he died just before 5 o'clock.[39] A coroner's inquest determined that he had indeed taken strychnine in a drink, and that had caused his death.[40] His body was moved to the Park Hotel, and he was buried in Ross Bay Cemetery.

Despite being in ill health, Henrietta Lush continued running the hotel, successfully obtaining liquor licences until 1877. In April 1878, she leased the hotel to William Ritcheson, who seems to have only run the establishment for a short time as the liquor licence was transferred back to Mrs. Lush in December 1878.

Mrs. Lush sold the hotel to Samuel Adams, as he is listed as the owner in 1879. He came from a hotel background, having operated the Lake House at the head of Dease Lake.[41] He renovated the property and re-opened it on April 26, 1879 noting in his ad that it had "choice liquors and everything of a first-class character."[42] Mr. Adams offered dancing parties at the hotel with free admittance to ladies.[43] He operated the hotel in partnership with Mrs. Catherine Hotz. She assumed sole ownership of the hotel under its new name, Colonist Hotel, in 1889 when Samuel apparently left town for Washington State, where he died in May 1891.[44] Mrs. Hotz, undoubtedly recognizing the impact that the development of Beacon Hill Park would have on the area, announced plans in January 1891 to erect a new brick building to replace the old frame one. It would "be equipped with all modern improvements, including electric light, billiard halls, salt and fresh water baths, tennis courts, etc. There will be 70 or 80 bedrooms, and the new hotel will be managed by a well known local caterer. The new hotel will aim principally to meet the demands of tourists, and, when completed is expected to be one of the best and handsomest summer hotels on the Pacific Coast."[45] Unfortunately, Mrs. Hotz died on January 22, 1892, before any work could occur, and the new building never came to fruition.

The Colonist Hotel and the corner lot opposite it fronting on Beacon Hill Park were offered for public auction by the executors of Mrs. Hotz's estate in May 1892.[46] On June 14, 1893, the *Victoria Daily Colonist* reported that The Colonist Hotel with one acre of ground adjacent had sold to J. Coigdarippe for $11,250 while the lot adjacent, with a frontage of 51.6 feet on Beacon Hill Park, and 150 feet on Simcoe Street was sold to W. Barns, for $1,200[47]. Nothing is known about either of these purchasers, and they do not appear in any further records. Charles Muriset reopened the hotel in July 1893, but ownership soon passed to John Gavin and then to "Denver Ed" Smith, an American fighter whose real name was Edward Corcoran and who had more desire to win a prize fight than run a hotel.[48] The address at this time shows as Katherine Street, which ran from the waterfront to Belleville Street. Alfred Wood operated the hotel for two years; then ownership passed to Frederick Weldon (former proprietor of the Senate Saloon on Government Street) and Peter Usher about whom nothing is known.[49] In 1902, Weldon partnered with Charles Stewart to operate the hotel and a year later, with Fred Weldon's death on September 5, 1903,[50] Stewart became the sole proprietor. Subsequent owners included W. A. Gatt and James Van Tassel, but its days as a hotel were over. After the lands were drained to permit the construction of the Empress Hotel, the street address of the building changed to Douglas Street at it now went right through to Dallas Road.

Mrs. Mary Bullock ran the hotel as The Park Tea Rooms for some years, but the building was deteriorating and had nowhere the glamour of its former years. It was, for a while, headquarters for the James Bay Troop Boy Scouts and Wolf Cub Pack and briefly a corner store, but it was demolished in 1924.

A three-storey, 24-unit apartment block, was built in 1955 and named the Emily Carr. It is a reminder of the prominence of the Carr family; I'm sure Emily would have been pleased with the new use.

2022 UPDATE

Unfortunately, the Emily Carr Apartments were demolished in 2014 and replaced by 200 Douglas Street, a six-storey luxury condominium project.[51]

1119 Government Street, 1122 Broad Street, 613 View Street – Arcade Building

Sometimes the Heritage Detective is inspired by different things to explore. This time it is photographs that I discovered in the course of research for my book on the history of professional hockey in Victoria.

As many people know, the Victoria Cougars won the Stanley Cup in 1925. The team entered the 1925–26 season with high expectations, but all did not go well at the beginning of the season. In December, coach Lester Patrick returned to playing – at the age of 42 – and led his team to a place in the playoffs; the team finished third behind the Edmonton Eskimos and the Saskatoon Sheiks. The Cougars won the first series against Saskatoon in overtime and earned the right to play Edmonton for the league title. The photographs that I found in the Victoria City Archives show the lineup for tickets for the March 20, 1926 game.

Line up for hockey tickets for a Victoria Cougars game in 1926 vs. the Edmonton Eskimos M06824, COURTESY CITY OF VICTORIA ARCHIVES

Few people held season tickets in those days, so all had to line up. The crowd is overwhelmingly male, all well dressed – many in suits and almost all with a hat of some sort – with a few women in fur coats. Tickets were sold at the Victoria Chamber of Commerce office in the Arcade Building, a massive edifice that faced on Government, View, and Broad Streets. The time on the clock at the corner of View and Government Streets reads 9:37 am, and the lineup extended two entire city blocks. It is the businesses that were in the Arcade Building that I will write about.

In 1910, disaster struck this area when a massive fire destroyed almost every building in the area bounded by Trounce Alley, Government, Fort and Broad Streets; only the Times Building at the northeast comer of Fort and Broad survived. After the fire, the City decided to continue View Street from Broad Street through to Government, creating new street frontage and forming the street we have today. There was quite a debate about what the newly extended road should be called; some called for View as the original View Street had run from the harbour to Cook Street before being permanently closed off in 1858. Others opted for Bastion to continue the street that existed then from Wharf Street to Government.

The Arcade Building was first occupied in 1916. It was home to several prominent Victoria firms. In later years, it formed part of the T. Eaton Co. complex and was demolished to make way for what is now the Bay Centre.

On the Government Street side, the photographs clearly show the storefronts of Mitchell and Duncan Jewellers and Cyrus Bowes, chemist, while the storefronts of their neighbours to the south – A.P. Blyth, optometrist; H.E. Munday, shoes; and Heintzman Co. pianos are obscured somewhat.

On the View Street side, the storefronts of Plimley and Ritchie Ltd., bicycles and sporting goods, and People's Cash Hardware are visible; those of The Lingerie Shop, Macey-Abell Co. Ltd., picture framers, stationers, and office furnishers; Crown Millinery Parlours; and W.J. Clubb, cigars, are not well seen.

The Arcade – Government Street, 1959
M04089, COURTESY CITY OF VICTORIA ARCHIVES

Also visible in the background are the buildings on the west side of Government Street, most of which are still there today.

Various enterprises occupied the upper floor, including doctors, lawyers, manufacturer's agents, and political parties. But, perhaps the most intriguing tenant was the SSKTP Reading Room. This room was the headquarters of the Society for Spreading the Knowledge of True Prayer, founded in 1917 by Frederick L. Rawson.

The method of prayer was to be that of the realization of and conscious communion with God. Rawson lectured to large audiences throughout the British Isles and, in 1920, made an extended tour of the USA and Canada, talking and giving class instruction and treatments. As a result, many SSKTP centres were established in American and Canadian cities. The Victoria office opened around 1922.

Long-time Victorians will recall that Plimley and Ritchie progressed from selling bicycles to becoming a successful automobile dealership, eventually moving to a new building on the corner of Yates and Vancouver Streets. Likewise, Munday's shoes moved to a new storefront on Douglas Street and remained in business for many years.

1406 Government Street

I researched this building as it has always fascinated me. The history proved to be more important to Victoria than I had originally thought.

The history of the Hotel Victoria is one of the more interesting tales in Victoria's history. The Wilson-Dalby Block was built in 1892 as three stores, designed by Victoria architect Thomas Hooper. In 1894, it was converted to the Hotel Victoria with P. T. Patton as the first lessee. He was born in Montreal on

1406 Government Street, 2022

July 15, 1875. His father had been in the hotel industry for years as the proprietor of the St. Lawrence Hotel in Montreal. Leaving home in 1879, Mr. Patton went to Denver, Colorado, where he worked in the hotel business for twelve years before coming here. The virtues of the hotel were described in detail in the local newspaper just before it opened,

> "From top to bottom the place is furnished actually regardless of expense and throughout it is apparent that the aim of the proprietor is to make it a thoroughly first-class house. In the basement are fine club rooms, pantries, wine cellars and billiard room, two of the best billiard tables ever seen in the city. On the ground floor is the entrance hall, the largest in the city, surrounded by big pot plants and ferns, which leads the visitor into the hotel office. This portion of the building is fixed up sumptuously in solid carved oak, every part of the work including desks, counter, chairs, tables, etc. being finished in that splendid wood. The ceilings and walls have been frescoed very artistically with splendid views, while the hall ceiling is also painted with large clusters of yellow roses.

> "One of the doors takes the visitor into the bar-room which is garnished with mahogany and black walnut. Next to this is the short-order restaurant, the entrance to which leads off Government Street. On the other side is the hotel dining-room, a great deal larger, and, if anything, more complete. A spacious flight of black walnut stairs takes the guest up to the first floor, where are situated the reception parlors for ladies and gentlemen, and 30 of the 75 bedrooms. The parlors are furnished with the best furniture procurable, and contain pianos, expensive oil paintings, lounges, the whole of the floors being covered with the finest in Brussels carpets. The Victoria has been furnished by the Sehl Hasile-Erskins Co. The chef was for eight years chef in the Palace Hotel in San Francisco."[52]

According to an article in *The Victoria Colonist,* fresco artists were at work on the hotel in March 1892 and later that month, the new hotel acquired a liquor licence. When it was time for the hotel to open, P. T. Patton advertised, "The Hotel Victoria is now open for the reception of guests, on the American and European plans. The café is an adjunct to the hotel and will be open from 6 a.m. to 12 midnight. Merchants' lunch will be served in the café from 11:30 am to 2 pm. Table d'Hote dinner from 5 to 6 p.m., $1, including wine." The hotel proved to be very popular with the local community, and several events were held here including, The British Columbia Amateur Lacrosse Association, a bonbon social dance with music by the Bantly Family, a billiard tournament, and a ministerial dinner. Among the noted guests was the Earl of Onalaw, Governor of New Zealand. It was also popular with businessmen as there were fine sample rooms which were furnished for free to commercial travellers. Throughout its early years, the Hotel Victoria was in competition with the Driard Hotel. Despite the popularity of his hotel, for some reason, in late 1894, Mr. Patton left the hotel and took his family to live in Fairfield. He built a fine home at the northeast corner of Burdett and Cook called "Firwood Lodge." Later he and his family left for Mexico City to reside.

The *Colonist* of October 7, 1894, announced: "Mr. Ernest Escalet, succeeding Mr. P. T. Patton as the proprietor of the Hotel Victoria, will take charge on Tuesday morning. He will have with him as steward, Mr. Chas. Browne, well known for excellent services in that capacity in the city. The Victoria is to be thoroughly renovated and run on strictly first–class principles." Among the interesting events held at the Hotel Victoria were the visit of Professor J. Martines, the great South American herbalist "who has gathered herbs from east and west India and is now in the city for the purpose of introducing those wonderful remedies for all complaints applicable to male or female". He was operating from rooms 32 and 33 at the Hotel Victoria. In room 31, Miss Franciesa, late of San Francisco, California, has opened her "Massage, Magnetic and Alcohol Treatment."[53] On a different note, Ernest received a viceregal commission in November 1894 (GG Marquess of Lansdowne 1894, Lord Aberdeen in 1896) when he catered the luncheon on the train during the Governor-General's visit to Duncan and to Wellington. On the last occasion, both His Excellency and the Countess expressed themselves as delighted with the delicious luncheons, and Lord Aberdeen presented Mr. Escalet with a diamond pin as a memento of the occasion.

Ernest Escalet, a chef by trade, was born in Marseilles, France, in about 1846 and moved to Lyon, France, by 1886.[54] He came to Canada in 1864 and married Swedish immigrant Matilda Alsan, in Victoria, February 10, 1887. They had three children, Ida Harriet, born December 8, 1887; Edith Marcella, born December 26, 1889; and Lillian Josephine, born January 3, 1892. In the 1891

Canada census, Ernest was listed as a restaurant keeper with 13 employees. He ran the Hotel Victoria for only two years, and by 1901, the family was in the Cariboo.[55] By 1903, he was back in Victoria as the owner of the Escalet Café at 56 Langley (later 1224 Langley) Street. On April 10, 1909, Ernest died in Reno, Nevada, and Matilda died in Victoria September 18, 1909.[56] Ida Harriet moved to the United States in 1915 and married Edward Joseph Nordhoff in Chicago, Illinois, July 21, 1917. By 1930, they were living in Beverley Hills, where her husband died January 29, 1973. She died in Los Angeles May 25, 1982 and is buried in Calvary Cemetery, Seattle, Washington. Edith Marcella moved to China and married Edwards Charles Ford, April 12, 1933, at the Shanghai Community Church in Shanghai, China. She died there April 11, 1935. Lillian Josephine married Commander Edward Sparrow, USN, in 1920. She died May 14, 1961, in Burton, Washington, and is buried in Arlington National Cemetery with her husband, who died in 1951.

Management of the hotel was assumed by John C. Byrne on February 1, 1896; he was in this position for two years. He was born in 1861 in Ontario, but little is known about his life. In 1898, Joseph Claus Voss assumed the proprietorship of the Hotel Victoria and was here until 1900. Born in 1859 at Holstein, he became a naturalized Canadian citizen on January 16, 1897. He is perhaps best remembered in Victoria for his voyage in a native whaling canoe, the *Tilikum*. In 1901, newspaperman Norman Luxton challenged Captain Voss to better the 1898 feat of Captain Joshua Slocum, who had sailed his 12-ton Spray around the world single-handed. Captain Voss eventually sailed the 11 ½-metre *Tilikum,* some 65,000 km from Victoria, through three oceans, taking three years, three months and ten days. He then went to Ecuador for a business venture, but Civil War drove him back to Victoria in 1905, where he bought the St. Francis Hotel on Yates Street. He married Mary Anna Grath, at St. John's Church, April 18, 1906. Their reception was held at his hotel. She died months later, August 21, 1906.[57] Three years later, he left for Japan as captain of a sealer until 1911. In 1913, he left for the south seas but was never heard from and presumed to be lost at sea. It wasn't until 1922, that Victorians got word that he had died in Tracy, California, where he drove the town jitney.[58] The *Tilikum* was sold and an engine installed, but the boat was later abandoned on a mud flat. It was shipped to Victoria in 1930 and, 30 years later, was restored and displayed at the Maritime Museum of BC.

The next proprietor of the Hotel Victoria was Edward E. Leason. He advertised the hotel as "this well-known and widely popular hostelry – conducted on both European and American plan – rates for the latter being $2 per day and upwards." Born April 2, 1859, in Kent, England, to William Henry and Jane Leason, he was in Victoria by 1901. He married Dora Fiddelia Dunaway in Seattle March 4, 1902. The couple had eight children, all born in Victoria.

Edward died April 13, 1935, having left the hotel industry to work as an assessor for the provincial government.[59] Dora lived until October 26, 1972.

In 1905, Frederick L. Wolfenden and Walter Millington were the proprietors of the Hotel Victoria. Frederick was born in Yorkshire, England, November 12, 1880, to Lieutenant-Colonel Richard Wolfenden and Felicite Caroline Bayley. By 1903, he was in Victoria, where he married Alice M. Anderson June 30, 1903. The couple had two children. In 1919, the family moved to California, where Frederick died February 13, 1965. Walter Millington was born in Victoria July 31, 1899, to Walter Millington and Sybil Backus. He signed Attestation Papers May 30, 1916 and was assigned to the 103rd Overseas Battalion. However, he was discharged from the Canadian Expeditionary Force July 6, 1916, when it was determined he was a minor.[60] He married Annie McLeod January 15, 1934, at St. John's Church. Annie died in New Westminster February 16, 1956, and Walter died June 23, 1983.

From 1908 to 1910, Charles Tulk operated the hotel. He was born about 1860 in England and came to Canada in 1890. He operated the Omineca Saloon before becoming the proprietor of the Hotel Victoria. He died April 25, 1932.[61] In 1911 and 1912, Thomas N. Graham and George Grant operated the hotel, and A. E. Brooks ran it in 1913. By 1914, the hotel added a pool parlour and cigar stand with Joseph Balgno as proprietor. During prohibition, which ran in BC from October 1, 1917 to June 15, 1921, the hotel sat vacant. The building was operated as the Wah Que Hotel in 1926 and 1927, then was vacant for another year before it became the headquarters of McLennan, McFeely and Prior, popularly known as Mac and Mac. The business was a wholesale hardware store which also carried sporting goods, radio supplies, bar iron and steel, tank plate, and wire rope. Located immediately to the north was the de Cosmos Block, built in 1885 by Amor de Cosmos. It was originally two storeys, with a third storey added in 1896. It was demolished in 1941 and replaced by a new two-storey building for Mac and Mac, designed by C. Elwood Watkins, architect. A third storey was added shortly after construction, and further alterations made in 1949 under the supervision of McCarter and Nairne. The original appearance was altered over the years, including the addition of stucco and removal of storefront and entrances, upper storey windows, and cornices. For several years, the buildings were home to provincial government offices and presented an empty stuccoed wall to the street. During this time, the cornices were removed, and the buildings generally deteriorated. There was little evidence of what had once been a dynamic architectural gem.

In 2006, the building was rehabilitated. The most dramatic phase of this work was the removal of stucco from the main floor, revealing original cast-iron pillars and the original splayed entrance. The building was seismically strengthened, and all services were upgraded. The main floor became the home of

Mountain Equipment Co-op, with merchandise clearly visible from the street. The residential component of the project produced bright suites, and the capacity was increased by an additional storey, set back from the street to minimize the impact. The building is once again a landmark in Victoria's downtown and demonstrates that rehabilitation can produce a useful building while retaining the historic fabric.

City Hall News, right, 2005

1500-block Douglas Street

This short article was published in the Spring 2005 issue of *Preserve* along with two small photographs. I have done additional research to produce a more detailed story of all of the east side of the 1500-block of Douglas Street.

This building at 1511–15 Douglas Street, designed by prominent Victoria architect C. Elwood Watkins sometime before 1933, has been the home of City Hall News for years; the adjacent (to the north) Royal Bank of Canada was "modernized" by the Canadian Imperial Bank of Commerce; this branch has recently been closed. The façade features fine examples of terracotta with a greenish tinge, still in fairly good condition. As the CIBC branch has been closed, there will be pressure to redevelop the entire block. The property is now listed with an international real estate firm. There are rumours that the Royal Bank of Canada will abandon their 1950s branch to the south, providing a larger parcel for redevelopment. The area to the east is currently parking lots.

2022 UPDATE

The corner of Douglas Street and Pandora Avenue was known as the home of the BC Electric Railway Interurban depot. From here, streetcars travelled the area, transporting citizens to numerous destinations. For years, a tobacconist occupied a portion of the building, selling his wares to travellers. In the 1940s, the tobacco shop was replaced by a firm that offered groceries and confectionery in addition to tobacco.

In 1930, a building permit was issued for a "brick bank and stores" with street addresses of 1511, 1513, 1515, and 1517 Douglas Street, between Pandora and Cormorant Streets. The estimated cost of construction was $33,000, and the permit fee was $19.50. Once construction was complete, the Royal Bank of Canada, which had previously been located at 1601 Douglas Street, moved into its new location at 1517 Douglas Street with A. Watson remaining as the manager. Small's Bakery occupied 1513 Douglas, Charcuterie Français, a delicatessen, moved into 1515 Douglas. The Canadian Bank of Commerce moved into the former location of the Royal Bank.

In 1941, City Hall News, a firm that had been established in 1915 under a different name, moved into 1509 Douglas. The business was sold in 1950 to George Streeter. His son Bob joined the business in 1949, worked with his father until 1987, and operated it in that location until 2004, when redevelopment of the site made a move necessary. A new location at 1607 Douglas Street was not profitable and, when the owner developed cancer, he decided to retire.[62] Robert (Bob) Streeter died in Victoria on March 14, 2022, leaving behind memories of a long-term business and the friends he had made over the years.[63]

Small's Bakery was replaced by Arnold's Victoria Bakery in 1947 but the remainder of the businesses remained the same for years.

In August 1955, the old BC Electric Railway building was demolished to make way for a $250,000 state-of-the-art building for the Royal Bank of Canada. BC Electric staff moved into the recently completed $1,000,000 structure at Pandora Avenue and Blanshard Street. Architects for the new building were Wade, Stockdill & Armour. Working plans were drawn up but until the existing building, which had no basement, was demolished, there was no way to

Royal Bank of Canada, Douglas and Pandora, 1960
M03683, COURTESY CITY OF VICTORIA ARCHIVES

determine if extensive drilling into bedrock would be required.[64] Farmer Construction was awarded the contract for the one-storey building in November,[65] and the new branch opened to the public on January 21, 1957. Despite earlier concerns about excavation, it featured a basement that held the furnace room and fire-safe record storage. On the main floor, traditional tellers' cages were replaced by wickets, and customers could access safety deposit boxes through a "16,000-pound door that opens at the touch of a finger." A mezzanine above the Douglas Street entrance was set aside for special jobs and possible expansion of banking services as well as a fully functional staff room.[66]

As it had years before, the Canadian Bank of Commerce (it became CIBC in 1961) moved into the old Royal Bank offices, this time at 1517 Douglas, and remained there until 2005.

Douglas and Pandora, 2022

In February 2015, development of two office towers on the site was approved. The proposal was unanimously approved with no opposition from the public. The project is an attractive example of what can be developed after extensive consultation at all levels.[67] Both towers have now been completed and the revitalized site is vibrant and full of energy.

William Harbeck and his fantastic movie of downtown Victoria

This is one of the most complex research projects I have ever worked on, but due to space limitations on the resulting website, much information couldn't be presented. A short report was printed in the May/June 2009 issue of Moss Rock Review and is presented here, followed by information for each building on the route that the streetcar took in 1907, with updates. The website, as created, can be found at http://williamharbeck1907.ca/.

Saturday, May 4, 1907, was a special day in the history of Victoria. That was the day that William Harbeck produced a cinematograph of downtown Victoria. Using a streetcar loaned by the British Columbia Electric Railway Company, he travelled the streets, turning the hand crank of a camera fixed to the front of the car. He began at City Hall, travelled down Douglas Street, turned right

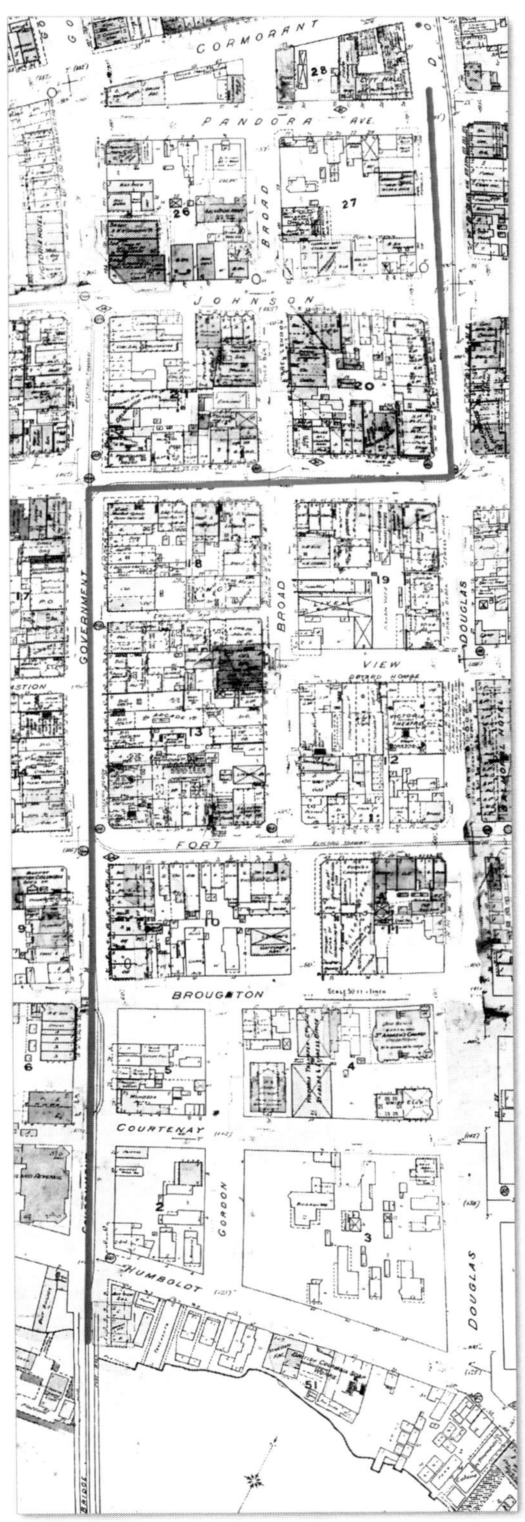

The route marked on a 1891 Fire Insurance Plan

on to Yates and then left on to Government, where he concluded his journey at the Post Office.

He was so taken with the view of the Empress Hotel being built on the former mudflats that he took a panoramic view of the harbour, including the Empress Hotel site, the Legislative Buildings, and the CPR terminal.

In the afternoon, he travelled by water to the Point Ellice Bridge, where he photographed the upper harbour and the sealing fleet. He then transferred to an electric launch and travelled up the Gorge Waterway as far as the Gorge Bridge. On the return trip, he captured the Isle of the Dead and the sawmills, conveniently in full operation.

The *Victoria Daily Colonist* of May 5, 1907, documents the experience and notes that Mr. Harbeck would be travelling "along the line of the E & N to Nanaimo: Stopping at Shawnigan Lake for photos of the glittering sheet of water and the pretty little hotel." He then made his way to Vancouver, where he shot 400 feet of film and planned to then travel up the CPR as far as Lytton. From this trip, only the footage of Victoria and Vancouver remains. It was found in the Australian archives a few years ago and brought back to Canada. What is interesting about the film is the number of buildings that are shown along the route that can be identified today – over a century later.

William H. Harbeck was born in Toledo, Ohio, in September 1863. He married Catherine (born in 1863) in 1886, and they had two sons, John (born April 1887) and Stanley (born February 1892). He gained his reputation in 1906 when he filmed the aftermath of the San Francisco earthquake. He was subsequently hired by the Canadian Pacific Railway to "put Western Canada on the motion picture screen." He produced 13 one-reelers designed to show Canada at its best and to attract Europeans to Canada. The Victoria and Vancouver reel was obviously one of these.

In 1912, the CPR sent him to Paris to study with Leon Gaumont, who had mastered the outdoor location shoot. According to the *Weekly Advocate* for Newark, Ohio (January 23, 1913), Harbeck had been in Europe "arranging for the disposition of 110,000 feet of motion picture film which he had made on a trip to Alaska, together with his motion picture machine valued at $600."

Mr. Harbeck had notified relatives that he would sail for New York on the *Titanic*. He was likely hired by the White Star Line to film the maiden voyage of the ill-fated vessel, and it is thought that he would be taken off the ship to film the arrival in New York. Strangely, Mr. Harbeck was travelling on the *Titanic* with Henriette Yrois, a 24-year-old model he had met on his European trip. Both died in the sinking; he was identified by his membership card in the Moving Picture and Projecting Machine Operators Union.

On Saturday, April 20, 1912, a very grainy photograph was published in the *Calgary Herald* with the caption: "Well known in Calgary, who is said to have been on the Titanic. Mr. Harbeck was engaged, it is said, to take a series of pictures of the Titanic's first voyage." He took many pictures in Alberta in connection with CPR advertising.

Harbeck's widow, Catherine, of Toledo, Ohio, filed a claim against the owners of the *Titanic* for damages for the loss of her husband and considerable property. She claimed $25,000 for her husband's death and $55,000 for the loss of property. His business partner, Mrs. Katherine George of Seattle, claimed $41,000 for the films that had been lost.

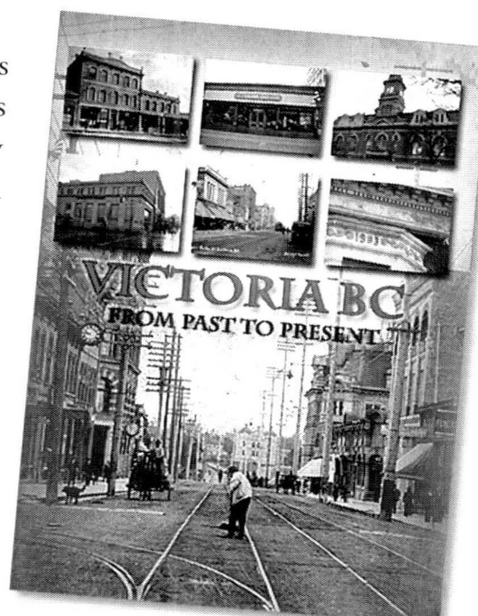

The cover for the CD of the project

The Hallmark Heritage Society received funding from the HBC Foundation and the BC150–Heritage Legacy Fund to produce an interactive website, including the original video. There is extensive information on the buildings that would have been on the route in 1858, then in 1907, and what was there when the project was completed in 2009. New research unearthed many stories and cleared up some misconceptions about buildings along the route.

Fort Victoria

Any discussion of old buildings in Victoria must commence with the construction of Fort Victoria. Some of the buildings the streetcar passed by were built on the site of the old fort. This essay on the fort was part of the original report.

In 1842, James Douglas of the Hudson's Bay Company selected the port of Camosack (the harbour where Victoria now stands) as a new fur-trade post, eventually to replace Fort Vancouver on the Columbia River as the company's Pacific headquarters and to bolster the British claim to Vancouver Island. It was obvious that the international boundary would be set at the 49th parallel, and Fort Vancouver would be firmly in United States territory. Charles Ross noted in his private correspondence:

> "The Fort is a quadrangle of 330 by 300 ft. The buildings on for the present to be eight in number, exclusion of bastions – and their dimensions – 60 by 40 by 30 feet. Posts and Pavilion roofs of these edifies we have already thoroughly completed three, and two more (main and officers house) are up but as yet unprovided with covering or inside work. One octangular Bastion of three stories was built. In the farming line we have not as yet done much, there are about three

acres broken up and prepared for the plough. The soil appears excellent being composed of decayed vegetable mould with a strong clayey bottom, it is however a good deal growth of fern. The landscape is beautiful and strongly reminds one of some of the noble domains at home – water alone being [wanting] to complete the picture. The climate is perhaps too fine, of which you may judge, when I tell you that from June to November we had scarcely anything else but bright sunny days."

The entrance to Bastion Square, 2022

On June 10, 1843, the new fort was officially christened Fort Victoria after Queen Victoria. The crown colony of Vancouver Island was established in 1849, and Richard Blanshard, who became its first governor in 1850, resided at Fort Victoria. In 1847, the fort walls were extended to include a post office, a stable, and another warehouse. The town site was surveyed adjacent to the fort in 1851–52.

With the discovery of gold on the British Columbia mainland in 1858, Victoria became the port, supply base, and outfitting centre for miners on their way to the gold fields, mushrooming from a population of 300 to over 5,000 literally within a few days. One morning in July, some 2,800 men arrived from San Francisco en route to the gold rush, and that year, 30,000 people passed through Victoria on their way to the Fraser River goldfields. Victoria also became the outfitting centre for miners on their way to the Cariboo gold fields.

Commemorative bricks create the outline of the original fort, 2022

As the town of Victoria grew – it was incorporated in 1862 – the fort was slowly dismantled to make way for the expanding town. In 1864, the last part of the old fort was demolished, the lots were auctioned off, and brick commercial buildings went up. The north bastion of the fort was at the corner of what is now Bastion Square and Government Street, and the south bastion was at Fort and Government Streets. The original outline of the fort is now marked on Government Street by a row of bricks containing names of Victoria pioneers.

Of the buildings seen in the Harbeck video, there are several that are built on the old fort site. 1108 Government Street, the current location of Munro's Books, was originally part of Fort Victoria and is almost exactly between the chief factor's residence and the men's quarters. The Promis Block at 1006–1010 Government Street occupies what was once the southeast corner of the fort. The Hamley Building, named after its original owner, Wymond Hamley, Collector of Customs for British Columbia from 1864–1871, was constructed on the site of the fort's garden. The site on which the former bank is located at 1022 Government Street is where the bachelors' quarters stood.

Buildings and sites along the streetcar route

#1 Centennial Square, City Hall

The February 2, 1876, *Daily British Colonist* contained a statement of income and expenditures for the City of Victoria for the year ended December 31, 1875, that showed an expenditure of $50 for City Hall design. Up to then, there had been no City Hall, and council meetings were held in the police barracks on what is now Bastion Square. In 1876, Council spent $300 on City Hall Design. City Hall was finally constructed in 1878 – with additions in 1880 and 1891 – to a design by John Teague. Its Second Empire style reflects the post-confederation usage of this style for public buildings across Canada. In 1962, Centennial Square was developed, including an addition to the original City Hall and rehabilitation of the

Victoria City Hall, 1973
HALLMARK HERITAGE SOCIETY ARCHIVES

McPherson Playhouse. At that time, the Victoria Police Station was part of the site, but a new police station was built at the corner of Quadra and Caledonia Streets in the 1990s. Since then, a new building incorporating the old police station has been built, and now houses Capital Regional District offices.

1402 Douglas Street – Porter Block

DATE OF CONSTRUCTION: 1900

ARCHITECT: WILLIAM RIDGWAY WILSON

This late Victorian two-storey commercial building features rusticated stone piers on the main floor that visually link the building to the ground. On the second storey, architectural highlights include a balustrade cornice and a nameplate on the Douglas Street façade in unglazed terra cotta, decorative multi-coloured brick detailing, and round-headed windows with stone on the upper portions. The building was noted as "among the larger and more costly structures which have been erected ... during the year" in the *British Daily Colonist* of September 14, 1900. The cost of construction was $13,000.

The original owner, Robert J. Porter, was born in Dorset, England, in 1834. He sailed to Vancouver Island to work for the Hudson's Bay Company on a trip that took 6½ months. Once in Victoria, he worked as a farmer, surveyor, brick maker, and butcher. He opened this wholesale and retail butcher shop and later had two shops in Victoria and two in Vancouver. His firm Porter & Sons was eventually purchased by P. Burns & Co. Between 1890 and 1928, Burns built one of the largest packing and provisioning businesses in the world. Robert Porter served as a Victoria City alderman from 1912 to 1916 and 1918 and was

The Porter Block, 1402 Douglas Street, 1959–1964
M01412, COURTESY OF CITY OF VICTORIA ARCHIVES

Mayor of Victoria from 1919–1921. His family home at 649 Superior Street was designed by Samuel Maclure.

The building has housed many diverse businesses over the last century but has retained its architectural integrity and is still a landmark on the downtown Victoria streets. For many years, it was the home of the Aveda Institute, and in 2022, it is the home of the Original Farm cannabis outlet.

1328 Douglas Street

DATE OF CONSTRUCTION 1878; ADDITIONS 1910

This early Victoria building was built in 1878 for Thomas Nicholson to house his grocery and liquor business. It is the oldest surviving building on Douglas Street and was built when masonry buildings were uncommon. Local contractors Hayward and Jenkinson were the builders. For more information on Charles Hayward, see the article on 1003 Vancouver Street. Thomas Edward Nicholson was born September 6, 1842, in County Kerry, Ireland, to Thomas Nicholson and Elizabeth Maybury. He came to Canada while still in his teens and studied medicine in Ontario for two years. He then went to California and became a professor of mathematics at the San Jose Normal School, a position he held for three years. In 1862, he came to Victoria and became a teacher at the Collegiate School until 1872, when he moved to Oregon City. On returning to Victoria, he began his downtown business. In 1888, he was appointed the first principal of the newly opened Victoria West School and was later appointed principal of the Lampson Street School. He married Sarah Eleanor Jenkinson in Victoria August 3, 1870; the couple had nine children. Thomas died in Victoria February 25, 1914.[68] By 1885, the building was used as a CPR hotel with a dining room on the second floor. From 1887, it was the home of the Regent Saloon, where notorious owner Bill Anderson was known to jump up on the bar and referee fights. On the second floor was Barney Levy's cigar factory, where his crew rolled "Pride of Victoria" cigars.

1328 Douglas Street, 2022

The building has been changed substantially over the years with an addition to the rear in 1910, designed by noted Victoria architect Thomas Hooper, and the addition of stucco to the brick façade. Several windows on the second floor have also been altered. For many years, this was the home of Dorman's Men's Wear, and in 2022, it is the home of a Burger King Restaurant.

1319–1329 Douglas Street – Craft & Morris Block

DATE OF CONSTRUCTION: 1888

ARCHITECTS: FISHER AND WILSON

Built originally for William Craft's dry goods business, this was once one of the most highly decorated façades in the area. The Victorian Italianate structure, built of brick, had decorative window hoods, finials and parapets, and a splayed corner entrance. It has been severely altered over the years, including a stucco application over the brick façade and removal of parapet details. The street-level retail use continues, although the store fronts have been altered so drastically that little of the original remains. William Craft was born in Rochester, England, May 28, 1838. He came to Canada in the early days of the gold rush and mined and prospected for many years in the Cariboo. He moved to Victoria, where he married Ellen Bickford December 12, 1877. William died suddenly November 11, 1986.[69]

In 1907, it was the home of the Direct Importing Tea & Coffee Company, J. Bray, manufacturer's agent, W. Jackson and Co., druggists, and F.E. Hewartson dry goods.

In 2009, the lower floor was occupied by a 7-11 Convenience Store, the upper storey was consolidated with the second storey of the IOOF hall (1307–1315 Douglas) and was used for Lodge activities. The 2022 use is the same as it was in 2009.

Craft & Morris Block, 2022

The Doane Block, 2022

1314–1324 Douglas Street – Doane Block

DATE OF CONSTRUCTION: 1891

The two-storey brick commercial building was built for Miss Margaret Doane, the daughter of Joseph Homer and Charlotte Elizabeth Doane, at a cost of $10,000. She had inherited her parents' properties on the death of her mother in January 1899. Featuring five bays, the conformity of the roofline is relieved by the central section with its slightly raised roofline and round-headed windows. Pilasters define the divisions between the bays, and a corbelled cornice draws the eye up to the skyline. Margaret died suddenly at Mill Bay May 25, 1911.[70] Her ownership of a business was unusual for her time.

In the 1890s, it housed a variety of businesses, including A. Bruce's Veribest & Co. fruit and tobacco dealers, McMillan Bros. grocers, and J.M. Nagona & Co.'s Oriental Bazaar that featured Japanese "fancy goods."

By 1907, the businesses were: George William McNeill, picture framer; William Duncan, harness shop; Oriental Bazaar, now owned by Wanibe and Matsouka; Pullman House lodging run by Mrs. Bessie van Sicklin; Yet Sing and Co., Chinese silks; and G.H. Bissell, tailor.

The site was acquired by the Morgan family in 1927. William Lloyd Morgan was born in Oakesdale, Washington, June 12, 1895, to Daniel Morgan and Jessie May Smith. On July 23, 1917, he married Mary Ellen O'Brien, born in Spokane, Washington, on January 23, 1896, but who had lived in Victoria since 1909. She attended St. Ann's Academy, Victoria High School, and the Provincial Normal School. She taught at Willows School for a year and then moved to Spokane, where she married. They then returned to Victoria, where she was known as a poet, penning "Our House." The family owned a fuel company for years and lived at the Priory at 729 Pemberton Road, which Mary ran as a guesthouse during World War II. William served on Victoria Council for about ten years.

William died February 28, 1969 and Mary died September 1, 1969.[71] Both are buried at Royal Oak Burial Park.

The diverse use continues today with a variety of tenants offering goods and services. The property is currently part of a redevelopment project with the Watson & McGregor Building, which is adjacent to it at the rear.

1313–1319 Douglas Street – IOOF Hall

DATE OF CONSTRUCTION: 1878
ARCHITECT: JOHN TEAGUE

In 1877, the Independent Order of Oddfellows outgrew their original premises at Wharf and Langley and purchased this site next to the Clarence Hotel. The contract was awarded to Hayward and Jenkinson contractors, and the cornerstone was laid on December 30, 1878. The upper floor contained a large ornate meeting hall which was illuminated by gas and heated by wood and coal.

Architect John Teague was instructed to draw plans "in accordance with the Fraternal Order's basic requirements" with the proviso that the Hall "was not to conflict with, but should complement, the existing Clarence Hotel." The total cost, including the architect's fee, was $16,317.42. The Hall was finished on time, by October 31, 1879, and dedicated on March 11, 1880.

A subsequent fire necessitated the removal of the original front face of the building, so none of the original façade remains. However, the upper meeting

Oddfellows Hall, 2022

hall was painstakingly restored during a three-year period ending in 1987. The geometric designs on the moulded plaster ceiling were repainted in their original brilliant colours, and the water-colour frescos in the cove of the ceiling, which had been covered with chicken wire to prevent falling plaster, have been brightened with a dry cleaning process. The chandeliers were taken down and restored to their former beauty, the old wallpaper was replaced, and the ornamental wainscoting and the great entrance doors were refinished.

The retail outlets on the main floor have varied over the years. In 1907, the firms were: William Wilby, fancy goods store; William B. Hall, grocer; Hallam and Wyndham Ltd., tea and coffee importers; W.H. Adams, sporting goods; and James Maynard, boots and shoes. The latter was the nephew of Richard Maynard, who had come to Victoria in 1862 with his wife Hannah and family and also operated a boot and shoe business (his wife Hannah ran her photography business from the same location). They were first located at the northeast corner of Douglas and Johnson, then moved to their new building at 723 Pandora in 1891.

1317 Douglas Street was known for years as Rose's Jewelers. The storefront was considered a good example of Commercial Modern architecture, having been remodelled in the 1920s. It featured black vitrolite panels and plate glass with metal mullions.

1313 Douglas Street was, for many years, the site of Paul's Restaurant, one of a chain of fine eating establishments owned by Paul and Lydia Arsens.

In 2009, there were a variety of outlets, including a restaurant, a hair salon, and a dollar store, with the IOOF Hall still upstairs. In 2022, the building houses Hope Key Restaurant, ARQ Salon, and Illusionz Bazaar Co.

1308–1312 Douglas Street – Victoria House

DATE OF CONSTRUCTION: 1891

This Italianate commercial building was built for Miss Pauline Lange, a popular Victorian socialite. It features triple bays with double-hung windows and cast-iron columns that define the lines of the bays. Bay windows, extending over the street, were popular in the 1890s as they allowed occupants of the rooms better access to light and fresh air. A strong cornice with brackets marks the skyline. Miss Lange (she is shown in several City Directories as "Mrs." Lange, but she never married) operated the upstairs as a small lodging and rented the downstairs storefronts to businesses.

In 1907, the spaces were occupied by Oscar Lucas City Fair, a dry goods business, and R. Kawai, who sold bamboo furniture. The lower space was later used as a liquor store by the Hudson's Bay Co.

In 1934, the building was purchased by Walter W. Cross for $10,000. He operated a butcher shop there. He had started in Victoria West in 1920 on Craigflower Road and would eventually own a chain of six stores. After World War

II, Walter handed over the business to his son Bob Sr. and his son-in-law George Saul. In 1974, Bob Sr. transferred his ownership in the business to his son, Bob Jr. and his son-in-law Arthur Baird. With the growth of supermarkets, Cross' Stores consolidated itself into one retail/wholesale outlet on Douglas Street and added a gourmet deli bar.

Victoria House, 2022

Bob Cross Jr. served as City of Victoria Alderman from 1991 to 1993 and Mayor from 1994 to 1999. In 2000, facing declining red meat sales and a demand for downtown housing, he decided to close the business and to restore the building. Following a seismic upgrade and careful restoration of heritage features, the upper two storeys that had sat vacant for years were converted to eight character suites. The main floor was transformed into two commercial storefronts.

1301–1305 Douglas Street

DATE OF CONSTRUCTION: 1923

ARCHITECT: A. ARTHUR COX

Once the site of the Clarence Hotel (see drawing), which influenced the design of the adjacent IOOF Lodge building, it is now the location of the Bank of Nova Scotia. Designed in a Classical Revival style, this stone-faced bank shows a late interpretation of the Temple Bank style. It is a prominent landmark in downtown Victoria and is part of the historic character of Yates Street.

The Clarence Hotel
UNIVERSITY OF WASHINGTON, SPECIAL COLLECTIONS

Scotiabank, 2022

1300–1306 Douglas Street

DATE OF CONSTRUCTION: 1889

ERECTED BY THE CANADIAN PACIFIC LAND & MORTGAGE COMPANY

The design featured brick masonry and plaster ornamentation, classic detailing, a large traditional storefront and upper storey windows with stained glass, a built-up parapet and pediments, a prominent corner tower with curved glazing, and relatively ornate decoration such as iron fencing. The storefront, cornice, parapet, top of the tower and ornate details have since been removed, and the brick and plaster have been painted in an unsympathetic colour.

The first tenant in the main ground floor space was druggist Edward C. Kellogg. Born in Seattle, Washington, in 1866 to Gardiner and Sarah Kellogg, he married Mame C. Cramsie in Victoria on May 23, 1889. He did not operate his business here for very long as on July 9, 1890, a notice appeared in the *Victoria Daily Colonist* advising that "Notice is hereby given that the business which has from some time past, been carried on at the corner of Yates and Douglas Streets, by E.C. Kellogg as a druggist, has this day been sold and disposed of to J. Cochrane & Co., who will in future carry on the business under the firm name."[72] There is no further record of Mr. Kellogg, so it must be assumed he returned to the United States where his family lived. John Cochrane was born August 12, 1867, in Huntingdon, Québec, to Reverend William Cochrane and Christina McKinlay. He spent his childhood in Lanark County and Kingston, Ontario. He graduated as a gold medallist in pharmacy from the Ontario College

1300–1306 Douglas Street, 2022

of Pharmacy in Toronto in 1887. Coming west in 1898, he followed his profession in Seattle and was there during the fire that practically wiped out the city. He married Edith Veronica Simon in Seattle September 14, 1892.[73] He then moved to Victoria, where he carried out business at this location until shortly before his death. He was one of the founders of the BC Pharmaceutical Association and represented British Columbia at the formation of the Canadian Pharmaceutical Association. For more than 35 years, he was one of the board of examiners on the BC Pharmacy Board. He was also one of the oldest and most active members of the Canadian Club, having held almost every office in the organization. In honour of his work, he was given a life membership in 1942. He died in Victoria July 31, 1949.[74]

Other early tenants included R.A. Brown Hardware and H.A. Potts, Merchant Tailor.

The tower was removed at some point between the 1920s and 1940s, although the exact date is unknown. In 1907, the tenants were John Cochrane, druggist; Postgate Fowler, fancy goods store; R.A. Brown and Co. Hardware; James L. Forrester, paints; William Russell, dentist; Dr. A.E. McMicking, physician; and Mrs. C. Cameron, lodgings (upstairs). Every upstairs room had its own fireplace, accounting for the seven chimneys seen in old photographs.

The building was occupied by Coles Books, Cunningham Drugs, and a leather wear store for many years in the 1980s but was left vacant in 1990. At one point, the City of Victoria was considering suing the absentee owner for the condition of his "filthy heritage building." One city councillor noted that "Paper coverings over the windows often fell down revealing the filthy interior." Eventually, the building was rehabilitated and was open for business again.

The main store space is occupied by a Circle-K convenience store with a language training school on the upper storey. Smaller businesses use the remaining street level retail.

648–652 Yates Street – Hotel Wilson

DATE OF CONSTRUCTION: 1893

What now appears as a very plain-Jane brick two-storey building was once a striking four-storey hotel. The main floor storefront had high stained-glass clerestory windows that blended well with the adjacent (1280 Douglas Street) styling. Built in 1893, it featured high-ceiling upper storey levels, arched fanlights, intricate brick detailing, and a prominent upper parapet and cornice. The original owner, J. Keith Wilson, also operated a popular saloon at this location. James Keith Wilson was born August 2, 1846, in Aberdeen, Scotland, to James MacAllan Wilson and Jane Smart. He came to Canada in 1872 and married Mary Kennethina Munro in Victoria July 19, 1877. In 1892, they built a Queen Anne home at 730 Burdett Avenue, which was the centrepiece of one of the most

648–652 Yates Street, 2022

luxurious estates in Victoria, stretching from Blanshard Street to Douglas Street. Interior fixtures included Venetian glass chandeliers, a hand-carved staircase, and elaborately ornamented ceilings. The leaded-glass windows rivalled those at the Parliament Buildings for quality. Sited atop a prominent rise of land, the local landmark was also the home of Victoria Jane Wilson, born May 27, 1878. On her fifth birthday, her parents gave her a ten-year-old parrot named Louis, who would eventually outlive her by many years.[75] The story of her will, which made special provisions for "my said birds and pets" including her favourite pet, Louis, became a tale of mythical proportions and was featured in numerous periodicals, including "Life" magazine.[76] When Victoria Jane Wilson died in 1949, the building was converted to rental suites, while Louis continued to occupy a place of honour. The residue of her considerable estate would be distributed to local charities "at the time of the last bird's death",[77] and her lawyer Howard Harman was instructed to employ a caretaker to care for the collection of birds. Louis received special treatment from Wah Wong, Miss Wilson's gardener, with his diet augmented by hard-boiled eggs, walnuts, and a tot of brandy daily. As long as Louis survived, the building could never be demolished. The property soon became a battleground between contractors who wished to develop the six lots of prime downtown real estate. Eventually, five lots were sold, with those on either side of the house turned into parking lots. The unsuccessful fight to try to save the mansion led to the formation of the Hallmark Society, now the Hallmark Heritage Society, in April 1973.

Mr. Wilson purchased the land from Miss Margaret Doane in 1891; the building permit was dated January 3, 1893, and noted "Central Ward – J. K.

Wilson, Yates Street; 3 4-storey brick stores – $17,000." The hotel was also the home of Bancroft's Candy Factory.

By 1907, the building had been sold to Louisa Gordon who renamed it the Gordon Hotel. Louisa Emily Walker was born November 12, 1856, in London, England. She married John Aberdeen Gordon and had three children. At one point, she operated the Aberdeen Private Hospital at 951 McClure Street. Her husband died April 24, 1914, and Louisa died July 24, 1922.[78]

It was also the site of one of Diego Zarelli's many cigar stores and shoeshine businesses; Mrs. Ethel J. Tripp, millinery; A. B. Oldershaw, watchmaker; and the Wilson Bar. Diego Tony Zarelli was born in Carolei, Italy in 1860 to Natale Maria Zarrelli and Rosa Bastone. He came to North America as a young man, spending two years in Pittsburgh, Pennsylvania, then moving to Tacoma, where he lived for a year before coming to Victoria in 1890. Tony's first shoeshine was at Yates and Government. He then moved to the old Horseshoe stand on Government and finally to Trounce Alley, where he claimed to have polished more boots and shoes than any man in the northwest. At that time, Tony's was the only exclusive shoe shining parlour in the city, and he had thousands of patrons.[79] He died in Victoria January 4, 1943.

At some point, the top two floors were removed, taking along with them the intricate parapets and the distinctive nameplate. All that remains of the original design is the articulated vertical piers. The façade has been stuccoed and the storefronts altered beyond recognition. However, this building is still important as it is part of the historic streetscape of this side of Yates Street; most of the other buildings remain much as they were constructed.

In 2009, the building housed a Korean grocery store, an internet café, and a Korean and Japanese food restaurant. It is used by a variety of businesses in 2022.

644 Yates Street

DATE OF CONSTRUCTION: 1888

Built for Thomas Houghton, this two-storey brick building continues to be used as a retail store. In 1907, it was the premises of M.A. Vigor, a millinery store. It has been covered with stucco, the cornice removed, and the shop front replaced.

In 2009, it was the site of a tailor shop, a use which continues in 2022.

644 Yates Street, 2022

640–642 Yates Street – Williams Block

DATE OF CONSTRUCTION: 1888–1889

These two storefronts have a long history in Victoria. The current buildings were erected around 1888 to replace wood frame structures that had been on this site from the early days of the city.

The first mention of a business at this location was in 1874 when James Crossman had his general store in what is now 640 Yates Street. He was born May 11, 1888, in Durham, England, to William Crossman and Elizabeth Burton. He married Violet May James and came to Canada in 1914. The couple had no children. William died November 4, 1949, and Violet died December 9, 1974.

By 1877, John James Wilson had opened The Central Bakery in the adjacent storefront. The *Colonist* from September 24, 1885, advises that: "Mr. John Partridge has leased one of the stores in Williams Block, Yates Street and in a few days will open with a choice stock of staples and fancy dry goods."

In the *Colonist* of September 29, 1887, John J. Wilson advised, "The undersigned takes this opportunity of thanking his customers and patrons for their very liberal patronage in the past, and would beg to announce that, on account of rebuilding on the premises now occupied by him, he is compelled to move, and that pending his return to this present site his bread will be kept constantly on hand at Messrs. Bossi and Geisselman's, Mr. Jos. Wrigglewsworth's, also at Geo. Collins' Bakery, cor. Store and Discovery Sts." When the building reopened, The Central Bakery returned to its original location, and the second storefront was occupied by John Partridge's dry goods store.

In 1907, when the streetcar went by, the bakery was owned by Robert Morrison and the dry goods store was owned by George W. Robinson. Today, these storefronts are occupied by a series of small businesses.

640–642 Yates Street, 2022

639–641 Yates Street – King Edward Hotel

DATE OF CONSTRUCTION: 1891; TOP FLOORS ADDED C. 1904

The top two floors were built over an existing one-storey block of stores which included the Dawson Hotel, when this building was converted to a luxury hotel. A building permit dated January 1, 1905 notes: "BC Land & Investment Agency – Remodeling Dawson Hotel (now King Edward) Yates Street – $10,000." The third storey has Romanesque windows with stone arches and lintels.

In 1907, it was still known as the King Edward Hotel and also housed Wescott Bros., dry goods and S.A. Stoddart, jeweller. However, by 1922, it was rented out as housekeeping rooms. Prohibition in 1917 had forced the closure of many hotels.

In 1997, A&B Sound moved into the building and undertook extensive renovations. With the demise of the business in 2008, the building underwent further modifications, and it was the home of Atmosphere, outdoor equipment and clothing, in 2009. In 2022, the building houses an electronics firm.

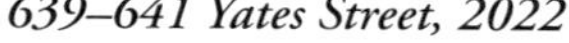

639–641 Yates Street, 2022

Lobby of the King Edward Hotel, postcard from 1907

636 Yates Street – Deluge Fire Company

DATE OF CONSTRUCTION: 1877

ARCHITECT: JOHN TEAGUE

The Deluge Fire Company was one of the City's earliest volunteer fire companies, formed at the American Saloon on August 6, 1858. Along with the Union Hook and Ladder Company (1859) and the Tiger Engine Company (1860), they fought fires in the young city of Victoria. There was much rivalry between the companies as they raced to burning sites hoping for "first water" and bragging rights. Deluge used this site until 1900; the tower formerly used for the alarm bell and for drying the hoses was dismantled by 1904.

When the streetcar came by in 1907, the building was home to G.A. Richardson's dry goods firm.

In 1995, the building was restored to accommodate retail on the main floor with offices above. The restoration included: replication of the finial urns above the parapet; washing and painting of the existing brick work; repair of existing second-floor wood sash windows; replacement of wood window sills; replacement of the wood cornice above the ground floor; removal of ceramic tile on existing brick piers; removal of the cast iron column in the centre of the ground floor; fabrication of new brick piers; new fibreglass arches to simulate the original stone work; all new granite bases; and new wood framed storefronts and doors. The project won a commercial restoration award from the Hallmark Heritage Society.

Deluge Fire Company building, 2022

632 Yates Street

DATE OF CONSTRUCTION: 1878, 1885, 1888

This simple, vernacular commercial brick structure was built for Alfred Bossi, a nephew of the noted Bossi family who built many of the structures in Market Square. It replaced a wood structure on the site and was intended to house the A. Bossi and C. Giesselmann grocery (also licensed to sell liquor). The building has a handsome corbelled brick cornice and originally had cast iron pilasters on the ground floor and a wooden arcade along both street frontages. The brick has been painted, obscuring the original signage. Additions were made to the store in 1885 ($2,000) and a one-storey addition in January 1888 ($1,500). By 1892, the building housed the Mirror Saloon and A.J. Rowbotham, grocer.

In 1907, it was the premises of C.H. Tite and Co., painters and C.W. Blackstock and Co. real estate, financial and loan agents. When Blackstock moved to Fort Street the following year, his former space was occupied by John Ringshaw's delicatessen. His new neighbour was Direct Importing Tea and Coffee.

The building was repainted to highlight its architectural detailing and in 2009 was the home of a coffee shop. In 2022, the lower floor is vacant.

The Surrey Building, 2022

631–637 Yates Street – Surrey Building

DATE OF CONSTRUCTION: 1878; ADDITIONS 1890, 1906, AND 1912

Originally built as a two-storey structure for Burns & Edwards, this building has undergone many renovations. James Burns, a hardware merchant, operated his business here for four years. In 1884, the building was purchased by Thomas Dixon Galpin, an important British investor, through the BC Land & Investment Agency, of which he was the Chairman. Nicholles & Renouf rented the premises as a hardware warehouse from approximately 1885 to 1904. One floor was added in 1906 to the design of Francis Mawson Rattenbury.

By 1907, the tenants were Robert Watson, boots and shoes, and British Columbia Hardware Co. In 1912, the storefronts were altered by James & James architects. At some point, the corner entrance was changed from rounded to angled.

In 1977, this building was consolidated with its neighbour to the east, 639–641 Yates, by A&B Sound who undertook massive renovations then, 1979, and 1982. With the demise of the business in 2008, the building had further modifications. In 2009, it was the home of Atmosphere – sports equipment and clothing. In 2022, it houses Giant Victoria, a bicycle store.

615–627 Yates Street

In 1907, the streetcar passed by Dean & Hiscocks, druggists; Adams Edwards, stationery; F.P. Watson, grocer; the Hotel Davies; and the Poodle Dog Restaurant. By 1912, 615 Yates was the home of the Delhi Café. By 1921, it was again the home to the Poodle Dog, this time under the ownership of Frank E. Graham and Joseph Chamberlain. They sold to H.A.W. Beer who moved the business to 706 Yates. The Poodle Dog Restaurant moved to the corner of Government and Yates (1239–1245 Government) in 1948 and was very popular in that location until the 1970s.

The buildings at 615–627 Yates Street were destroyed by fire in the last part of the 20th century, and a new building was erected on the site.

615–627 Yates Street, 2022

607–611 Yates Street

DATE OF CONSTRUCTION: 1882

Built as a grocery store and saloon for John Boyd, this simple two-storey vernacular structure has had its storefronts altered, and the window openings on the second storey have been enlarged to accommodate double sashes. Initially, there was a corner entry with a window above. The façade has been stuccoed. Boyd operated his successful wholesale and retail, wine and spirits, tea and cigar business from this location.

607–611 Yates Street, 2022

The British Colonist of April 2, 1890, carried the following advertisement:

> "Andrew Tolmie, having leased the premises occupied by me for so many years at 45 and 47 Yates Street, will carry on the business in conjunction with Duncan Stewart, under the name TOLMIE & STEWART and by a careful selection of liquors and strict attention to business will keep up the well established reputation of the house. Thanking my friends for their patronage in the past, I would request a continuation of the same for my successors.
> (signed) JOHN BOYD."

Further changes were made, as noted in the *British Colonist* for November 19, 1904:

> "Notice. We hereby give you notice that we intend to apply at the next sitting of the Board of Licensing Commissioners for a transfer of the license now held by us to sell wines, spirituous and fermented liquors by wholesale and retail on the premises known as 45 and 47 Yates Street, in the City of Victoria, B.C., to Duncan Stewart. (signed) Tolmie & Stewart, November 16, 1904."

In 1907, Duncan Stewart was still in business and apparently rented out the upstairs to tenants, including James D. Robinson, bookkeeper.

In 2009, the building was the site of an internet cafe with offices above; in 2022, the main floor is occupied by a Pierogi Bar.

604–628 Yates Street

When the streetcar travelled past this block of Yates Street between Broad and Government, it still boasted vintage buildings. Among the businesses housed on the north side of this block were Arthur Holmes, clothing; D.F. Sprinkling, tailor; F.G. Moody, dentist; E.J. Eyres, photographer; International Correspondence Schools; W. Henry Pennock, jeweller; H.P. Winsby, real estate; McFadden & Mould, meat market; S.M. Okell & Co., manufacturer's agents; J. and F. Hepworth, tailors; Coast Locators; B. Williams and Co., clothing; Empire Realty; Diego Zarelli, cigars and shoe shine; the Manitoba Bar; Drake & Horn, hardware; and the Turfman's Club. At the corner of Yates and Government was the Imperial Bank Chambers with Aikman & Courtney, barristers; Albert C. West, dentist; and Moresby and O'Reilly, barristers above the main banking floor.

The scene is quite different in 2009. At the corner of Yates and Broad is the Legacy Art Gallery and Cafe housed in the former Bank of Toronto (William Frederick K. Gardiner, Architect, 1950). The corporate heraldic shield is sculpted in low relief above the entrance and remains as a visual key to the building's history. Further on, new buildings have been built next to old ones, housing clothing outlets, interior design firms, and an architectural office. At the end of the block, at the corner of Yates and Government, is a complete remodelling of the 1883 Pritchard House, of which all visible traces have been removed. Built for the Imperial Bank of Commerce in 1946 by D.C. Frame and Douglas James, Associated Architects, it was the home of Starbucks coffee in 2009. In 2022, it's the home of Bubby Rose Bakery.

604–628 Yates Street, 2022

As the streetcar travelled down Yates Street and made the turn to Government Street, the 500-block of Yates Street was clearly seen *(see photo oveleaf)*. This block, with its wholesale outlets and numerous saloons, hotels, restaurants, and offices, was the heart of the commercial district in early twentieth-century Victoria.

Yates Street, looking west from Government Street, c. 1900
M06983, COURTESY OF CITY OF VICTORIA ARCHIVES

578 Yates Street

578 Yates Street, 2022

Located at 578 Yates Street in 1907 was the Palace Saloon. The *Colonist* of February 22, 1901, noted: "Mr. Ralph Borthwick has disposed of his Government and Yates Streets property to Mr. H. Siedenbaum for $17,000. The property has a frontage of 20 feet on Government Street and the same on Yates Street, being L-shaped. The Palace Saloon, of which Mr. Siedenbaum is proprietor is located on the property." The saloon is long gone, and the site was vacant in 2009. In 2022, it is the home of Quesada Burritos and Tacos.

576 Yates Street

Next door to the Palace Saloon was the Steitz Restaurant at 576 Yates, a popular meeting place for sporting groups and men's clubs. In 2009, it was the home of a shoe store. In 2022, the storefront is empty.

576 Yates Street, 2022

564 Yates Street

DATE OF CONSTRUCTION: 1860?

The building at 564 Yates Street has undergone several radical façade changes during its lifetime. It may be as old as 1860, built as Nathaniel Moore's Dry Goods Store, although the front façade dates from a renovation done in 1917 by C. Elwood Watkins. In 1909, shortly after the streetcar travelled by, it was renovated as the Majestic Theatre by Thomas Hooper. When the streetcar made its journey, the site was the home of the Women's Christian Temperance Union, the voice against alcohol, ironically in the heart of the alcohol-consuming district. It was later a kitchen supply store and Hughes Clothing, which relocated to Oak Bay. In 2022, it the new home of Luxe Home Interiors and Adventure Clothing, with suites above.

564 Yates Street, 2022

566–570 Yates Street

DATE OF CONSTRUCTION: 1891

Known as the Lewis Building, 566–570 Yates Street was built in 1891, although there had been a hotel on the site since 1885. During the 1890s, it contained one of Victoria's most popular saloons. The building is noted for its elaborate brick detailing and granite lintels. The front façade is crowned by an ornate cornice with a false front. When the streetcar travelled by, the lower floors were inhabited by B.C. Hughes' real estate office; Hugo Boss Realty Co.; General Agency Corporation; the Province Cigar Co.; Imperial Life Insurance Co.; James H. Greer Ship Brokers; and B.C. Saddlery Co. Ltd. Sarah Flemming ran a "boarding hotel" on the upper storeys. The hotel was renamed the Kings in the late 1940s and, in 1975, was the first beer parlour on Vancouver Island to introduce dancing with live music. The building has been restored on two occasions, both of which respected the heritage character. It is still operational today.

566–570 Yates Street, 2022

560–562 Yates Street

DATE OF CONSTRUCTION: 1883

560–562 Yates Street was built by Thomas Hooper for Mrs. Mary Hannah Watkins in 1883 when lot 184 was subdivided. She was born in Bowmanville, Ontario in 1854 to James Eliphalet McMillan and his wife, Louisa. By 1874, she was living in Victoria as she married Charles Richard Watkins here December 12, 1874. Her husband died of typhoid November 1, 1884, leaving her with five children, including noted Victoria architect Charles Elwood Watkins, who began his career in the office of Thomas Hooper. Mrs. Watkins ran a dressmaking shop out of her building; then, it was the location of William J. Jeffree's outlet. His business had been established around 1858 in a wooden building at the northwest corner of Government and Yates and moved to the newer brick building. According to directories, the firm carried "gentlemen's furnishings, trunks, goods, etc." William Jeffries died on March 18, 1885, and the business was carried on by his son, also named William Joseph. In 1894, he moved the store up the street to the Jewell Block on the corner of Douglas and Yates and appears to have gone out of business by 1896. He appears in the 1901 Vancouver City Directory. 560–562 Yates was the home of F. R. Stewart & Co. Fruits & Provisions from the mid-1890s and that business was in this location when the streetcar made its journey.

560–562 Yates Street, 2022

550–560 Yates Street – Oriental Hotel

DATE OF CONSTRUCTION: 1883

Perhaps the most intriguing building on Yates Street is the Oriental Hotel, named for its location adjacent to Oriental Alley (alley access from Yates no longer exists). In 1883 William McKeon commissioned the eastern half of this structure adjacent to his Oriental Saloon. Designed by John Teague, the hotel was "a brick hotel of three stories … The front is supported on arches resting on iron columns, and bay windows run through the upper stories" according to the *Daily Colonist* report of January 5, 1884. An addition in 1888, also by Teague, doubled the frontage on Yates Street and replaced the old saloon building.

550–560 Yates Street, 2022

A feature of this addition was an ornate cupola-like tower that once graced the southwest corner of the hotel. From sunset to sunrise, a light was kept burning in the tower; mariners used the light as an aid to navigation. The name was changed to the St. Francis Hotel in 1906 and retained that name for several years, although it suffered a severe loss of business during Prohibition from 1917–1921. It survived by renting rooms and, in 1958 was acquired by Goodwill Enterprises for the Handicapped, who used it as a second-hand store and warehouse; they sold used materials to raise funds to help their disabled clientele. It was then acquired by LeFevre and Co., who did a complete restoration and adaptive reuse project.

546 Yates Street

DATE OF CONSTRUCTION: 1880S

Directly across Oriental Alley (now closed off) from the hotel was Hickman Tye Hardware Co. Ltd. at 546 Yates Street. Established as the firm of Matthews, Richards & Tye in the 1880s, the company took the name of Thomas Hickman Tye around the turn of the twentieth century. It was still in this location when the streetcar made its journey. The building also featured a tower on the southwest corner that served as an aid to navigation. In later years the business was located on View Street near Quadra, not closing until the 1970s. There is now a modern building on the Yates Street site. It was a BC government liquor store outlet for many years.

546 Yates Street, 2022

538 and 536 Yates Street

DATE OF CONSTRUCTION: 1880S; 1860S?

The buildings at 538 and 536 Yates have now been legally consolidated but were separate entities in the early days. 538 Yates was built by A. Gilmore in 1888. T.B. Pearson & Co. Wholesale Woollens were the tenants by 1892. The building was vacant in 1907. A striking feature of the building is the decorative work over the windows, the metal cornice and brackets, and the iron pillars at the entrance. Its neighbour at 536 Yates was first mentioned in an 1860 city directory listing for Webster & Co. Wholesale and Retail Dealers in Boots, Shoes, Leather and Findings. It was the first brick building on Yates Street. James Webster was murdered in 1862 in a case of mistaken identity that was the talk of the town for several days and was front page news in the *Daily Colonist.* The buildings have been recently restored to bring them up to modern codes and to highlight the historic architectural features.

536–538 Yates Street, 2022

534 Yates Street

DATE OF CONSTRUCTION: 1896

534 Yates Street, 2022

The Smith, Davidson & Lecky Building at 534 Yates Street was built for Thomas Earle's firm of wholesale grocers in 1896. Architect Thomas Hooper's design features two large bullet-like finals on the upper edges of the upper storey. The high arched front façade allowed the maximum penetration of light into the workspaces. The building illustrates the introduction of steel to building technology and the new commercial styles gaining popularity in Chicago and the American mid-west. In 1907, it was the home of Cammel Laird & Co. of Sheffield who were steel manufacturers specializing in mining drill and tool steel, steel rails, shoes, and dies. In 1909 the firm, the British Columbia branch of a well-established Sheffield, England enterprise, gained a licence "To carry on business as builders of ships and vessels of all kinds, whether for warlike purposes or for other purposes whatsoever; to carry on business as manufacturers of armour plates and all other descriptions of armour and all accessories thereto and of ordnance of all kinds, including guns, gun carriages, torpedoes and of ammunition, missiles and explosives of all kinds , and all kinds of apparatus for use in connection with the same." This building was restored in 2008 and converted to residential units with retail on the main floor.

524 Yates Street – Simon Leiser Building

DATE OF CONSTRUCTION: 1896

One of the most striking buildings on lower Yates Street is the Simon Leiser Building at 524 Yates. This warehouse, designed by architect Alexander Charles Ewart in 1896, is richly embellished with terra cotta rosettes and a corbelled and bracketed cornice. The interior featured the latest in technology with an electric freight elevator. To facilitate the handling of goods, two lines of track were laid on every floor; they crossed on the elevator itself, which was fitted with a turntable so that a loaded truck could be run into the elevator from any direction then be moved to any part of the building with a minimum of labour. After the sinking of RMS *Lusitania* on May 7, 1915, this building was damaged during the anti-German riots that ensued. Most of the windows were broken, and glass littered the street. For many years in recent times, this was the home of the Capital Regional District but was declared unsafe due to seismic concerns. After their move to a new building on Fisgard Street, the building was sold and was restored and converted to residential units with retail on the main floor in 2008.

524 Yates Street, 2022

516 Yates Street

DATE OF CONSTRUCTION: 1883

Architect H. O. Tiedemann built a two-storey L-shaped brick and stucco warehouse at 516 Yates Street for Sidney John Pitts in 1883. The Italianate-style structure was built to accommodate "the requirements of his rapidly increasing business." Pitts was a wholesale grocer and importer of provisions. His building had frontages on both Yates Street and Waddington Alley, wrapping around its neighbour at 518 Yates. He was born March 14, 1850, in London, England, to John Henry Pitts and Marian Hopkins. Sidney was educated in France and London. Soon after the discovery of gold in California and British Columbia, the family moved to Victoria. Then 15 years of age, he completed his education at the Collegiate School in Victoria and entered the law office of John Copeland. After Mr. Copeland moved away from Victoria, Sidney Pitts entered commercial life as a wholesale commission merchant. His firm became one of the largest wholesale importing houses in British Columbia. He was president of the Victoria Board of Trade for a number of years prior to his retirement in 1907. He married Margaret Williams in 1881, and their first child was born in 1882. He was a familiar figure in Victoria in the early days. He was fond of horses and drove a dog cart. He brought from England a Daimler car, one of the first autos on the island. Sidney and his wife Margaret had five children at the time of the 1891 Victoria census. She died in Victoria in 1900 while he lived until August 1, 1942.[80]

516 Yates Street, 2022

Pitts owned several properties around Victoria and lived on St. Charles Street, so his business must have been very profitable. This building, like its neighbour at 518 Yates Street, was used by the Salvation Army Harbour Lights program for years until the organization built a new structure at the other end of Waddington Alley. It was restored in 1990 by the Canadian Hostelling Association.

510–512 Yates Street

DATE OF CONSTRUCTION: 1891

The last building on the north side of the 500-block sits at 510–512 Yates. Built in 1891 by Alex Phillips on the site of his early soda water factory, it was for years the home of Henderson Bros. wholesale druggists. This firm had been established in

1858 as Charles & Alfred John Langley (Victoria & San Francisco) and, as noted in the *Victoria Daily Colonist* of June 2, 1896, business would be carried on under the firm name of Langley & Henderson Bros. following the death of Alfred Langley in April. Joseph Newlands Henderson moved to Vancouver to take charge of the firm's business there, while Thomas Morrison Henderson and his brother William remained in Victoria. Shortly thereafter, on June 13, 1896, the firm decided to "withdraw from the retail business" and directed their former customers to Charles E. Jones for their future prescription needs. They continued the wholesale business in the two cities for many years. Around the turn of the twentieth century, the firm became known as only Henderson Bros. When the streetcar turned onto Government Street, Henderson Bros. was still in the Yates Street location. It would last there until a move to Fort Street in 1910. The building was for many years the home of Chez Pierre restaurant. It is now the home of Chimac Korean Pub and Fried Chicken restaurant.

510–512 Yates Street, 2022

503–527 Yates Street

DATE OF CONSTRUCTION: LATE 19TH CENTURY

Although most of the south side of the 500-block of Yates Street is not visible in Harbeck's movie, it is nonetheless historically important. This side of Yates Street was cut into small portions by a series of alleyways and streets, some of which remain today. In 1907, businesses were Joseph Boscowitz & Sons, fur dealers at 503 Yates; Harry Donkin & Son, commission agents at 507 Yates; Paterson Bros. wholesale fruits, at 511 Yates; and Lenz & Leiser Ltd. wholesale dry goods at 517 Yates. The buildings that housed these businesses between Wharf Street and Commercial Alley were demolished and replaced by modern structures beginning in 1947.

503–507 Yates Street, 2022

533 Yates Street, 2022

533 Yates Street

DATE OF CONSTRUCTION: 1887

East of Commercial Alley at 533 Yates Street was the Boucherat & Company Building, built in 1887. This two-storey brick structure was home to their liquor merchandising business. Luke Pither took over the business, changing the name to Pither & Leiser. By 1916, the building housed the Turkish Sulphur Baths and was later used by Smith, Davidson & Wright Paper Company. It was also used by Switzer Frozen Foods in the 1970s.

During the 1990s, the Victoria Native Friendship Centre was located on an upper floor of the building, serving as an important hub for Indigenous peoples in Victoria.[81]

In later years, the storefront became a fish and chips restaurant, and then a Pizza Hut outlet. In 2009, it was a Caribbean restaurant, and in 2022, it houses El Furniture Warehouse restaurant.

535 Yates Street

DATE OF CONSTRUCTION: 1900

The Pither & Leiser Building at 535 Yates was built by John Hepburn in 1900. Hepburn was a successful Klondiker who invested in property development. The *Victoria Daily Colonist* of January 13, 1900, notes that: "the rapidly increasing business of Messrs. Pither & Leiser necessitated a larger premises and work will be at once commenced on a modern warehouse and office building for them on the premises immediately adjoining their present quarters, now occupied by the old American hotel and smaller wooden stores. The property on which these buildings stand was recently purchased by Mr. John Hepburn. The contract for the new building has already been let by the architect, Thos. Hooper and as stated before, work will be commenced at once and pushed to early completion. The brick and stonework will be in the hands of Messrs. Elford

533 Yates Street, 2022

and Smith." By 1908, Pither & Leiser had moved their main office to the corner of Wharf and Fort Street. Although the building has lost its cornice and pediment with nameplate, it is still a handsome structure. It was restored in 2009. In 2022, it is called the Arcade with several outlets including Cinnaholic, Saint Cecelia Coffee, and IllusionXR.

555 Yates Street

The next building up the block, at 555 Yates Street, was occupied by John Piercy & Co. wholesale dry goods in 1907. At that time, this was on the corner of Court Alley and Yates Street. The land between Court Alley and Langley Street was home to the Bank Exchange Saloon and Restaurant that at one time was owned by H. Siedenbaum, the owner of the Palace Saloon. It seems to have changed ownership on a regular basis and was constantly in the news for liquor infractions during the years around the turn of the twentieth century. These buildings were demolished when the Bastion Square Parkade was built.

555 Yates Street, 2022

565–579 Yates Street

DATE OF CONSTRUCTION OF ORIGINAL BUILDINGS: 1880S

565–579 Yates Street, 2022

The block between Langley Street and Government Street was home to a variety of businesses in 1907. They included Bissenger & Co., hides; the Bank of British North America; Martin Mitchell & Co, brokers; Arthur R Sherwood, real estate; Leonard McLeod Gould, stenographer; Alfred Caiss, barrister; William B Smith, undertaker; and W. G. Allen's newsstand. All these buildings, along with their counterparts along Government Street, were demolished in preparation for the construction of the new Dominion Post Office that was completed in 1949.

When the streetcar came down Yates Street, it made a wide turn onto Government Street. This allowed the viewer to see the northwest corner of the 1300 block of Government Street. As these areas were very important to the commercial core of Victoria in 1907 – and are integral structures in the early history of Victoria – they are included in our coverage of the journey.

1312 Government Street

DATE OF CONSTRUCTION: 1892

Perhaps the most visible building from this corner is the New England Hotel at 1312 Government Street. The Steitz brothers, Fritz and George, built the original New England Restaurant in 1858 and sold it in 1876 to Henry and Louis Young, immigrants from Bavaria. In 1892, they demolished the building and built a new luxury hotel designed by John Teague. The design used iron structural piers throughout, while the interior featured hot water, electric heating, and full-length windows with red plush drapes. There was a restaurant on the main floor, a richly decorated dining room, and rooms for private parties. Michael Young died in 1934 and the hotel went into liquidation. It was somewhat restored in 1968 and was the home of Ivanhoe's Restaurant for years. However, in February 1978, the hotel was closed for good when the owner could not afford to make the building comply with the fire regulations of the day. The lower storey was used for commercial enterprises, but the upper storeys were vacant until the building was acquired by Chris LeFevre in 2010. It has since been redeveloped into rental accommodation with retail on the main floor.

The New England Hotel, 2022

1308 Government Street

DATE OF CONSTRUCTION: 1900

At 1308 Government Street was the Excelsior Saloon built for Dr. F.W. Hall in 1900 by noted Victoria architect Thomas Hooper. It is a very sparsely decorated building but does sport a decorative brick cornice. In 2009, it was home to a bookstore and in 2022, it's a gift shop.

1308 Government Street, 2022

1306 Government Street

DATE OF CONSTRUCTION: 1902

The building at 1306 Government Street was built in 1902 for Hy Siedenbaum, owner of the Palace Saloon at 578 Yates Street. In 1907, it was home to Frank LeRoy tobacconist and John Dean real estate. It is still used for commercial purposes and serves as a link to early Victoria. In 2022, it is the site of a jewellery store.

1306 Government Street, 2022

1300 Government Street

DATE OF CONSTRUCTION: 1896

1300 Government Street, 2022

The building on the corner of Government and Yates Streets is the Adelphi Block. Designed by Thomas Hooper and built in 1896, it takes its name from the Adelphi Saloon that had formerly been on this site. It was built by the BC Land Company as a speculative store and office space. H L. Salmon, tobacconist, occupied the main floor for many years while the upstairs was used as the BC Electric Railway employees' room in 1907, as the streetcar travelled by. In 2009, the building was the home of Field Shoes. It was completely renovated in 2021–2022 and is now an eyewear outlet.

We now return to the buildings on Government Street that the streetcar passed by. These represent the heart of the city's commercial district at that time.

1239–1245 Government Street – Colonial Hotel

DATE OF CONSTRUCTION: 1875
ARCHITECT: JOHN TEAGUE

The British Colonist of July 7, 1875 reported that the plans for the new Colonial Hotel, designed by John Teague, had been released to reporters. The article outlined the lavish appearance of the new building which was to replace the old wood structure that had been destroyed by fire on June 7, 1875. It is one of the oldest surviving masonry commercial structures in downtown Victoria. Along with a corner entrance for the hotel, the streetscape also featured storefronts. One of the first to occupy was the San Francisco Baths. This new building is a good example of Italianate commercial architecture and is a visual landmark, even in modern Victoria.

1239–1245 Government Street, 2022

By 1892, the BC Cattle Co. had its meat outlet here, and by 1902, it was the home of the Victoria Printing & Publishing Company, Barber Bros. Novelties, and BC Candy Kitchen. In 1907, when Harbeck's streetcar made it way past the building, it was occupied by Victoria Printing & Publishing Co.; Anton Zarelli, bootblack; and the British Columbia Market Co. Ltd. For many years in the 20th century, it was the home of the Poodle Dog Restaurant which had moved down the street from 615 Yates.

In 2009, the building housed a retail clothing outlet and a small restaurant. In 2022, Street jeanswear is housed on the Government Street façade, while Honey Bun is on the Yates Street side.

1223–1245 Government Street

In 1907, the buildings along this portion of Government Street were occupied by: Fletcher Bros. musical instruments; Senate Saloon, bar; H.E. Munday, boots and shoes; Maryland Restaurant; Diego Zarelli, bootblack; and the Horseshoe Saloon. It is interesting to note that both Fletcher Bros. and H.E. Munday later moved their businesses to Douglas Street.

1223–1245 Government Street, 2022

In 2009, a modern building here housed Sasquatch Trading, Roots – shoes and clothing, Rocky Mountain Chocolate Factory, and a jewellery outlet. By 2022, the tenants are Sasquatch Trading, Roots, Out of the Mist Gallery, and Migration.

1221 Government Street

W. & J. Wilson is Victoria's oldest firm of clothiers, founded in 1862, the year the City was incorporated. They always conducted business from this location. This building was the result of a complete rebuilding of an earlier one, that may have dated to the late 1870s. The building reflects the growing confidence in the City of Victoria at a time when many older buildings were being replaced by Edwardian-styled masonry and stone structure.

1221 Government Street, 2022

When the streetcar came past in 1907, the older building was still here.

In 2009, the firm was still operating from the historic location, but it closed at the end of summer 2021 as the company moved its operations solely to the suburbs.[82]

1204–1244 Government Street

In 1907, the west side of Government Street held a collection of late–19th-century commercial buildings. Government Street was still the heart of the business district, although there had been some movement to Douglas Street.

The list of businesses illustrates the diversity of this portion of the street.

1244 Government – Royal Guarantee and Trust Co.
1242 Government – Northern Pacific Railway Co.
1240 Government – Robertson and Griffith – real estate
1238 Government – Glass & Mailing – real estate
1236 Government – F. Proctor – dentist
1236 Government – Ernest Hall – physician
1236 Government – William Blair – photographer
1234 Government – Swinerton and Oddy – insurance
1232 Government – Hall Goepel & Co – insurance
1232 Government – Hall & Walker – coal
1230 Government – Liberal Association Rooms

1230 Government – George H. Hayes – dentist
1228 Government – Cyrus H. Boyes – druggist
1226 Government – Arthur E. Bowers – tobacconist
1224 Government – McPherson & Fullerton Bros. – real estate
1222 Government – Pacific Coast Steam Ship Co. – ticket office
1220 Government – Standard Stationery Co. – stationery
1218 Government – Danes & Ruckhaber – barbers
1216 Government – E. Andernach – jeweller
1214 Government – Jens Sorensen – tailor
1214 Government – Grubb & Cayzer – real estate
1214 Government – Albert Toller – real estate
1214 Government – Joseph Peirson – auditor
1212 Government – George W. Dean – real estate
1212 Government – Great North West Telegraph Co.
1212 Government – Western Union Telegraph
1210 Government – B. C. Permanent Loan and Savings Co.
1208 Government – B. C. Permanent Block
– Week Publishing
– William C. E. Blakemore
– A. Maxwell Muir – architect
– Canadian North West Oil Co. Ltd.
– Mitchell's Realty – real estate
– W. C. Sheldon – real estate
– YWCA
1206 Government – National Finance Co. Ltd.
1204 Government – Northern Bank

This entire block of buildings was replaced by the new federal Post Office (Percy Leonard James, James & James, Architect, 1948–1952). This five-storey complex was originally conceived as a make-work project in 1936 but was delayed due to depression and war. The project was not completed until 1952 due to its size and complexity. Ironically, this was also the site of the first post office and is the third at this location. The Post Office had previously been located at the corner of Government and Wharf Streets.

1204–1244 Government Street, 2022

The Post Office was diversified in the late 20th century and the building redeveloped to include offices and retail on the main level. It was renamed P. L. James Place to honor the architect responsible for the design. In 2022, the storefronts on Government Street are Running Room and Eddie Bauer.

1200 Government Street – Bank of Montreal

DATE OF CONSTRUCTION: 1897
ARCHITECT: FRANCIS MAWSON RATTENBURY

Although he was not yet finished with the Parliament Buildings, Rattenbury won the competition to build the first new premises in Victoria for the Bank of Montreal. The site was once occupied by the home of Thomas Harris, Victoria's first mayor. The bank was the architect's first work in the Chateau style, a blend of Renaissance English and French architecture, that he would use to advantage in the later Empress Hotel. The walls were sheathed in Nelson Island ashlars of granite and Haddington Island stone. The interior featured intricate plaster and fine woodwork. Located at the termination of View Street, it was a landmark then and remains one today.

1200 Government Street, 2022

When the bank moved its headquarters to Douglas Street in 1925, this became an office for the BC Bond Corporation (H.E. Boorman, manager). In 1931, the premises were renovated and enlarged to serve as a branch of the Bank of Montreal to relieve the stress on the Douglas and Yates Street branch.

After use as a clothing store, the building was converted to the Irish Times Pub in 2004. At that time, the plaster work was restored, wood finishes were renewed, and period lighting installed. This use continues today.

1150 Government Street – Bank of Montreal

DATE OF CONSTRUCTION: 1878

This two-storey commercial building was built for John Wilson who also owned the Garrick's Head Saloon (located behind this building on Bastion Square). In 1907, it was operated as a saloon.Over the years, it has housed may different businesses, including barristers due to its proximity to the law courts.

The front façade was altered in 1910 when the windows were changed from arched to square openings.

In 1986, this building was one of six that were consolidated into the Alhambra Project. The interiors were gutted, façade material that had been added over the years was removed, recessed entrances were reinstated, and recycled materials and reproduced architectural detailing was used wherever possible.

In 2009, it was the home of Breeze Clothing Store but in 2022, it is part of an expanded Garrick's Head Pub.

1130–1140 Government Street

Thomas Napier Hibben, who had been a San Francisco bookseller came to Victoria in 1858 and later formed a partnership with Mr. Bone. The firm, which retailed books and stationery, acquired this three-storey structure in the 1890s when the Colonist newspaper moved to Broad Street.

1130 and 1150 Government Street, 2022

In 1907, the tenants were: J. Howard Champion, manufacturer's agent; Chartres C. Pemberton, real estate; J.C.M. Keith, architect; George Morphy, barrister; Universal Brotherhood & Theosophical Society; Federal Life, insurance; and Charles D. Miller, draughtsman. In 1913, Hibben hired architect Thomas Hooper to add two storeys to make it an office building.

In 1986, this building was also part of the Alhambra Project as noted above.

1116 Government Street

DATE OF CONSTRUCTION: 1882; ALTERATIONS 1909
ARCHITECT FOR ALTERATIONS: THOMAS HOOPER

John Smeaton had this two-storey brick shop built at a cost of $2,000. The building was noted as a dry goods store in a plumbing permit dated February 28, 1895. The name at this time was the Westside.

In 1907, this was the home of the Ideal Shoe Store and Sea & Gowan – men's furnishings. The December 3, 1908 *British Colonist* reported that "an important deal has just been consummated whereby E.A. Morris, tobacconist, has purchased the premises now occupied by the Ideal Shoe Company, on Government Street, between Fort and Bastion Streets. As soon as the latter concern moves out, Mr. Morris will proceed with the fitting up of his new premises, which will compare favorably with the elaborate and expensive fittings of his Vancouver store."

The Ideal Shoe Store's last day of business was October 30, 1909 and the extensive renovations began thereafter.

The interior was designed to emulate a High Victorian gentleman's club. The doorway is of Mexican onyx and the domed leaded window above blends with the interior ceiling mirrors, making the store seem larger than it is. In the centre of the floor is an electrolier on an onyx pedestal. During the renovation, the original counters were replaced with mahogany ones. The exterior features glazed brick on the upper storey and a fine name plate. The interior is still remarkably intact, virtually unchanged since 1910. A visit is like walking into an early 20th century store.

1116 Government Street, 2022

Today, E.A. Morris Tobacconist still occupies this space, although changes to local bylaws have made some signage changes necessary and there is an age restriction for entry.

1110 Government Street – Mahon Building

DATE OF CONSTRUCTION: 1907
ARCHITECT: WILLIAM RIDGWAY WILSON

This two-storey Edwardian Classical Revival brick structure was built for Edward Mahon, a real estate agent and member of the firm Mahon, McFarland & Proctor. He was involved in much of the planning of North Vancouver. This building, clad in glazed brick replaced an earlier structure that had burned.

In 1907, Ogilvie Hardware Co. Ltd. occupied the main floor with Homer Burgess, dentist; Globe Agency Ltd.; A.B. Ellis, real estate; Canavan and Mannell, real estate; William Blair, photographer; and Griffen W. Jones, financial agent in the upper storey offices.

1110 Government Street, 2022

It was known to generations of Victorians as the home of Spencer's Department Store, the place to find obscure items that were not stocked by any other outlet. Spencer's specialized in camping gear, tools, footwear, and clothing.

In 1986, this building was also part of the Alhambra Project as noted above.

1108 Government Street – Royal Bank of Canada

DATE OF CONSTRUCTION: 1909–10
ARCHITECT: THOMAS HOOPER

In 1907, when the streetcar travelled down this part of Government Street, there was a different building here. The long-time home of Jacob Sehl's BC Furniture outlet was occupied by W. Bownass Hardware Store. The building site was originally part of Fort Victoria and is almost exactly between the chief factor's residence and the men's quarters. Following the dismantling of the fort in 1864, the land was sold, and brick commercial buildings went up.

1108 Government Street, 2022

In July 1909, citizens of Victoria learned of the "fine premises for Royal Bank that would soon grace Government Street, immediately south of the premises occupied by E.A. Morris." This Edwardian Classical bank building combines a Roman entrance-arch with Tuscan columns and Renaissance pilasters in a glorious interpretation of the dignity of the Edwardian bank. Built with two storeys, the basement contained a shooting gallery where bank employees could be prepared to cope with a hold-up. The second storey was removed in the 1980s and the main features of the original banking hall obscured.

Bookseller Jim Munro purchased the bank in 1984 and, within seven months, had restored the former banking hall for use as a bookstore. During the process, he uncovered original plaster that had been hidden in the 1980s and uncovered other fine features. The bookstore continues in the same location today.

1102 Government Street Southgate and Lascelles Building

DATE OF CONSTRUCTION:
C. 1869; ADDITIONS 1887

1102 Government Street, Southgate and Lascelles Building, 2022

This building was originally built as a one storey structure for J. J. Southgate and H. D. Lascelles' general merchandising firm. Southgate was a local politician, real estate speculator, and businessman. The second storey with elaborate window surrounds was added in 1887. At that time the building was occupied by Lenz & Leiser Wholesale Dry Goods. The building features a bracketed cornice, brickwork, pilasters, and strong lines.

In 1907, the building was the home of the Canadian Pacific Railway office. Victorians will remember this office, which remained open for several decades. In 2009, the storefront was vacant and in 2022, is the home of Lugaro Jewellers.

1101–1211 Government Street

In 1907, the east side of Government Street between Trounce Alley and Fort Street held a collection of late–19th-century commercial buildings. The list of businesses illustrates the diversity of this portion of the street.

1211 Government – Lewis and Evans Hub Cigar Store
1209 Government – J. Wenper – jeweller
1207 Government – Heisterman and Co. – insurance
1205 Government – Great Northern Railway Line – railway office
1203 Government – Miss E.L. Coffey – dressmaker
1203 Government – Mrs. T. Campbell – chiropodist
1203 Government – Skene Lowe – photographer
1201 Government – Allen and Co. – Fit Reform Wardrobe – quality men's clothing
1127 Government – T.N. Hibben & Co. – stationery
1123 Government – H. Young & Co. – dry goods
1117 Government – David Spencer – dry goods
1113 Government – Victoria Book and Stationery Co. Ltd.
1111 Government – William Langley – barrister
1111 Government – William Foxall – photographer
1109 Government – Baker Shoe Co. Ltd. – shoe store
1107 Government – Finch and Finch – men's furnishings
1105 Government – George Morison & Co. – druggists
1101 Government – Five Sisters block: Royal Bank of Canada

Fort Street frontage and office in upper storeys of the Five Sisters Block

1. F. M. Rattenbury – architect
4. Norah Laugher – advertising writer
5. Samuel Maclure – architect
6. John Nicholson – real estate
8. Thomas Parr – surveyor
11. Hooper and Watkins – architects
15. Mason and Mann – barristers
17. Harry Dier – dentist
21. Sedger and Pounall – architects

22. Gavin H. Burns – broker
22. William Wallace Grime – broker
23. Victoria Chess Club
24. John Adair – commission agent
25. John Savannah – photographer
28. Vernon G. Forbes
32. Mrs. Leonore Munoz – domestic
35. Canavan & Mannell – timber and mines
36. Joseph L. Forster – vocal teacher
38. James Patterson
42. V. I. Fire Underwriters
44. R. H. McMillan – commission agent
45. Mrs. Amelia Haggert
46. Miss Woolridge – dressmaker
49. Leonard C. Harris – manufacturing jeweller
+ 22 other tenants using building as a residence

In 1910, disaster struck this area when a huge fire destroyed almost every building in the area bounded by Trounce Alley, Government, Fort and Broad Streets; only the Times Building at the northeast corner of Fort and Broad survived. David Spencer who had lost his retail outlet in the fire, seized the opportunity to buy the damaged Driard Hotel and Victoria Theatre for $370,000, giving Spencer's store frontage on Douglas, View, and Broad Streets. The growing business was sold to the T. Eaton Co. in 1948. After the fire, the City decided to continue View Street from Broad Street through

The Bay Centre, Government Street façade

to Government, creating a new street and the frontage we have today. There was quite a debate about what the new extended street should be called; some called for View as the original View Street had run from the harbour to Cook Street before being permanently closed off in 1858. Others opted for Bastion to continue the street that existed at that time from Wharf Street to Government. A new six-storey commercial building rose on the site between Trounce Alley and the new View Street. Designed by A. Arthur Cox for the Union Bank, and built in 1912, it featured white-glazed terra cotta on the main floor, as quoining blocks, window surrounds, and for the Beaux-Arts cornice. This is now the site of retail on the main floor along both frontages with offices above.

A notable loss in the 1910 fire was the Five Sisters block which had been built in 1891 on the northeast corner of Government and Fort Streets. In a calamity for several local architects, all the plans drawn by a virtual who's who of Victoria architecture were destroyed.

New buildings arose along this street as well, and all were demolished in 1989 when Cadillac-Fairview built the Eaton Centre (now the Bay Centre) on two complete city blocks, bordered by Government, Fort, Douglas, and View (and encompassing Broad Street) in downtown Victoria.

1023 Government Street – Brown Jug Saloon

DATE OF CONSTRUCTION: 1861

Opened on January 23, 1861 by John D. Carroll, this was one of the finest public houses in Victoria. He served beer in brown bottles with a label that said "Brown Jug." In 1912, the owner took over the adjacent Albion Hotel (built 1880) to comply with the new liquor act and named the complex the Brown Jug Hotel. In 1917, the Brown Jug Saloon was closed, a victim of prohibition. For 56 years, it had been BC's most exclusive pub. About 1918, Mr. F.J. Williams turned the building into a drug store.

1023 Government Street, 2022

The building has suffered many renovations over the ensuing years and there remains little of its proud history. In 2009, it was the home of Birks Jewellers. Unfortunately, that business was permanently closed on March 26, 2022, bringing an end to the jewellery firm's presence in downtown Victoria.[83] It is still vacant.

1022 Government Street – Bank of British Columbia

DATE OF CONSTRUCTION: 1885

ARCHITECT: WARREN H. WILLIAMS

The Bank of British Columbia was an international organization and was backed by British capital. This building was their headquarters and was also the largest office building in British Columbia when it was built. Warren H. Williams was a Portland, Oregon architect who also designed Craigdarroch Castle. Built in the Renaissance Revival Style, its design is derived from the 16th century Florentine banking palazzos.

To emphasize the corner entrance of the main banking room, a Greek gable is mounted above the entrance. Above that in a roundel hovers Mercury, the Greek god of commerce. Opened on March 1, 1886, the bank featured cast iron pillars, lintels, and windows sills made by Albion Ironworks. Total cost of construction was $50,000. The site on which the bank is located is where the former bachelor's quarters of Fort Victoria stood.

1022 Government Street, 2022

Soon after 1900, the Bank of British Columbia was absorbed by the Bank of Commerce. In 1903, the Bank's most famous employee, Robert W. Service – the Bard of the Yukon – worked at a salary of $50 per month and lived above the bank vault that he guarded. He transferred to Kamloops in 1904 and then to Whitehorse.

In 1907, the offices above the bank were occupied by T.J. Jones, dentist; BC Development Association; E. Crow Baker, financial agent; Victoria Bank Clearing House; L.M. Mills, art studio; and BC Deposit and Loan Co. Ltd.

The Bank of Commerce closed this branch on January 15, 1987. It was then turned into a Christmas store. In 2008, the vacant building was acquired by publican Matt McNeill who transformed the former bank into the Bard and Banker Pub.

1017–1021 Government Street – Galpin Block

DATE OF CONSTRUCTION: 1884

ARCHITECTS: HARRIS & HARGREAVES

This was the first in a series of commercial buildings erected in the City for London-based Thomas Dixon Galpin. He was born on November 15, 1828, in Dorchester, England. He married Emma Amelia Pare in Dublin, Ireland on October 18, 1851. Although he never resided in Victoria, he invested in real estate here including buildings occupied by BC Land & Investment Agency, Challoner & Mitchell, John Cochrane, and the King Edward Hotel. He also bought large tracts of land on the mainland and owned several ranches there at the time of his death. He was a member of Cassell, Petter, & Galpin, at that time the largest publisher in the world. Through Victoria realtor and financial agent Thomas Alsop, who visited him in England, Galpin made substantial investment in mortgages and real estate in our city. He eventually bought out Alsop's firm and re-organized it into the BC Land & Investment Agency, with its head office in London. Two of his daughters married Victoria residents: Mabel Clare married the Honourable John Douglas Prentice, former Minister of Finance for the province, and Beatrice Maud married Cuyler Armstrong Holland.[84] From 1900 to 1911, the second floor of the Galpin Block was home to the Alexandra Club, formed by local women who were unable to access the Union Club, which was reserved for males only.[85] Galpin died on April 25, 1910, leaving family around the globe.

1017–1021 Government Street, 2022

The ground floor contained Pennock & Clayton Jewellers from 1890–1895 and Challoner & Mitchell from 1895–1914. In 1912, the owner of the adjacent Brown Jug Saloon took over this building known then as the Albion Hotel to comply with the new liquor act and named the complex the Brown Jug Hotel.

In 1907, the tenants were John R. Mackie, engraver, and Challoner & Mitchell, with the Alexandra Club upstairs.

One long-time tenant is the Irish Linen Store, first established in Victoria in 1910 by Scotsman John Norrie. The store moved around downtown until settling here in 1917, where it has been ever since. In 2009, the other half of the main floor was occupied by Jock and Jill, a sports clothing outlet, with government offices upstairs. In 2022, visitors can find Glam & Fam and the Irish Linen Store.

1016–1020 Government Street

In 1907, this was the home of the BC Funeral Furnishing Co. Then a two-storey building, it is now one storey and the home of Lusl cosmetics.

< 1016–1020 Government Street, 2022

1012–1014 Government Street

DATE OF CONSTRUCTION: 1890

This simple two-storey Edwardian building was originally a store and photographic gallery for Joseph Sommers. By 1907, he was sharing the premises with Fleming Bros Photographer.

Over the years it has lost its architectural details, but it is nevertheless a visual link to the Edwardian commercial buildings along Government Street. In 2009, it housed a restaurant while in 2022, it is a souvenir shop.

1012–1014 Government Street, 2022

1009–1013 Government Street – Greenwood Building

DATE OF CONSTRUCTION: 1884 DESIGNER: DENNIS HARRIS

When first built, this building contained a realtor's office and a jeweller's shop. Levi W. Myers, United States Consul, maintained a suite of offices on the second floor. Charles Redfern, who owned the jewellery store, was Mayor of Victoria in 1883 and again in 1897–1899. He was born in London, England, on October 23, 1839 to Charles Edward Redfern and Martha Allen. He was in Victoria by October 5, 1877, when he married Eliza Arden Robinson. He died March 26, 1929. One of the features of his store was a chiming clock, clearly visible in the 1907 video, and clearly audible throughout downtown.

1009–1013 Government Street, 2022

In 1907, in addition to Redfern, the tenants were A. Bancroft, confectionery, and dentists Richard Nash and A.A. Humber. For many years in the mid–20th-century, this was the home of Brand's Restaurant.

In 2009, the building was home to a gelato shop and a coffee shop, with offices upstairs. In 2022, the gelato shop is still there, with Cool as a Moose souvenirs next door and Brun Body Bar upstairs.

1007 Government Street – Bridgman Building

DATE OF CONSTRUCTION: 1863

This was one of the first brick buildings built on this block. The ground floor was built in 1863 for Christian J. Hein and the second storey was added in 1886 for Lowenburg & Harris, realtors. Dennis Reginald Harris, who was also an engineer, designed the addition. The present storefront is believed to be the work of architects Hooper & Watkins and was built about 1905 for Arthur Weaver Bridgman. The building has Italianate windows on its upper storey, as do its neighbours, adding to the rhythm of the streetscape.

1007 Government Street, 2022

In 1907, A.W. Bridgman's real estate office occupied the building. By 2009, the building was restored and housed a wine shop. In 2022, Little Blue House, a children's clothing outlet, is at this address.

1006–1010 Government Street – Promis Block

DATE OF CONSTRUCTION: 1905

ARCHITECTS: HOOPER AND WATKINS

1006–1010 Government Street, 2022

Oscar Promis was born in San Francisco April 24, 1855, the son of French immigrant Geraud Promis who had arrived in the USA in 1848. Geraud was a grocery retailer, and the family came to Victoria in 1858, undoubtedly drawn by the gold rush. They lived here until 1873, accumulating downtown property. Although Oscar returned to the USA, taking up residency in San Jose, California, at age 18, his family retained their ownership of land in Victoria until shortly before his death. In his profession as a real estate developer, he made many trips to Victoria during his lifetime.

This two-storey structure was originally named the Promise Block, a corruption of the owner's name. It occupies what was once the southeast corner of the original Fort Victoria. The upper storey features glazed brick, moulded terra cotta, and a heavy bracketed cornice.

In 1907, the tenants were Samuel G. Clemence, dentist; Pacific Loan Co., Henry S. Griffiths, architect; Charles J. Ellacott, civil engineer; Maggie Wilson, dressmaker; British American Timber Co.; B.C. Dental Supply Co.; H.H. Jones, real estate; William C. Stewart, real estate; H.J. Rous Cullin, architect; and Griffin W. Jones, real estate. For many years in the 20th century, it housed Paulin Travel.

In 2000, the building was restored and many of the original features that had been obscured in unsympathetic renovations, were revealed. In 2009, the building housed an Aboriginal Arts outlet and a souvenir shop. In 2022, Black Goat Cashmere and Chocolats Favoris are the tenants.

1001–1005 Government Street – Hamley Building

DATE OF CONSTRUCTION: 1885; ADDITIONS 1912

1001–1005 Government Street, 2022

The Hamley Building, named after its original owner, Wymond Hamley, Collector of Customs for British Columbia 1864–1871, was constructed on the site of the old Fort Victoria garden. The round-headed windows and detailing are identical to those on the Bridgman, Greenwood, and Albion Hotel buildings, so it is possible that Dennis Harris designed them all. The fourth floor was added in 1912 to a design by William Ridgway Wilson when the building was owned by Mrs. Diana Irving, daughter of Wymond Hamley.

In 1907, the tenants were A.W. Harper, surveyor; E.P. Colley, surveyor; J.M. Whitney, jeweller; and Dominion Express.

In 2009, the building housed a souvenir outlet and a soap factory. The souvenir shop is still there in 2022 and the second storefront is now the home of a candy shop.

1000–1002 Government Street – Pemberton Building

DATE OF CONSTRUCTION: 1899
ARCHITECT: THOMAS HOOPER

1000–1002 Government Street, 2022

This massive brick building features dramatic arched bays and decorated terra cotta cornice. Like the terracotta spandrels in Maclure's Temple building (525 Fort Street), some of the capitals of the piers support small faces. This was probably to show off the wares of the owner, Charles A. Vernon, who founded the BC Pottery Co. The ground floor housed the Waitt & Co. piano warehouse and Erskine, Wall & Co. grocers.

In 1907, the piano warehouse and grocers were still tenants. In 1947, the property was purchased by Pemberton Holmes Real Estate who had their offices there until the late twentieth century. When the real estate office moved to the suburbs in 1999, the building was restored and converted for retail use on the main floor with office above.

In 2009, the lower storeys were occupied by Artinas Jewellers and Out of Ireland that retails Irish imports. The same retailers are there in 2022.

921 Government Street – Weiler Building

DATE OF CONSTRUCTION: 1899

Weiler Building, 2022

Victoria's first department store and, at the time of its construction, one of the largest retail stores in Canada, was built for Weiler Brothers Home Furnishings. John Weiler came to Victoria from California in 1862 and established a furniture manufacturing business in which quality was the byword. Each of Weiler's four sons was responsible for different functions of the business.

The new building boasted 109,000 square feet of well-lit display and storage areas that were serviced by two elevators. Construction of the interior was an engineering feat which utilised a massive post and beam interior frame within a brick shell. Other features included ground floor windows floodlit at night, moulded interior ceilings, native wood wainscotting, and fire hydrants on each floor. Weiler's had a reputation for fine imports including the Liberty of London line, Voysey & Morris-designed carpets, and Turkish and Indian rugs.

George Straith Ltd., retailers of fine clothing, occupied the building from the 1940s.

The building has been well maintained over the years and remains a landmark retail presence on Government Street. In 2022, it is the home of Moose Crossing Gifts.

909, 911 and 913 Government Street

DATE OF CONSTRUCTION: 1903

ARCHITECT: THOMAS HOOPER WITH JOHN TEAGUE

What appears from the street to be one building is actually three separate buildings for three separate owners.

909–913 Government Street, 2022

913 Government Street

Charles W. Rogers established a confectionery shop on the west side of Government Street in 1885. In 1891, his original shop was torn down along with other buildings on the block to make way for the new BC Land and Investment Agency Building. Rogers resumed his business in a new shop located in this building; he remained at this location until 1917. The Rogers building formed the left site of the symmetrical three-part composition.

911 Government Street

The two outside blocks featured metal clad bay windows projecting from the second storey; the centre structure rose three feet higher than the adjoining blocks in order to accommodate a higher first-storey ceiling; all three were unified by a common metal cornice and frieze design. All three buildings contained retail facilities on the first floor, with living accommodation above.

909 Government Street

Rogers rented his building to Brown & Cooper, fish and fruit merchants. By 1905 this firm had moved to 27 Government and been replaced by W.B. Shakespeare, a jeweller. In 1909 a second jeweller, W.B. Wilkerson, was listed as occupant; he remained until 1916.

In the following year, C.W. Rogers moved his own business into the building from his former premises across the street. The building has received commemoration by the Historic Sites & Monuments Board. The interior is valued for its intact "original surviving interior fixtures and decorative detailing, including glass-fronted cabinets, curve-topped glass counters, tall wall mirrors, the ornate broken pediment above the mirrors, and the turned wooden spindle design below the mirrors."

The centre section was built for F. Moore of the Victoria Chemical Company, and the third, for Brown & Cooper, fishmonger and fruiterer. By 1907, the occupants of the three buildings were: 913 – W.B. Shakespeare jeweller; 911 – W.B. Hinton electrician; and 909 – Brown & Cooper, with H.E. Newton living above.

In 2009, Rogers still occupied 913, while 911 was home to Jade, jeweller, and 909 to Collections by 5th Avenue, fine clothing. In 2022, 911 is vacant and 909 houses The Nooks, which retails handmade Canadian products. Rogers Chocolates is still in its location and likely will be there for the foreseeable future.

910 Government Street – Harbour Centre Mall

DATE OF CONSTRUCTION: 1974

In 1891 the new BC Land & Investment Agency Building rose on this block. Among the tenants was Charles Rogers with his candy manufacturing business. The BC Land & Investment Agency was founded by London publisher Thomas Dixon Galpin who bought several parcels of land in Victoria, then bought out Alsop & Mason, realtors. The company was Victoria's principal marketer of land during the 1900–1914 boom. At one time, it owned or controlled half of the land in the Victoria area. The new building joined smaller ones in this block.

Harbour Square Mall, 2022

In 1907, when the streetcar travelled by, the businesses on this side of Government Street included the BC Land and Investment Company; Peden Bros., bicycles; Bodwell & Lawson, barristers; George Hargreaves, civil engineer; Drury & MacGum, real estate; C.W. Rogers, confectionery; George A. Fraser, druggist; BC Fur Manufacturing Co. Ltd.; and, R. Porter & Sons, butchers.

Amid great controversy in September 1974, the entire city block was demolished and replaced by the Harbour Centre Shopping Mall.

907 Government Street – London Bakery

DATE OF CONSTRUCTION: 1908 (ASSUMED)

This building is either a new building or a rebuilding of the earlier two-storey brick structure that stood on this site. In 1907, the tenant was A.W. Simmons delicatessen.

In 2009, the main floor was occupied by a souvenir store, and the upper storeys were vacant. Northwest Origins had the main floor location where it retails First Nations artwork and remains there in 2022.

907 Government Street, 2022

901–905 Government Street – Windsor Hotel

DATE OF CONSTRUCTION: 1858–59

Built in response to the gold rush by George Richardson, this was originally called the Victoria Hotel. It is said to be the first brick building in BC. It would appear that this was a popular meeting place; meetings of the IOOF were held here in 1859, and of the Pioneer Cricketers in 1860. In the 1890s when a more grandiose "Hotel Victoria" was built elsewhere in Victoria, the name of this building was changed to the Windsor Hotel.

901–905 Government Street, 2022

In 1907, the streetcar travelled by the

Windsor Hotel, John Emery tobacconist, and the Windsor Restaurant. At some time in the mid-twentieth century, the façade was given a "Tudor" treatment with stucco and black beams. In 2009 we could see Save on Souvenirs and Victoria Ice Cream and Fudge Factory. In 2022, the storefronts are occupied by the Ice cream shop and Goodfellas Cigar Shop.

809–815 Government Street – Rostein Building (now Metropolitan Building)

DATE OF CONSTRUCTION: 1903
ARCHITECTS: HOOPER & WATKINS

Joseph and Lewis Albert Rostein had this two-storey commercial block erected in 1903. It featured a series of arched bays on two street fronts and large storefront windows on the main floor. By 1904, it had acquired its new name and rented premises to Thomas Plimley's Bicycle Shop, the American consulate, and the Windsor Grocery.

809–815 Government Street, 2022

In 1907, the 1904 tenants were still there with the addition of Baxter and Johnson, office supplies; C.S. Baxter, customs broker; and M. Tsingloy, fruits and vegetables. Alterations were made in 1946 by architects Birley Wade & Stockdill. At some point, the second storey cornice was removed, and the storefront altered considerably.

In 2009, the building was home to Mirage Coffee, Pier 815 imports, and Spirit of Victoria souvenirs. In 2022, the name of the coffee shop has changed to Milano Coffee, but the other tenants are the same.

816 Government Street – Federal Building

Queen Victoria's Diamond Jubilee produced two imposing new buildings, the Parliament Buildings and a new post office. This site was the home to the new post office, opened on July 1, 1898 after three years of construction. Designed by Department of Public Works architect, Thomas Fuller, it was an imposing site appropriate for Her Majesty's government.

By 1907 when the streetcar travelled by, the building housed the Post Office with Noah Shakespeare as postmaster; the Public Works Department with William Henderson as architect; the Inland Revenue office with William Gill as district inspector; the Post Office Inspector's Office and Dead Letter Office,

Post Office as seen from the new Empress Hotel, postcard, 1907

with Evarard Hyde Fletcher as inspector; the Weights and Measures Office with Hugh Findlay as inspector; the Meteorological Office with Reid E. Baynes as superintendent; the Government Telegraph Service with Dee William in charge; and, the Dominion Customs House with William Marchant as inspector.

In 1952, postal services moved up Government Street to the 1200 block and this building was replaced in 1956 for Customs and Immigration use. The new building was devoid of ornamentation and unsympathetic to the original building, of which a section was retained to the rear.

In the 1980s, a group of local merchants petitioned the federal government to rework the design to more accurately reflect its origins. In an editorial dated April 30, 1988, the *Times Colonist* noted: "It is time to make amends for the heritage violation wreaked by Ottawa decades ago to provide once again a grand, stately entrance from the waterfront to Victoria's charming Old Town." The resulting alterations to the façade of the building was an improvement and did contain Edwardian elements.

In 2017, it was announced that the building on Government Street would be demolished, and the remaining original post office would be transformed into a set of 57 residences, which, it was claimed, would be some of the most expensive real estate ever sold in Victoria. In 2022, the project is complete and has become a modern landmark.

801 Government Street – Belmont Building

When the streetcar passed this site in 1907, it was the location of the Belmont Saloon. It originally opened as the John Bull Hotel in 1859. Jarvis Longhurst owned the Saloon from 1872 to 1891. In 1909, *The Daily Colonist* noted that

"The Belmont site is considered one of the choicest and most valuable business properties in the city. It was formerly owned by the Loewen and Erb estates, by whom it was sold to a Winnipeg syndicate about two and a half years ago. There is talk that a luxury hotel may rise there, even though the property faces the new and splendid Empress. Tourist promoters here say that Victoria is facing a tremendous influx of visitors each summer and that there will soon be need for two commodious and elegant hotels."[86] The Belmont property was eventually bought by the O'Reilly family of Point Ellice House.

In August 1911, the Belmont Saloon was demolished to make way for the Belmont Hotel tower, but plans changed, and the project became the office building with retail space on street level that we see today. The building was so expensive that the family lost a great deal of money on it. It was credited as Victoria's first reinforced concrete office building. The original building permit, issued to The Belmont Ltd. by the City of Victoria in March 1912, describes a "new reinforced concrete building, eight storey, 180 rooms, purpose: offices and stores" with an estimated construction cost of $400,000. The architect was Samuel Hoult Horton, who was active in Victoria from 1911, at first under his own name, and later in partnership with Paul Phipps. This was their best-known work. The building was described as "a substantial Edwardian commercial block constructed using the Hennebique System of ferro-concrete, a patented construction method invented by Louis G. Mouchel in 1897." It is important to note that Robert Butchart's business office was on the third floor, and it is likely that his Vancouver Portland Cement Company supplied the concrete for the construction. When I began working for the federal government in 1965, many of the floors contained the office of what was then the Income Tax Department. My desk was located on the east side of the main floor. When the department moved to 1409 Vancouver Street in 1967, various businesses were located here.

Belmont Building, 2022

In 2009, the site contained Sam's Deli, Roger's Sweet Shop, and other retail with offices on the upper floors. There have been many changes to the businesses since 2009. Today, they are Tractor Everyday Health Foods; Merchant Quarters General Store; Merchant Quarters Blacksmith Shoes; a currency exchange; and 10 Acres Commons restaurant.

Empress Hotel, 2022

721 Government Street – Empress Hotel

DATE OF CONSTRUCTION: 1904–08; ALTERATIONS: 1910–12; 1928

The Empress Hotel is an early–20th-century stone hotel, constructed in the Chateau style. It is prominently located at the head of Victoria's inner harbour. Built for the Canadian Pacific Railway (CPR), the Empress is one of a series of Chateau-style hotels built by Canadian railway companies in the early 20th century to encourage tourists to travel their transcontinental routes. Popular with the travelling public for their elaborate decor and comfortable elegance, these hotels quickly became national symbols of quality accommodation. The Chateau-style vocabulary used by the railway hotels evolved as a distinctly Canadian architectural type. The Empress signals the beginning of this evolution from a strictly Chateau-style design towards one that incorporated contemporary forms.

Built in 1904–08 to designs by Francis M. Rattenbury, the Empress was enlarged in 1910–12 to designs by W.S. Painter and in 1928 to designs by J.W. Orrock.

It is an important visual clue to the harbour – the reason that Victoria was chosen for the Hudson Bay Company Fort north of the new American border – and its proximity to the Parliament Buildings (Rattenbury, 1897) illustrates the architect's grand plan for this important harbour. Built after the draining of the James Bay mudflats and the construction of the Inner Harbour Causeway, the hotel would be the first thing that travellers arriving by water, presumably on a Canadian Pacific ocean liner, would see.

William Harbeck was said to be so impressed by the site of the hotel rising from the ground that he stopped in his tracks and rotated his camera to catch a panoramic view of the entire harbour.

835 Humboldt Street – St. Ann's Academy

DATE OF CONSTRUCTION: 1871; ADDITIONS: 1886, 1910

When the streetcar made its journey in 1907, we can catch a glimpse of the original St. Ann's Academy with its 1886 addition as the streetcar makes its way past the Empress Hotel building site.

St. Ann's is comprised of a monumental brick-clad building and formal gardens occupying approximately 6.25 acres of land within Victoria's original urban core. The garden contains a formal processional allée created with tree rows and hedges, an orchard containing approximately 100 original fruit trees, a novitiate garden, a formally landscaped area containing several historic trees, structural remnants, formal gardens, hedges, historic paths and walkways, and additional plantings established by the Sisters of St. Ann around the Academy building and along sections of the site perimeter, and a perimeter wall and gates.

Arriving in Victoria in 1858, the Quebéc-based Sisters of St. Ann responded to the educational and nursing needs of the West Coast by opening a succession of convents, hospitals, and mission schools throughout British Columbia, Yukon and Alaska. Their success created a demand for larger accommodations in Victoria which was met by construction of the first section of the present building in 1871, then by further additions in 1886 and 1910. From 1871 until its closing in 1973, St. Ann's retained its stature as an important educational institute and continues to symbolize the Sisters' contribution to education and social service in Western Canada.

The distinctive architecture of St. Ann's Academy reflects the strong influence of French-Canadian religious orders during a formative period in the history of British Columbia. It was the largest building in the province in 1871 and remained the tallest masonry building in Victoria for most of its history. While the 1871–86 and 1910 sections of the building embody the neo-baroque

St. Ann's Academy, 2022

characteristics of 19th-century Quebéc convent design, the chapel is a unique transplantation of traditional 17th- and 18th-century Quebéc ecclesiastic design tradition to the west coast. Built as the original Roman Catholic cathedral in Victoria in 1858 by Brother Charles Michaud, the original timber framed building was moved to its current site and incorporated into the academy complex in 1886. The heritage value of the chapel resides in its well-preserved interior massing and design features.

The building was rehabilitated in 1997, with the main portion of the building seismically upgraded and converted for office use. The original chapel and the 1871 portion were restored as an interpretive centre and administrative offices for the national historic site.

501 Belleville Street – Parliament Buildings

DATE OF CONSTRUCTION: 1897; ADDITION: 1915
ARCHITECT: FRANCIS MAWSON RATTENBURY

The BC Parliament Buildings dominate the architectural landscape of Victoria's Inner Harbour. Construction of a new parliament building was first authorized by an act of the provincial legislature in 1893, the Parliament Buildings Construction Act. The province, anxious to show its growing economic, social, and political status, engaged in an architectural competition to build a new legislative building in Victoria, after outgrowing the previous wooden buildings, colloquially known as "The Birdcages" (built in 1859 for the Colony of Vancouver Island).

The Parliaments Buildings, postcard, 1907

Parliament Buildings, 2022

Francis Mawson Rattenbury, an English immigrant, won the competition over 64 other architects, despite being only 25 at the time. Rattenbury and his crew focused the construction of the BC Parliament Buildings using, as much as possible, local materials, resources, and expertise. Features include gold and silver leaf, murals, ornate plaster details, and wood mouldings ornamenting the richly hued walls and ceilings. Visitors also encounter marble columns, statuary, stained glass, as well as unique architectural flourishes. The original budget was $500,000; the final cost was $923,000. Although completed in 1897, the buildings were not officially opened until February 10, 1898 to commemorate Queen Victoria's Diamond Jubilee.

Over 3,000 light bulbs that outline the building were turned on in June 1897 and some did not require replacement until 1976. The gilded statue atop

The Inner Harbour, postcard, 1908

the dome is Captain George Vancouver, the first European to circumnavigate Vancouver Island.

In 1901, a visiting King George V (then the Duke of Cornwall) praised British Columbia's Parliament Buildings as one of the finest examples of architecture in the Dominion. Phase two was completed in 1915 at a cost of $1.2 million. Over $40 million was spent to restore the buildings in 1973.

Inner Harbour and the Gorge

In the afternoon, William Harbeck travelled by sea through the Inner Harbour and the Gorge Waterway and back to just past the Empress Hotel. The sites and buildings he passed are documented here.

The Sealing Fleet

Early Victorians took advantage of the natural resources of the area, including the seas teeming with different species. The sealing industry was well established and driven by the European demand for seal pelts. In 1889, 32 sealers left Victoria and brought back pelts valued at $247,170. The entire sealing industry was Victoria-controlled.

Coincidentally, sealers' wages were a main source of revenue for hotels, rooming houses, eating houses, saloons, and the retail trade. City ship chandlers fitted out not only Victoria-based sealers but also those from Nova Scotia, Newfoundland, and U.S. Pacific ports which chased the seals to Alaska.

Postcard of sealing, 1907

The 1901 census listed sealers, the majority of which were young single men. By 1905, the industry was in decline largely due to a drop in the price for sealskins in 1897, largely due to over harvesting. The Americans were alarmed at the drop in the seal population and took action to decrease the catch. The May 7, 1907 *Victoria Daily Colonist* reported that the sealing fleet had returned from its coast cruise and noted that the catch was a very low one. There were only 9 ships with "1,039 skins which at their present value will be worth about $25,000." The heyday of the sealing industry was over for Victoria.

When the Americans declared the entire Bering Sea to be their territorial waters and limited the sealing season, the Victoria and British vessels could not operate profitably, so left the majority of the business to the Japanese and Russians. The seals still continued to decline in numbers as those countries took too many. The result was the 1911 Pelagic Sealing Treaty, where the U.S., Russia, and Japan agreed to limit hunting and to turn over a share of the sale proceeds to Canada in return for a complete abstention of Canadian vessels from sealing.

The Gorge

The Gorge is a historical inland sea where past generations of Victorians would spend summer days swimming, sunbathing, canoeing, rowing, and generally lazing around.

Swimming in the Gorge

The photographer travelled under the Point Ellice (Bay Street) Bridge. In 1896, this was the site of a horrific accident when a streetcar, designed to carry 60 people was drastically overloaded with 142 passengers, caused the bridge to collapse under its weight. Fifty-five people died in what still stands as North America's worst streetcar incident.

In the past, the houses of the wealthy lined the Gorge, and some remain today, although most are gone. Point Ellice House, the home of the O'Reilly family, is still served via water today. Visitors can be dropped at its dock just as happened over a century ago.

The reversing falls was a tidal phenomenon located at the narrowest point in the Gorge Waterway. During certain tides, large volumes of water attempted to flow through a narrow, shallow opening, creating a "reversing falls" with a current of up to 6 knots (11 kilometres per hour/6.5 miles per hour) and up to 5.75 feet (1.75 metres) difference in the water level on either side. The rocks that caused the tidal phenomena were removed in the mid-20th century.

The Gorge swimming area once had diving towers and was the site of several competitions. Recreational boating such as kayaking, canoeing, and rowing is practiced in the Gorge, with rowing limited to the lower portion. Many of

Postcard of activities on the Gorge, 1907

the historical industrial sites in the Selkirk Water of the lower Gorge have been replaced with residential housing, except for a scrap metal recycling operation. The Selkirk train trestle has been converted to a pedestrian and cycle bridge that forms part of the highly used Galloping Goose multi-use trail.

The Selkirk waterfront is located at the north end of the trestle and was once a working sawmill, one of many along this body of water. Today it is home to the Victoria Rowing Club as well as a newly developed residential area with office buildings, restaurants, businesses, and a school.

The Gorge waterway, 2021

Johnson Street Bridge and E&N Railway

The Johnson Street Bridge spans the gap between downtown Victoria and Victoria West and defines the entrance to the Upper Harbor. It has for years been the major land link to Esquimalt and the naval base there.

The bridge that we see in the 1907 video was replaced in 1924 by a bascule-type bridge. The Strauss Bascule Company Limited who held the patents on the design, prepared the design for the bascule spans and the operating machinery. Joseph Strauss later went on to design the Golden Gate Bridge in San Francisco. The superstructure of the bridge was fabricated in Walkerville, Ontario, and contained 100 tons of steel. The City of Victoria Engineering Department built the sub-structure of the bridge. It required 10,000 cubic yards of concrete. The main opening span was 148 feet in length and when in the open position, was balanced over a 45-foot fixed span. It was opened in 1924, having cost $918,000 to construct. In 2018, a brand-new bridge was opened with bike paths and walkways.

Steaming over the bridge in the video is one of the Esquimalt & Nanaimo Railway locomotives. The history of the railroad begins when British Columbia joined confederation in 1871. Under the terms of union, the federal government was required to start construction of a railroad joining British Columbia to the rest of Canada. In return, the province of BC was to grant a band of public land of up to 20 miles (32 km) in width along either side of the railway line to the federal government for it to use in furtherance of the construction of the railway.

In 1873, Prime Minister of Canada Sir John A. Macdonald had stated that Esquimalt, British Columbia, the site of a naval base, would be the terminus of the "Pacific Railway." However, both the federal government and the Canadian Pacific Railway placed a low priority on construction, as it had low traffic potential and would duplicate an existing steamer service. Although construction began on the section between Yale and Kamloops in 1879, nothing happened on Vancouver Island despite personal intervention by prominent politicians.

Robert Dunsmuir was interested in taking on the railway project, and in the coal reserves, a railway land grant would provide. He went to Ottawa in 1882 and made his case. The government originally chose the Vancouver Land & Railway Company, controlled by Lewis M. Clement of San Francisco, for the job. When Clement and his company failed to come up with the necessary funds, the government quickly moved to accept Dunsmuir's terms.

In 1883, the British Columbia government signed a contract with Dunsmuir to build a railway between Esquimalt and Nanaimo in exchange for the same grant of land that Clement had negotiated, amounting to 800,000 acres (3,200 km^2) plus a cash grant of $750,000 from the federal government. That amount of land, almost 20% of the entire island, included all known coal deposits. Shortly afterwards, Dunsmuir and three partners (Charles Crocker, Collis P.

Huntington, and Leland Stanford of California) incorporated the Esquimalt & Nanaimo Railway with Dunsmuir president and owner of one-half of the shares.

Construction of the railway took three and a half years. On August 13, 1886, the last spike was driven at Cliffside, about 25 miles (40 km) north of Victoria. The spike was gold, and the hammer was silver. Prime Minister Macdonald drove the last spike during his only visit to British Columbia. The railway was extended to Dunsmuir's mine at Wellington in 1887 and into Victoria in 1888. It was extended west to Port Alberni in 1911, west to Lake Cowichan in 1912, and north to Courtenay in 1914.

The E & N Railway was originally to have been built all the way to Campbell River, but that plan fell through due to the outbreak of World War I. From 1905 to 1999, the E & N was owned and operated by the Canadian Pacific Railway. VIA Rail took over operation of CPR's passenger train service (called The Malahat) in 1978, while the CPR de-marketed its freight operation, claiming that freight traffic was declining. In 1996, the CPR reorganized the E & N as an "internal short line" named E & N Railfreight while its rail barge operations were sold to Seaspan Intermodal.

In early 1999, shortline operator RailAmerica purchased the route from Nanaimo to Port Alberni and leased the balance of the line. This RailAmerica subsidiary was named E & N Railway Company (1998) Ltd. and used the reporting mark ENR (the reporting mark EN was still owned by CPR), thus maintaining the historic name associations for the Vancouver Island line. The railbed is no longer used as it requires substantial upgrading to make it feasible.

Pendray House and Businesses

William J. Pendray started his soapworks in 1875 at the corner of Humboldt and Douglas Streets, on the north shore of the James Bay Mudflats. At one time, the factory turned out 40,000 pounds of soap a week. The first telephone line in Victoria was installed between the soapworks and Jeffree's Clothing Store (owned by his uncle) at the corner of Government and Yates Streets in July 1877.

The Pendray House, 2022

Following the construction of a stone retaining wall and the draining of the mudflats in 1900, Pendray sold his land to the CPR. At about the same time, he acquired the Canada Paint Company, changing the name to British

Topiary at the Pendray House, postcard, 1907

America Paint Co. (known as BAPCO). Jacob Sehl had founded a furniture factory at Laurel Point in the late 1870s, but when the building was destroyed by fire, Pendray purchased it for his expanding business and moved operations to Laurel Point, joining other industries in the area. It is likely that he chose the new site for its proximity to his home. BAPCO paint was still being produced into the 1970s.

In 1895, William Pendray and his wife Amelia commissioned architect Alexander Charles Ewart to build their family home. Located at 309 Belleville, it was an instant landmark. Rising two and one-half storeys from the ground, the home features a Queen Anne octagonal tower. The house is clad in different types of shingles in a variety of complex patterns. The entire structure contains voids and solids in a never-ending flow. The interior was as fine as the exterior with frescoes by German artists Muller and Sturn in the main rooms and fine woodwork throughout. The property was also known for its collection of late Victorian topiary in the extensive gardens.

Unfortunately these examples have been lost in the transition from one use to another. In 2009, the property was a bed & breakfast and restaurant, and that use continues in 2022.

CPR Steamship Building

After the Canadian Pacific Railway Bill was voted through the House of Commons in February 1881, the Canadian Pacific Railway Company was formed. They agreed to build the railway in exchange for $25,000,000 in credit from the Canadian government and a grant of 25,000,000 acres (100,000 km^2) of land. The government transferred to the new company those sections of the railway it had constructed under government ownership. The government also defrayed surveying costs and exempted the railway from property taxes for 20 years.

CPR Steamship Building, 2022

In 1884, the Canadian Pacific Railway Co. entered into ship ownership, and three steamers were built to operate Great Lakes services. Once the railway was completed to British Columbia, the CPR first chartered, then soon bought their own steamships. These sleek steamships were of the latest design and christened with the prefix Empress in a link to the Orient.

A Vancouver-Victoria service started in 1897, and in 1901, the ships and coastal services of the Canadian Pacific Navigation Co. were acquired. The company had a practical role in transporting immigrants from much of Europe to Canada. They also played an important role in both world wars, with many of them being lost to enemy action, including the *Empress of Britain.*

Service on the BC coast included the Vancouver-Victoria-Seattle Triangle Route, Gulf Islands, Powell River, as well as Vancouver-Alaska service. British Columbia Coastal Steamships operated a fleet of 14 passenger ships made up of a number of Princess ships, pocket versions of the famous ocean-going Empress ships, along with a freighter, three tugs, and five rail car barges. Popular with tourists, the Princess ships were famous in their own right, especially the *Princess Marguerite (II)*, which became the last coastal liner operating from 1949 until 1985.

In 1905, Francis Mawson Rattenbury built the first wooden terminal for the company, and that is what we see in the 1907 video. Later, in 1923, this would be replaced by what is considered to be Victoria's best example of Neoclassical Revival architecture, designed by Rattenbury in partnership with Percy Leonard James. Constructed of precast concrete, the new building is a temple to maritime commerce with intricate carvings. Generations of Victorians travelled via CPR Princess Ships through this terminal. In 1963, the CPR moved its head office to Vancouver, and this site was purchased by the Provincial Capital Commission. The Royal London Wax Museum moved into the main floor in 1971 and remained there until 2010.

The site is now the home of The Robert Bateman Foundation. Founded by renowned artist and naturalist Robert Bateman, it seeks to educate the public on the importance of human-nature connection.

On January 23, 2023, it was reported that the Maritime Museum of BC would be moving into the former CPR steamship building, and that the Bateman Gallery would be moving into the Douglas Street facility currently occupied by the museum.

Dominion Customs House

DATE OF CONSTRUCTION: 1876

When British Columbia joined Canadian confederation in 1871, Victoria became the westernmost point of entry to the new nation. Built in 1876 as the first Dominion Customs House, it was designed by Thomas Seaton Scott, a Department of Public Works architect. He used the Second Empire style, popular for government buildings across Canada. This building was intended to present the face of the Canadian Government to those who arrived by sea and to also provide tangible evidence to British Columbians of their new status.

Malahat Building, 2022

This is the last building that we see on the Harbeck video, perhaps fitting as the harbour is the reason that Victoria was chosen as the site of the Hudson's Bay Company fort. The building has been extensively restored and is currently in good repair. No longer used by Customs, with those facilities having been placed in later buildings, it is now home to lawyers and other professionals.

{ End of William Harbeck's streetcar journey }

821–825 Broughton Street

The Mellor Building is an Edwardian classical two-storey commercial building with main floor storefronts. Built in 1912, the building is an example of a small Edwardian classical commercial building with a residential component above. Once very common in Victoria, this is now a rare surviving example of the period.

It is an excellent example of the work of Charles Elwood Watkins, a native-born Victoria architect. With partner Thomas Hooper, he was prolific in commercial construction in the downtown area, responsible for many of the buildings that define Victoria's Old Town. The Mellor Building was built after his acrimonious split with Hooper in 1909 when he opened his own office.

821–825 Broughton Street, 2022

During the population boom between 1908 and 1913, Watkins was also one of a group of younger architects who developed modern school designs. His work began with George Jay School in 1908. He was appointed architect for the school board in 1912, constructing several examples extant in Victoria, including Victoria High School.

There is social value in the evolution of the building's tenants and merchants throughout its history. It was built by the Mellor Brothers, a well-known firm of painters and decorators, as a seven-suite apartment with a retail presence on the main floor. The firm occupied the lower storefront until the late 1940s. After the storefront was vacant for a year, Pacific Sign & Display Service moved into the main storefront.

In 1951, the lower storefront was divided into multiple units, with Gibson's Studio Photographers in one unit. Wilfred Gibson was born January 7, 1888, in Newcastle-on-Tyne, England, to William Hewison Gibson and Kate Lawson. The family came to Canada in 1889. Wilfred Gibson married Hannah Elizabeth Whitehead in Victoria April 5, 1909. She was born May 1, 1890, in Leadville, Colorado, to Matthew Whitehead and Ellen Ida Kinder. They had seven children before the marriage was dissolved on March 23, 1936. She died December 7, 1947, in Victoria. His second wife was Muriel Lily Gummeson, who was born to John Langley and Edna Brown January 17, 1904, in Brighton, East Sussex, England. She came to Canada in 1914 and married Gustaf Herman Gummeson in Swift Current, Saskatchewan, on February 18, 1926; he died in Victoria February 1, 1935. Wilfred worked as a professional photographer for 68 years, retiring in 1963. Countless school children had their individual and class photographs taken by this firm over a forty-year span during which he rarely missed an assignment. In his photographic work outside of the school duties, he specialized in children as well. He died in Victoria January 9, 1968,[87] and Muriel, February 18, 1998.

Another storefront was the home of Kool Vent Awnings, while Western Heating Products and Smith-Anderson Roofing Co. were in the others. By 1955, Alan Macey Sound had moved into the area previously occupied by Kool Vent Awnings.

In 1980, the building was extensively renovated, with the upper apartments changed to recording and broadcast facilities for C-FAX radio station; the eastern lower level was converted to a reception area, with offices to the west. Monday Publications, Trade Typesetting, and Real Estate Victoria then moved into the space. At other times, provincial government offices, a law firm, and a mortgage company shared some of the space. In 2008, C-FAX radio moved into a new facility on Broad Street, and the Nature Conservancy of Canada purchased the Mellor Building. It is now used by a dental clinic and other offices.

713 Johnson Street

THE BUILDING

Built in 1908 as a carriage factory for William James Mable, this three-storey Edwardian commercial vernacular structure features a finely detailed façade with shallow arched double-hung windows and a projecting horizontal cornice. It complements the other historic carriage works, William Grimm's carriage factory, down the street. It is part of an important grouping of heritage buildings along Johnson Street. It shares a cornice line with the 1912 Scott Block to the west, designed by L.W. Hargreaves and built for Robert Scott, a local landowner and developer.

This brick building designed by architects Thomas Hooper and C.E. Watkins replaced an earlier wooden structure that had been built on the same site in 1885. Early painted signage is still visible on the east façade, as are the chimneys.

Heritage value is found in the building's siting as part of a grouping of heritage buildings of a similar type and vintage. It represents the growth of Victoria during the Edwardian period when wooden structures were replaced with brick, reflecting the economic health and development at that time. The building is indicative of the move of Victoria from a late 19th-century trading post to a 20th-century city. As is customary in Edwardian commercial structures, the building is set right to the lot lines with no setbacks.

By the mid-1920s, William Mable changed the name of his firm to "Mable's Carriage and Auto Works," reflecting the growth of the use of the automobile in the early twentieth century. By 1929, there was no mention of carriages in his advertisement in the City directory. He had moved with the times to make his business viable:

William J. Mable
Auto repairing • Body building • Painting • Wheels
Tops Trimming • Auto Springs

After William died March 3, 1938, his widow, Loma, sold the property to Martin and Helen Boas, who rented the upper storeys to trade unions and other small enterprises; they named the building, Boas Block. Among the tenants were Victoria Labour Council, International Woodworkers, Machines Fitters and Helpers, S.J. Mott Upholsterer, James Bay Transfer, and Plan A. Home Drafting Co. The main floor was the home of Hub Furniture Company, dealers in new

Hub Furniture, 1960 M04366, COURTESY CITY OF VICTORIA ARCHIVES

If you've been following this series let me warn you that we are still on the nostalgic theme of the horse in our past. Which accounts for today's old time picture showing a carriage factory; and a tough one to ferret out. Mainly because I had to follow, through old street directories, the individual careers of G. F. Giles, carriage trimmer, and J. F. Beek, carriage painter, until I found them together. Which occurred in 1890 when they were associated with Mr. Mables' carriage factory on the south side of Johnson just east of Douglas. Which happened to be next door to Cameron & Calwell's livery stable and about opposite the Blue post Saloon.

With these facts in mind, and converting the old street numbers, one arrives at the site today. Occupied by the Hub Furniture Company.

Undated "Yesterday and Today"

and used furniture. By the mid-1950s, the furniture company was being run by Benjamin Louis, although the focus had now shifted to "second-hand goods." In 1974, Benjamin retired and sold his business to David Robinson, who made a shift in retailing to antiques and moved his business to Fort Street shortly after that. 713 Johnson then became the home of the Salvation Army Thrift Shop. By the early 1990s, the building had a new tenant, the 711 Bingo and Snack Bar.

The Mable Family

William James Mable was born in Thorvold, Ontario, November 23, 1858, the son of William and Johanna Mable. By the mid-1880s, William was in Victoria, constructing a wooden carriage factory. On March 25, 1891, he married Loma Ella Weldon, born September 29, 1868, in St. John, New Brunswick, to Loma Ella Sewell and Wilson Weldon. The family lived at 223 Russell Street in Victoria West, just down from Esquimalt Road. The couple had four children: Pearl Ethel, born May 24, 1892; Arthur William, born January 4, 1896; Loma Sewell, born November 15, 1900; and Marion Edith, born July 1907.

William worked at his business until he died March 8, 1938; Loma moved in with her daughter Pearl's family at 1301 Rockland Avenue, then to the Oak Lodge Private Hospital in Saanich, where she died June 22, 1951. They are buried at Ross Bay Cemetery.

Pearl married Henry Meadows Cowper, son of Captain Jesse Cowper and Susan Barr, in Victoria, October 30, 1914. She died October 13, 1961 and was buried in Ross Bay Cemetery.

Arthur was drafted for service during World War I on December 14, 1917. The extent of his overseas service is unknown. After the War, he became a Provincial Policeman. While stationed at Kamloops on active duty, he was killed in an automobile accident September 27, 1926. He was interred at Ross Bay Cemetery in the family plot.

Marion married William E. Nachtrieb October 19, 1929. She died in Victoria on March 6, 1964. Nothing is known about the fourth child, Loma Sewell Mable.

2022 UPDATE

In 2005, Cool Aid and AIDS Vancouver Island joined together to acquire the former Bingo Hall property for the future home of ACCESS. This was possible, in part, through a generous donation by the former owner, Fairline Foods, and a mortgage through VanCity Credit Union. In the spirit of cooperation, the building was provided as a temporary home for the Our Place drop-in site for the homeless while they were constructing their new facility. Without this support, Our Place would not have had a home and their critical services would have been lost from January 2006 through Fall 2007. This time also allowed Cool Aid to raise more funds to help bring the project to fruition.

713 Johnson Street, 2022

Throughout the rehabilitation process, careful attention was paid to the heritage aspects of the building. As the many commercial uses over the years had obliterated the original heritage features on the interior, it was gutted and seismically upgraded. New interior partitions and services were installed, custom designed for the new uses.

On the exterior, however, special attention was paid to the windows. All frames were refurbished or, when necessary, replaced by new ones, fabricated using the existing sash as templates. The work was carried out by Vintage Woodworks.

The rear courtyard was refurbished as a quiet oasis in the midst of downtown noise and congestion. Historic painted signage on the east façade was preserved.

On the front façade, care was taken to preserve the windows and the upper cornice, while the lower floor was configured for the new use.

The history of the building is celebrated with a historic plaque at the entrance so visitors will be aware of the building's rich past.

The ACCESS Health Centre brings together under a single roof the services of Cool Aid's Community Health Centre, AIDS Vancouver Island, VIHA Mental Health & Addictions Services, and other providers of health services for the Capital Regional District. Not only has this project provided long-overdue social services to those who need it most, but it also shows that a successful rehabilitation can celebrate heritage features at the same time.

845 Yates Street

THE DINSMORE BROTHERS AND THEIR BUSINESSES

This small article was published in the Spring 2005 issue of *Preserve* along with two small photographs. I have done additional research to produce a much more detailed story of the brothers and their lives.

Faded sign on brick wall, 2005

New building under construction, 2005

In the words from Canadian Joni Mitchell's song, *Big Yellow Taxi*, "You don't know what you've got till it's gone." It is pretty interesting to walk around neighbourhoods with a camera in hand. The discerning eye can detect subtle changes then record them. There are also hidden "gems" that only come to life when adjacent buildings are demolished. Such is the case of the building, which according to the painted signage on the rear of it, once housed Dinsmore Bros. The firm not only cleaned cars but also undertook repairs. A quick perusal of city directories shows that William Dinsmore began a sales career with National Motors on Yates Street in 1916; his brother James was a carpenter. By the following year, William is the manager of National Motors, and James is listed as a salesman. The brothers had learned much from their experience at National Motors. In 1928, they opened Dinsmore Bros. Garage at 845 Yates Street, just

Front of former site of Dinsmore Bros., 1965
M05607, COURTESY CITY OF VICTORIA ARCHIVES

up the street from their former employer and right in the heart of the "automobile row." Among the other businesses on this block were Auto Electric and Battery at 847 Yates as well as Whitaker and Revercomb wholesale auto parts at 843 Yates. In 1931, the company moved to larger quarters at 904 Yates Street but seems to have become a victim of the Great Depression, as the firm disappeared from the listings in 1933–1934, with William now working for Jameson's Electric and James with Shell Oil. But, of course, change is inevitable, and we can see in the 2005 photographs, the housing units on View Street are now complete, and the original building on Yates Street has been demolished and will soon be replaced by housing.

2022 UPDATE

William Hiram Eckert Dinsmore was born July 4, 1877, at Gore Bay, Manitoulin Island, Ontario, to Abraham Dinsmore and Mary Ann Spinks. His brother, James Alexander, was born February 1, 1881. The family moved to Victoria around 1897. On May 19, 1909, William married Martha Dwyer Andrews in Victoria. The next day, the *Victoria Daily Colonist* reported that the couple travelled to Vancouver on the *Charmer* for their honeymoon trip. William was a lacrosse player and referee. He was one of the officials in the 1912 Mann Cup championship, emblematic of supremacy in senior lacrosse in Canada.[88] In 1918, he played goal in a match to raise funds to support the war effort. The officials for this match were Lester Patrick of hockey fame and Fred White[89].

The family lived for many years at 1048 Princess Avenue. Around 1942, William changed his profession and became a grocer in Oak Bay. At that time, he moved to 2509 Estevan Avenue, living above the storefront. This structure had been built in 1931 as a grocery store operated by Harry O. Kirkham and later Harry O. Blakely. There were two apartments above the store, and the main floor also accommodated Sub Post Office #29. On April 12, 1951, a purpose-built

Super-Valu grocery store opened at 2510 Estevan Avenue, directly across the street from Dinsmore's store; it would have affected his business, and he retired shortly after that. He moved to 119 Moss Street and lived there for several years. William was residing at 1010 Queens Avenue when he died November 25, 1961. He left no children.

Site of William Dinsmore's grocery store, 2509 Estevan Avenue

James married Sarah Margaret Galbraith in Victoria August 20, 1913, at the home of the bride. It was a small wedding with only immediate relatives in attendance. The newspaper account of the wedding notes that the bridegroom who "is employed at Weiler Bros. received a handsome present from that firm." After a honeymoon trip to the Puget Sound area, the couple lived at 439 Belleville Street. After Dinsmore Bros. Garage was dissolved, James worked as a salesman for Begg Motors, then as an electrician for VMD and Yarrows for many years. He lived at 1028 Caledonia Avenue (demolished in 1966) from the 1920s to the mid-1940s when he moved to 442 Montreal Street. He was residing at 1422 Harrison Street (demolished May 6, 1981) when he died November 15, 1970, leaving no children.

Peacocks and ducks in Beacon Hill Park, which is opposite the first few blocks of Cook Street

Cook Street

In which the properties on this major north-south artery are presented.

1 Cook Street

Built in 1912, Dashwood Manor is a two-and-one-half-storey Arts and Crafts Tudor Revival mansion located on Victoria's Dallas Road waterfront at the corner of Dallas Road and Cook Street, across from Beacon Hill Park. The estimated cost of the home was $15,000.[90]

H.T. Whitehead, who at the time was in a partnership with E. Stanley Mitton, used the Tudor Revival style firmly associated with Samuel Maclure. These buildings feature stone foundations, half-timbering, cedar shingles, bay windows, prominent entrances, and dormer windows, and are usually considered landmark buildings. The draining of lands to allow the construction of the Empress Hotel led to the land boom of 1907–1913, when much of the Fairfield Farm estate was surveyed into building lots for middle-class housing. The homes built in the vicinity of Dallas Road (named for Sir James Douglas' son-in-law Alexander Grant Dallas) tended to be better constructed and more costly than those further to the east. No expense was spared with "slashed grain in the hall, dining room in oak, drawing room ... richly plastered cornice and ceilings." The foundation and lower floor have walls of solid granite and the interior features a built-in electric vacuum system.

The use of the British Arts and Crafts Tudor Style by the architect harkens to the origins of many Edwardian immigrants and their aspiration to create a house

1 Cook Street, 2022

from "home." Herbert Thomas Whitehead was born in England and arrived in Victoria in 1911, where he opened an architectural office with E. Stanley Mitton who was already well known in British Columbia for his designs in Shaughnessy, the newly created subdivision in Vancouver. The partnership generally produced houses in the Arts and Crafts style with English precedents.

The original owner was Arthur Lineham and his wife, Eleanor Madigan, whom he married in Victoria April 13, 1898. Arthur was born at Newark, Nottingham, England, January 27, 1871, to Francis Lineham and Eliza Trueman. After completing his education in England, he worked in South America and South Africa, spending time in the Kimberley goldfields. He came to Canada in 1889 and was one of the first employees of the BC Light and Power Co., subsequently called the BC Electric Railway Company, and managed the light and power department. He later was a realtor in partnership with Ronald Grant (Grant & Lineham). When J.S.H. Matson purchased *The News Advertiser*, Mr. Lineham moved to Vancouver as manager. After the formation of *The Sun* and the demise of *The News Advertiser*, he moved back to Victoria and resumed his real estate career. He served as a City of Victoria Alderman in 1921, but ill health forced him to resign his position. Once he had recovered, Arthur worked to bring tourists to the natural beauty of British Columbia, making trips to New Zealand and many points in the province of BC. He was an active member of the Chamber of Commerce, serving as a director and a member of the trade group, and retained his involvement with the Real Estate Board. Arthur died suddenly December 6, 1923, while on a trip to California.[91] Eleanor continued to live in the house until about 1937. She died in Victoria, June 23, 1952. Both are buried at Ross Bay Cemetery.[92]

The house sat empty for two years, and, in 1940, William and Caroline Munsie converted the property to the Caro-Line Apartments. William Harris Munsie was born to William Smith Munsie and Catherine Dunn at Victoria, March 6, 1889. He married Caroline Cecilia "Carrie" Helmann in Seattle, Washington, December 18, 1912.[93] William's father was the co-owner, with Theophilus Elford, of the Shawnigan Lake Lumber Company, the partners having purchased it shortly after William Lossee established it in the late 1880s. When William's father died, he assumed one-half of the company and operated it with Frank and Ray Elford. The company prospered until the Great Depression affected finances. There were also three fires, the latest in 1935, and after that, William sold his shares to Christopher Boyd. On August 14, 1943, the Shawnigan Lake Lumber Company closed permanently.[94]

The house remained as a rental operation until 1978, when Derek Dashwood purchased it and converted it into Dashwood Manor, a successful bed-and-breakfast inn. It is still a familiar landmark on the Dallas Road waterfront.

15 Cook Street

This house, built in 1913, is a two-storey cross-gabled Arts and Crafts residence located across from Beacon Hill Park and close to Victoria's waterfront. It is sited to take advantage of the views and sea breezes, particularly from the sleeping porch on the second floor, reminding us of Edwardian interests in health and quality of life. The building exhibits the pride in craftsmanship that is the hallmark of the Arts and Crafts movement, while its solid foundation anchors the building to the land. The home represents the building boom after the building of the Government Street causeway and the draining of the swamp land to the east to enable the construction of the Empress Hotel. It was during this time that much of south Fairfield was developed. The boom ended just before World War I when the world lumber market crashed.

John Grant Miller was the first owner of the property, although his family never lived there. He was born in Wick, Scotland, in 1881 to Donald Miller and Christina Sutherland and came to Canada about 1913. He worked as a stonemason and married Elizabeth Sutherland, who had also been born in Scotland, in Vancouver, March 29, 1919. The couple lived in Esquimalt until John's death September 8, 1922.[95]

The Johnston family was the first to live in the house. William Johnston was born about 1849 in Picton, Ontario, to James Johnston and Hannah Fleming. He married Rachel Herbert Hunt December 29, 1874, in Thornbury Village,

15 Cook Street, 2022

Collingwood Township, Ontario. She died March 26, 1895, at Brandon, Manitoba. A merchant, he came to British Columbia in 1915 and moved into this house with his nephew, William John Johnston, who worked as a bank accountant. During World War I, he served overseas with the 4th Battalion Machine Gun Corp and returned to Canada with the rank of Major. He worked with different branches of the Bank of Montreal, and from 1926, was in charge of the savings department of the Douglas Street branch here. That same year, the nephew married widow Esther Edge. William Johnston died November 4, 1931, and William John, April 15, 1939. Esther continued to live in the house until the late 1940s.

Elizabeth Jane Nash lived in the house by 1949. She was born Elizabeth Jane Symons November 15, 1859, in Cornwall, England, and came to Canada in 1885, where she married Frances Nash. She moved to British Columbia about 1927, living in Victoria and Vancouver, where she died September 13, 1952.

The home was designated as a heritage building in 1995, ensuring it will continue to be a local landmark.

25–27 Cook Street

This is an outstanding example of an English Arts and Crafts residence. It is located across from Beacon Hill Park. Stylistically, it combines elements of the American Craftsman Bungalow style and Victoria's Chalet style. The house is also representative of the boom years during which the bulk of the south Fairfield neighbourhood was developed. After the building of the Government Street causeway and the draining of the swamp land to the east to enable the construction of the Empress Hotel, Victoria coincidentally entered its most prolific building phase, ending just before the onset of World War I when the world lumber market crashed.

The building was designed by Harold Joseph Rous Cullin. Born in England, he came to Canada in 1904. After working in the office of Samuel Maclure for one year, he opened his own practice. Cullin worked in many styles, designing each building "to use every inch of space without loss of the artistic." He designed at least seven schools in the Victoria area, commercial blocks and apartments, and several residences, including this example, and 1134 Dallas Road for William Dobson.

Louis Sebastian Vancouver and Mary York were the original owners. Louis was born in Victoria July 29, 1878, to Joseph York and Martha Dickens. Between 1885 and 1894, the family moved back to England so the boys could be educated, but they returned after that. Louis married Mary Albert Lee at Victoria September 28, 1910. On returning from their honeymoon, they moved into a new house at 19 Cook Street but were living at 25 Cook Street a year later.

25–27 Cook Street, 2022

Louis was an auditor with the provincial government and later the boarding house manager of Miller Court. He was an outstanding athlete in soccer and cricket and a member of both the Pacific Club and the Victoria Golf Club. With his brother Will, Louis was a realtor with John E. Smart & Co. during the building boom. Will was connected with architect Cullin in 1910–1912, under which partnership, both 17 Cook Street and 25–27 Cook Street were designed. Louis died in Victoria on August 14, 1952 and is buried at Royal Oak Cemetery.

The next family to live in the house for more than a year was the Hollands. Walter Glen Cuyler Holland was born to Cuyler Armstrong Holland and Beatrice Maude Galpin September 13, 1889, in Surrey, England. He married Janet Miriam Grace Tupper, daughter of Sir Charles Hibbert Tucker, December 30, 1915, in England and moved to Canada. The family was involved in the BC Land & Investment Company for years, moving to the Vancouver area later. Janet died December 21, 1971, in Surrey, BC,[96] and Glen followed her April 5, 1972. They were survived by one daughter and three sons.[97]

William Arthur Patrick Garrard, a boat builder, lived here for three years. He was born at Victoria to Major William Garrard and Violet Downes in 1906. His father served in the South African War and World War I, being twice wounded in the Battle of the Somme and was well-known for his regular attendance at Remembrance Day ceremonies.[98] After moving to Vancouver, William married Mary Margaret Hope September 18, 1934.[99] He died suddenly May 12, 1937, leaving behind his wife and infant son and was buried at Ocean View Burial Park.[100]

Alfred Howard Hebb called 25 Cook Street home for five years. He was born December 3, 1886, at Lunenburg, Nova Scotia, to William Howard Hebb and Ada Sarah Heisler.[101] He married Marie Juanita Roman about 1911, and his son Harry was born in 1914. Alfred worked as a general agent for the Great Northern Railway while he lived here. The family moved to Vancouver, where Maria died December 3, 1969.[102] Alfred followed her January 5, 1971.

Lawyer Arthur John Patton lived here from 1934 to 1939. He was born in Markham Township, Ontario, November 20, 1880, to William Francis Patton and Martha Lamoureux. The family moved frequently over the next 30 years, residing at The Dalles, Oregon; Scarborough, Ontario; Victoria, BC; and Seattle, Washington. Arthur married Myra Shakespeare in Seattle, December 3, 1906,[103] and brought her to Victoria, where they lived until his death September 24, 1958.

Gladys Dacre Jancowski was the next resident, living here until 1943. Born October 29, 1888, in Durham, Ontario, to William Barrett-Lennard and Margaret Lettia Boswell,[104] she had married Richard Frederick Jancowski in 1909 at Wabamun, Alberta.[105] Richard was born in Ontario and came west in 1908, residing in Alberta before he came to Nanaimo in 1912. He was a pioneer resident of Nanaimo and Gabriola Island. From 1912 to 1928, he operated a "passenger and excursion boat between Nanaimo and Gabriola Island." He was well known on the coast and also at Stewart, BC, where he was engaged in mining. He died January 9, 1953, leaving Gladys with three sons and two daughters.[106] Gladys continued to live in Victoria and died there April 15, 1970.

From 1943 to 1958, siblings Robert, Thomas, and Agnes Linn owned the property and lived here. They were all born to Thomas Brown Linn and Agnes Orr in Scotland. The family came to Canada, where their father homesteaded in Mannville, Alberta, with the first application made May 2, 1904.[107] He died in Mannville in 1928, aged 90. When Agnes died December 12, 1952, she still had property in Scotland to the value of £658.17s.1d.[108] The family continued on the family farm until they moved to Victoria. Agnes, born August 2, 1871, died November 21, 1954; Thomas, born April 5, 1877, died January 17, 1958; and Robert, born March 3, 1873, died June 4, 1962.

The home at 25–27 Cook Street was designated a heritage building May 8, 2003. The designation also includes an inglenook fireplace in the living room and the entry foyer, including the original lamp, radiator, waterglass stained glass, wood beams, burlap panels, and woodwork.

59 Cook Street, 2022

59 Cook Street

One of the most in intriguing homes in Fairfield is 59 Cook Street. The building, designed by noted Victoria architect Thomas Hooper, is best known for its semicircular front porch with double-storey classical columns. The house has fourteen rooms, including a finished basement, panelled and beamed dining room, living room, den, and six fireplaces. The interior also features oak floors, two sets of pocket doors, and four bathrooms. Exterior features include a porte-cochère and two verandahs. In addition, plans show a "Chinaman's apartment" (accommodation for a live-in Asian servant) in the basement. The building permit with a value of $15,000 was issued on June 6, 1912, right at the height of the building boom in Victoria.

Development of the land in this area was enabled when municipal authorities decided to drain the Fairfield marsh and culvert the Fairfield streams. The construction of the causeway on Government Street in 1904 began the process of drying out the land. In 1908, James Douglas' grandsons, one of whom maintained a home near Moss Rocks, overlooking the neighbourhood, began selling large parcels through the BC Land and Investment Agency Ltd. At one time, the company owned or controlled half of the land in the Victoria area. Smaller lots of the Douglas land were sold up to 1909. The creation of a residential infrastructure during this period, with development along a strict rectilinear grid, similar to that in downtown Victoria, reminds us of speculative confidence in the early years of the twentieth century in the anticipated growth of the city population.

Thomas Hooper was born in Devon, England, in 1857. His family moved to Canada in 1871, settling in London, Ontario, where Hooper apprenticed as a carpenter and joiner after completing his education. The family followed the booming Canadian economy to Manitoba and finally to Vancouver in 1886, arriving months after the fire that destroyed much of the city. Establishing a private practice in 1887, he was responsible for significant commercial, religious, industrial, and domestic commissions throughout the province. In the 1890s, Hooper established a Victoria office, although he maintained offices in both centres. Hooper is known for residential work in Victoria, including Pinehurst (Battery Street, 1890) and Haterleigh (Kingston Street, 1902), his own home. By this time, Hooper was well established as an architect and had changed his focus to large-scale commercial and institutional projects, calling himself a "specialist in steel-framed structures." Major commissions included E.A. Morris Tobacconist (Victoria, 1909), Revelstoke Courthouse (1911–1913), Chilliwack City Hall (1910–1912), Vernon Courthouse (1911–1914), ice arenas in Victoria and Vancouver (1911–1912), later additions to St. Ann's Academy (1910), the Carnegie Library (1904), and several buildings for the Royal Bank of Canada.

The first owner was Miss Christina Louise Haas. She appeared in Victoria City Directories for a few years. Passenger records indicate a person of this name travelled from Victoria in 1900 and 1902 to California to visit a brother, Charles. Research by several historians has now established that Christina belonged to a farming and merchant family that settled in Solano County in the 1850s. Their youngest child was named Charles. A daughter named Christina appears in the US census listing in 1870 and 1880, disappears in 1900 and 1910, then reappears in 1920. Christina Haas was born April 5, 1862, in Dixon, Solano County, California. The 1870 US census shows her aged 8 and living with her father, Matthew Haas (born in Prussia in 1821) and her siblings, Henry (13), Amelia (11), Annie (10), Josephine (9), and Charles (6).[109] Her mother, Johanna Seidel, who had been documented on the 1860 census, does not appear in future records, so it must be assumed that she died between 1860 and 1870. Matthew Haas, who had become a naturalized US Citizen on September 1, 1857,[110] died November 8, 1875, from an accidental gunshot wound in Mendocino County, California. His minor children were placed under the guardianship of William E. Gerber with the sum of $150 per month to be paid from November 11, 1875, for their support.[111] Christina was aged 13 at this time. By 1880, she was living with her sister Josephine in Ukiah, Mendocino County, California, with an occupation of "keeping store."[112]

When she came of age in 1883, she received her share of her father's estate and later used those funds to purchase two properties in Victoria. According to travel records, Christina had travelled from Victoria to San Francisco on the

Umatilla on November 25, 1902, and the record notes that she had previously made this trip in October 1900 and was meeting her brother there.

She arrived in Victoria about the time that Stella Carroll, the city's notorious madam, was leaving and, as Stella had done, Christina took over an established brothel, acquiring Alice Seymour's house at 715 Broughton Street that drew clientele from the nearby Union Club and the Driard Hotel. However, she wanted to have an exclusive property outside of downtown. Thus, Christina commissioned Thomas Hooper to design the magnificent house at 59 Cook Street. It is said that her girls were well groomed and well dressed, and some were even married with children.[113] Their occupations were often listed as salesclerk or dressmaker, all for a sense of respectability in early 20th century Victoria. Christina operated her high-class operation until 1919 when she sold the property and moved back to California. There is no record of her anywhere in Canada after that. She died November 14, 1938, in Westport, Mendocino County, California and is buried in Rose Memorial Park Cemetery in Fort Bragg, Mendocino County, California.[114]

John Edward Day was the next owner of the property. He was a fascinating character who exemplified the entrepreneurial spirit of the late 19th and early 20th centuries. Born in Gibraltar, the son of Englishman John Edward Day and his wife Catarina Fasha, November 22, 1862, he entered the Royal Navy in 1880. He served aboard *HMS Express* from February 7, 1880 to October 7, 1881, then between November 1, 1881 and May 17, 1882, he moved to *HMS Excellent*, a shore establishment in Portsmouth. Initially housed in a number of hulks named *HMS Excellent* since 1830, it was formally established in 1869; it moved ashore in 1891 and remained active as a "stone frigate" until 1985, when it ceased to be an independent command. Several ships were renamed *HMS Excellent* while serving as homes or tenders of the establishment. Following his training, he moved to *HMS Jumna*, an iron screw troopship. His next posting would have been an interesting one as a crew member on *HMY Osborne* from July 20, 1883 to December 31, 1884. The vessel was a paddle steamer Royal Yacht, launched on December 19, 1870, to replace the yacht of the same name formerly known as the *HMY Victoria and Albert*. It was used for cruises to foreign countries and, later, on the short run to Queen Victoria's residence, Osborne House on the Isle of Wight. For the next four years, Day served aboard *HMS Triumph*, a Swiftsure-class battleship launched in 1870. His final posting with the Royal Navy was *HMS Amphion*, a Leander-class protected cruiser. This class of ships was used primarily for trade protection. When *Amphion* berthed at Esquimalt on July 9, 1890, he left the Navy "at his request" and began civilian life there. He would soon become a major player in the hotel and brewing industries.

Shortly after his arrival, John purchased the Esquimalt Hotel, which he owned until it was taken over by the navy in 1943. John married Jessie Wilson Price September 24, 1890. She was born in 1863 in Barrhead, Renfrewshire, Scotland, the daughter of Henry Price and Margaret Wilson, and had landed in New York April 30, 1875. She was accompanied on the trans-Atlantic voyage by her grandmother, Elizabeth Price, and her brother, Joseph, as well as her stepsister, Elizabeth Price. The family travelled across the continent, where they eventually settled in Metchosin. By 1881, she lived with her father, Henry; uncle, Richard; grandmother, Elizabeth; and her brother Edward.

By the 1891 Canadian census, John and Jessie Day were living in Esquimalt with her brother Joseph boarding with them. John Edward soon became involved in the brewing industry. In 1902, Robert Tate and his sons Frederick and Reginald had built a brewery on a one-acre lot on William Street, where his son Fred brewed Silver Spring Old English Ale and a fine stout. In November 1908, this business was sold to a former employee of the Victoria-Phoenix Brewery, Harry Maynard, and his associates John Edward Day and Philip Crombie. Their brewmaster was Adolph Brachat, who had been a brewer with Anheuser Busch in St. Louis, and whose father was a master brewer in Switzerland. Silver Spring Brewery acquired the old Fairall Brewery site at the corner of Catherine Street and Esquimalt Road and built a modern new brewery in Victoria West, donating their former location for a playground for students of Victoria West Public School. In 1910, when Adolph Brachat's son Victor was born (Vic would become a longtime brewmaster at New Westminster's Lucky Lager-Labatt's Brewery in later years), Silver Spring offered its first lager beer. By 1928, Silver Spring Brewery was amalgamated with the Victoria-Phoenix Brewery under the Coast Brewery's corporate flag. The company was dissolved in 1959 when Lucky Lager Breweries Ltd. absorbed it.

Over the next few years, John and Jessie lost six children – four stillborn and two daughters who lived for only a few days. The couple purchased a large plot of land on Esquimalt Road and, in 1907–08, they built a house which they named *Glenday* (now 1382 Esquimalt Road). They also built a small cottage on an adjacent lot called *Glen Cottage* (now 1376 Esquimalt Road). Jessie died February 4, 1909 and is buried in Ross Bay Cemetery. John then married Dorcas Lillian Pearson, the daughter of Charlton Pearson and Selena Pargeter, November 30, 1910. He was 44, and she was 21. John filed for divorce December 4, 1916, when Dorcas moved to Washington State. The divorce was finalized January 12, 1917. She married Jessie Swartz September 4, 1917, in Seattle and had three children. However, John did not stay single for long, as he married widow Eliza Amelia Hygh (née Pargeter) October 22, 1917; she was 43, and he was 53.

In 1919, the residence at 1382 Esquimalt Road received an extensive renovation that produced a Regency-style house. The house next door also was renovated at the same time when it was raised with a basement added. As well, the main floor was expanded, and a second half-storey was added. The Days did not live much in either house, instead renting them out to military personnel.

The following year, John Edward Day moved to 59 Cook Street. He lived there quietly with Eliza, remaining active in community activities, including the Navy League, the Naval Veteran's Branch of the Canadian Legion, Esquimalt Lodge No. 24, A.F. and M., Oddfellows order, and the Victoria Rotary Club. He was also an enthusiastic bowler and had served as president of the Victoria Lawn Bowling Club. He died unexpectedly at his residence January 30, 1944, being found slumped over a card table by his nephew, Lieutenant-Commander Ivan Day. He was survived by his wife, nephew, a stepdaughter Mildred, and a granddaughter Lola.

Shortly after John's death, Eliza moved to 911 Bank Street and died in Victoria March 30, 1954. Both are buried in Ross Bay Cemetery. From 1946, the house at 59 Cook Street was operated as a rooming house with five suites. It is still there with its trademark massive columns. Drive by and think about the fascinating people who lived there. If those walls could talk, what stories they could tell.

97 Cook Street

This excellent example of a Craftsman bungalow is located across from Beacon Hill Park in Fairfield. Built in 1911, the house illustrates the professional interest of the builder, John Avery, a contractor who pioneered the use of concrete block in home construction. Together with its neighbour to the north (139 Cook Street), it is one of the few early examples of concrete block construction surviving in Victoria. Of particular interest are the three different types of blocks used and the different colours of pointing. Craftsman bungalows expressed pride in craftsmanship, and the attention to detail in this example is remarkable, both inside and out.

The house is also representative of the boom years during which the bulk of the Fairfield neighbourhood was developed. After the building of the Government Street causeway and the draining of the swamp land to the east to enable the construction of the Empress Hotel, Victoria coincidentally entered its most prolific building phase, ending just before the outset of World War I when the world lumber market crashed.

John Avery was the original owner of the lot as well as the builder of the home and is an interesting character. He made the concrete blocks himself with the tradename, Ideal concrete building blocks.[115] He was involved in a controversy when the city expropriated land for the new Victoria High School. John Avery had his cement block plant on one of the lots on the Spring Ridge sand pits and had a contract with the previous owners of the lot for the supply of

97 Cook Street, 2022

sand and gravel. He felt he should be compensated by the city for the loss of his business operations and made a claim for $25,000. As a result, John Dean was named as Arbitrator.[116] At the hearing, John Avery made the case that he had been forced to move to a new location in the city and was thus "deprived of the privilege of getting his material, sand and gravel, at a low figure, this material being heretofore right to his hand." It was also noted by the city that Mount Tolmie Sand & Gravel Co., recently merged with the Worswick Paving Company, would provide Mr. Avery's needed sand and gravel provided that "he located his new plant at some point which could be reached by the street cars which haul the material from Mount Tolmie."[117] In the end, the claim for damages was reduced to $3,750, which was still more than the original offer of $1,500 from the city.[118] John Avery obviously found a new site as he continued to build residences around Victoria for some time.

The first owner to live in the residence was Captain William Henry Logan, known as one of the best salvage owners in the world. Born December 5, 1861, in Liverpool, to Scottish parents Charles Logan and Sarah Ann Allcot, he began his career on sailing ships, then joined the Royal Navy. William married Elizabeth Martha Bury in the early 1880s, and their three children were all born in England. He became a master mariner and sailed as captain on vessels for the Leyland Line in the Mediterranean and North Africa. The family came to Canada, where he served as a representative for the London Salvage Association, a department of Lloyd's of London at Montreal. In 1908, he was appointed special officer and surveyor in BC and oversaw salvage operations on countless shipwrecks from Panama to Alaska. He was responsible for the salvage of several notable vessels, including the CPR Steamer *Princess May* in Alaska and the SS *Kaikyu Maru* off the BC coast. Perhaps his most notable salvage was the SS *Sesostros* off Guatemala, which had been lying several yards from the shore for eleven years and was difficult to salvage as she was lying broadside to the sea. The crew excavated around the site, dug a channel into the sea, and pumped in sea water. The SS *Sesostros* was then turned around and finally pulled into the ocean and towed to Victoria.[119] Captain Logan designed the Pacific Salvage steamer *Salvage King*, and it was on this vessel that his remains were carried to Victoria for his funeral. According to a newspaper report, "The casket, which was carried on the deck, was covered with wreaths and floral offerings from shipping firms and friends in Vancouver and was carried down the gangplank to the waiting hearse, while the silent watchers stood bareheaded." Among those who accompanied the remains were Mr. and Mrs. W. H. Logan, Jr., Andrew Wallace, head of the Burrard Drydock Company, and A.C. Burdick, manager of the Pacific Salvage Company.[120] After Captain Logan's death, his widow, Elizabeth, lived in the house until her death October 8, 1945. Their daughter, Florence, whose husband John Ross McIlroy had died in Vancouver, moved to Victoria and lived in the house with her daughter, Patricia, in 1946.

Hugh Baldwin Pratt bought the house in the late 1940s. Born December 1, 1892, in Hyderabad, India, to Benjamin L. Pratt and Edith Amelia Ball,[121] he was schooled in London, England, and came to Canada in 1909. He signed up for the Canadian Expeditionary Force in Valcartier, Québec, on September 24, 1914, and was assigned to the Canadian Army Medical Corps, serving overseas in France. On June 8, 1917, he was admitted to No. 11 General Hospital, Carmiers, suffering from a gunshot wound in the right thigh which fractured his femur. He recovered from that injury but, on March 17, 1919, contracted the Spanish Influenza and pneumonia and was dangerously ill for one week. He was discharged from the service December 6, 1919. Hugh married Madeleine Barbara Heath in Guildford, Surrey, England, in July 1919. The family moved to Canada and was living in Winnipeg by 1928, where they had two children, Alan Heath and Denis Hugh. They were in Victoria by 1931, where Hugh worked as an assessor for the Canadian government. He and Madeleine were divorced, and he married Mona Patricia Barbara Weston, an aide at St. Joseph's Hospital, in 1953. Hugh died in Victoria November 8, 1970[122] and Mona followed him on May 2, 1979.[123]

Madeleine Pratt then married The Honourable Marcus Lowther Crofton, and he moved into the house at 97 Cook Street. Her two sons, Alan and Denis, lived there as well until Denis married in Ottawa in 1955.[124] Crofton had been a soldier and was then working at service stations and car dealerships.

The house at 97 Cook Street was designated as a municipal heritage site on January 19, 1995.

139 Cook Street

This building is an excellent example of a five-room Craftsman bungalow. It is located across from Beacon Hill Park in Victoria's Fairfield neighbourhood.

The house illustrates the professional interest of the first owner and builder, John Avery, a contractor who pioneered the use of concrete blocks in home construction. Together with its immediate neighbour to the south, 97 Cook Street, it is one of the few early examples of concrete block construction surviving in Victoria. For more information on John Avery, see the article on 97 Cook Street. Craftsman bungalows expressed pride in craftsmanship, and the attention to detail in this example is remarkable, both inside and out. Of particular note is the pergola on the south verandah, a feature that rarely survives Victoria's wet climate.

The house also represents the boom years during which the bulk of the Fairfield neighbourhood was developed. After the building of the Government Street causeway and the draining of the swamp land to the east to enable the construction of the Empress Hotel, Victoria coincidentally entered its most prolific building phase, ending just before the onset of World War I when the world lumber market crashed.

John Avery lived in this house with his wife Ellen and daughter May. By 1912, Charles Herbert Dickie owned the property but never lived there. He was born September 14, 1858, in Beachville, Ontario, to James Dickie and Lucretia Burdick. He came to Victoria in 1885 to work on the railway and married Eliza Ellen Calvert here September 22, 1888. Their only son, Herbert William, was

139 Cook Street, 2022

born January 14, 1890. He then worked in the mining industry, living in the Duncan area for years. Eliza died in Victoria January 15, 1926, and Charles married Edith Amy Bennett after that. Charles served as MP for Nanaimo from December 6, 1921 to October 1, 1935, representing the Conservative party.[125] He operated a mine for years and died in North Vancouver September 17, 1947.

Charles George Guy resided here in 1913. He was born in 1869 to John Guy and Agnes Mary deNormanville in New Granada, Colombia, South America, and served in the British India Service. When he came to Victoria, he worked as a department manager for A.W. Bridgeman Company, real estate and general finance. He married Lillian Elizabeth Hobbis June 17, 1911,[126] and died January 23, 1929, after a long illness.[127]

From 1914–1920, the resident was Chinese interpreter Sick Yew Lee. Nothing is known about his life. Cecil Sit-Shiu Lee moved into 139 Cook Street in 1919. Born in Victoria September 25, 1895, to Lee Cheong Lee and Seto Yee Chun, he married Grace Won Cumyow in Vancouver August 30, 1919,[128] and the couple moved into this house after returning from their honeymoon. Cecil worked as a teller at the Merchant's Bank in Victoria, then moved to Vancouver to work in the newspaper industry. He died there July 29, 1971.

The Kramer family moved into the house in 1929 and lived there until about 1960. Hyman Kramer was born in Kreitzberg, Latvia, March 2, 1893, to Herchel Kramer and Sprenze Chazan. His family immigrated to Canada in 1916. Hyman lived briefly in Seattle, where he married Lithuanian Etta Goffe June 17, 1918. By 1921, the family was back in Canada. For years, Hyman Kramer was the proprietor of Northern Junk. After his death May 4, 1967, his son, Allan Harold, took over the business. When Allan died February 26, 1978,[129] his wife, Clara Beatrice "Trixie," assumed control of the properties. Some have been redeveloped, and others are in the redevelopment process.

1005 Cook Street

This article was published in the September/October 2010 issue of *Moss Rock Review*.

1005 Cook Street, a 1½ storey Edwardian dwelling, was built in 1906–07 for Master Mariner Leonard Pye Locke. The house was designed to suit its corner location and position at the gateway to Rockland Avenue. It features a wraparound verandah with Tuscan columns, and the steps to the entrance off Cook Street are set to the left beneath a small gable. The building has been used for different functions over the years but has retained its architectural integrity.

Captain Locke was born in Halifax, Nova Scotia, in 1852 and took training there as a mariner. By 1895, he was living in BC, working for the Dunsmuirs.

1005 Cook Street, 2022

He joined the CPR in 1901, serving in their steamship fleet. By 1909, he was Captain of the S.S. *Princess Royal* on the Alaska run. He and his wife, Emily, lived at 1005 Cook Street with their children (Emily, William, Elizabeth, James, Frederic, and Leonard) until about 1912. Leonard Pye Locke is remembered as the Captain of the S. S. *Princess Sophia* that sank on October 25, 1918, a day after she hit the Vanderbilt Reef in Lynn Canal, Alaska. All 353 passengers and crew on board were lost in the frigid waters. The First Officer, Jeremiah Chivers Shaw, was also from Victoria, living at 69 Menzies Street. Emily Locke received a pension of $20 per month under the Workmen's Compensation Act; her son Leonard received $5.00 per month.

The subsequent owners of the property were Paul Raoul Chaney (of Heath & Chaney Real Estate) and his wife, Hilda. By 1917, the home was owned by Dr. Annie Cleland, listed in directories as Mrs. Hugh Mackenzie Cleland, although her lawyer husband had died unexpectedly at age 34, November 4, 1903, many years before. She lived here and operated her medical practice from the house until about 1920. The next owners were Dr. Joseph Douglas Hunter and his wife, Anita. They lived here until 1929, when they moved to 911 Linden Avenue where they remained for many years. His medical office was at 209–715 Fort Street.

Perhaps the most intriguing use of the house was from 1930 to 1954. Captain Wilfred Ord and his wife Marion owned the Victoria School of Expression. While Wilfred had a career in the federal civil service, Marion was the school principal. They offered courses in singing, elocution, and drama. It is said that Marion started the school to help her cope with the tragic loss of her four-year-old son, John Wilfred Michael Ord, in an automobile accident in 1921 when she was here visiting her mother. The family moved to Victoria after the tragedy, presumably so Marion could have her mother's company. After Wilfred died in 1954, Marion closed the school, although she continued to live in the house until 1958. From 1956, her daughter, Anne Clemency Perrins, her husband, and daughter, lived with her. In a strange coincidence, the daughter, also named Anne, was a school friend of mine. Little did I know, or care about, the history of the home when I used to visit her in the 1950s and played on the beautiful verandah. Marion eventually moved to Vancouver and died there on November 25, 1967.

1005 Cook Street is now home to Cook Street Community Midwives, several psychologists, and a lawyer. However, it is still an important part of the streetscape of this side of Cook Street, and every time I walk by it, I recall the fun I had playing inside and on the verandah. That makes it a part of my heritage; now, the story can be shared so others can learn about it.

1009 Cook Street

This article was published in the July/August 2010 issue of *Moss Rock Review*.

In this issue, we continue our journey along the west side of the 1000 block of Cook Street. 1009 Cook Street is an example of an Edwardian house, like its neighbours to either side. It was built in 1908, at the height of the building boom in Victoria and, in particular, Fairfield. Architect William D'Oyly Rochfort designed this imposing 2½ storey Tudor Revival dwelling for Victoria dentist Sigfried Moritz Hartman.

Prominent features of the house are the massive rock base and pillars that support the main entranceway with a verandah above. Ornate bevelled glass windows frame the main entrance, while examples of stained glass can be found beside the interior staircase. The upper storey is stucco with decorative half-timbering, while the lower storey is clad with shingles with some stonework around the entrance.

Hartman was born in Aldernau, Province Posen, Germany, May 26, 1858, and was apprenticed to his home physician at age 15. Among the skills he learned were minor surgery, dentistry, and the use of the razor. On his arrival at

1009 Cook Street, 2022

Vancouver Island in 1877, Sigfried did not know the English language, so he opened a barbershop. Once he had mastered the language, he bought out Dr. Cool's dental outfit. Interestingly enough, the first set of false teeth he made was for Judge Crease, who lived three blocks away at "Pentrelew" (later the site of the Victoria Truth Centre on Fort Street). Sigfried worked as a dentist in Victoria, with offices on Yates Street between Government Street and Oriental Alley, until 1882, when he went to San Francisco to work in the same field.

In 1885, he returned here and resumed his dental work. Like his neighbour and good friend, Isador Nodek, Hartman was prominent in the Victoria Jewish community, later serving as president of the Jewish Congregation. He married Ida Rostein (born October 1864) in Victoria April 8, 1888. They had three children: Albert Gustav (born July 27, 1890), Leo Roy – also known as LeRoy (born January 1, 1893), and Bertha (born September 18, 1898). By 1915, he was practicing dentistry at 203–1029 Douglas Street in partnership with his son LeRoy. Sigfried Hartman died in a Seattle hospital April 16, 1923, of complications from kidney troubles and stomach flu. He was buried in the Jewish Cemetery in Victoria.

David R. Macfarlane, the chief accountant for the Liquor Control Board, then bought the house. He lived there until 1935, when he sold to Mrs. Mary A. Haslam, widow of Victor George. She sold in 1938 to Henry Hudson, a porter with Spencer's Stores, who lived there with his wife Lillian until 1946. Arthur Charles Bancroft, a local builder, then acquired the property and converted the home to three suites. He, his wife Rose, and their family lived in one suite and rented the others. Rose died in December 1965, and Arthur a year later. At this time, their daughter Doris inherited the property. She continued to operate the apartments until 2000.

Over the years, the condition had deteriorated, and the interior was in poor shape when a firm of accountants took possession. They completely restored the property to its former glory, rebuilding the front porch and balcony to specifications on historic drawings, repairing the massive chimneys, and installing new services. Inside, the woodwork was refurbished, including stripping of many layers of paint, and the wooden floors of Australian Gum, Brazilian Cherry, and Fir were refinished.

The home now glows with renewed life and sits as a vibrant jewel on the street.

1015 Cook Street

This article was first published in the May/June 2010 issue of *Moss Rock Review*. A follow-up article was published in the Spring 2021 issue of *Preserve*.

As a long-time Fairfield resident, I regularly walk the streets of my neighbourhood. What is disturbing to me is the decrease in the original housing stock and the proliferation of condos. One recent example that has me angry is the removal of 1015 Cook Street. Although it was deconstructed and pieces of the original materials will be used elsewhere, I mourn the loss of the beautiful old house with an interesting history.

1015 Cook Street, 2021

1015 Cook Street was an early 20th-century Edwardian dwelling that was part of a cluster of similar buildings on the east side of the 1000 block of Cook. They were rare survivors in a sea of apartment blocks and condominiums

1015 Cook Street, being deconstructed, 2021

that have largely replaced the vintage homes south of Rockland Avenue.

Built in 1908 for Isidor Max Nodek, the house featured a hipped bell-cast roof, stone entranceway, and corbelling along the rear chimney stack. Along with its neighbours to the south – the Sigfried Moritz Hartmann house (1009 Cook, built 1908 by architect William Rochfort) and the Leonard Locke house (1005 Cook, built 1906) – it was an example of the type of houses built during Victoria's building boom from 1905 to 1912. Fairfield, in general, benefited greatly from increased transportation links, notably the 1891 extension of the Victoria Electric Railway & Lighting Company line through to Oak Bay and soon grew from a limited number of large rambling estates to a thriving, middle-class neighbourhood.

Isidor Nodek was born in Adeinau, Poland, in 1869. He came to Canada in 1885. In Victoria, he worked as a stockbroker. He purchased the land on Cook Street in 1907; by 1908, he was living in this house with his new wife, Cerline. She had come to Canada in 1887 and was the widow of Isadore Braverman who had worked as a "money broker" from an office in Bastion Square and lived at 172 Yates Street (between Blanshard and Quadra). Braverman, a well-respected member of the Board of Directors of Jubilee Hospital, died in Victoria March 14, 1905, at age 75, leaving his much-younger widow (she was 40 when he died). Dr. Siegfried Moritz Hartman conducted the funeral service at the residence, and, following that, the cortege made its way to the Jewish Cemetery for last rites. Cerline was a wealthy widow, having inherited substantial real estate holdings from her late husband.

It would appear that Isidor Nodek and Cerline Braverman were married quietly in 1906 or 1907, as they were living at 1015 Cook Street by the end of 1908. In later years, Isidore's niece, Helen Boas, and her husband Martin came to live with them. In the 1930s, Nodek served as president of the Congregation Emanu-el, Canada's oldest synagogue in continuous use. In that position, he was instrumental in securing the services of Rabbi Marcus Berner.

After Cerline's death October 16, 1935, Isidore and the Boas lived in the house until his death March 24, 1945. At this time, Helen Boas inherited the entire estate as the only living relative and continued to live in the house with her husband, Martin, and their son Cyril. During this time, the Boas became owners and proprietors of 713–715 Johnson Street and ran Hub Furniture. This classic three-storey Edwardian commercial building had been built in 1908 as a carriage factory for William James Mable, replacing an earlier wooden structure on that site. Helen and Martin ran the furniture store together until 1953 when Martin died. Although Helen continued to operate the furniture business until the 1980s, she decided to sell the home at 1015 Cook Street. The Johnson Street property went through several hands and has now been rehabilitated as the ACCESS Health Centre.

The Cook Street property was then purchased by Noel F. Lax, assistant trust officer at the Yorkshire Trust Company, who converted the building to suites. At some point, the exterior was covered with stucco, and all traces of the original cladding were obscured. However, many examples of fine stained-glass windows and interior finishes remained and added to the ambiance of the building. Over the ensuing years, the building was used for a variety of residential and commercial functions, including the Jungian Counselling Centre and Champagne Salon.

The site is now home to a new four-storey building. Another link to Victoria's past is gone forever.

1015 Cook Street, 2022

1017–1023 Cook Street

This article was published in the March/April 2010 issue of *Moss Rock Review*.

Sometimes the buildings on the streets we walk on our way to our daily tasks are the most interesting if we would only take the time to look. Since I was a tiny child, Cook Street has been part of my life. I have seen many changes over the years.

I decided to examine Cook Street between Rockland Avenue and Meares Street. Starting with old City Directories at the Greater Victoria Public Library in their Public History Room, I checked the east side of the two blocks. The amount of information I found was so detailed that I found enough material for a couple of articles. Most of the construction was done on this side of the block after 1903 and before 1910, as was common in many parts of north Fairfield.

The Heritage Week Theme for 2010 was the Heritage of Sports and Recreation, so I focused on the sports-related story I discovered. The apartment

1017–1023 Cook Street, 2022

block at the corner of Cook and Meares Street was, from the beginning, four separate addresses: 1017, 1019, 1021, and 1023. The address of 1021 was for the apartments in the three-storey building, while the others were for the main floor spaces. Among the many tenants in the main floor offices were the Patrick Brothers.

The name Lester Patrick is iconic in Canadian hockey. Born in Drummondville, Quebéc, December 30, 1883, he first came to prominence in 1900 when he played for McGill University. In 1904, he was a star for Brandon in the Northwestern and Manitoba Hockey Leagues and became the first defenceman to score a goal. He played for the Montreal Wanderers in 1906 and 1907, leading them to the Stanley Cup in both seasons. His father, Joe, moved the lumber business to Nelson in 1907, and Lester and his brother Frank moved to play there. In 1911, they undertook their greatest gamble, the formation of the Pacific Coast Hockey Association. Using Patrick lumber money, they founded the league, eventually building arenas in six cities. The Victoria rink on Cadboro Bay Road (see the memorial cairn on the grounds of Oak Bay Secondary School) was Canada's first artificial ice rink. The Victoria Arena Co. head office was located at 1019 Cook Street. The 1913 Victoria City Directory notes that Lester was the general manager of the rink (his brother Frank operated the Vancouver franchise).

In 1918, Lester was player-manager for the Victoria team, later given the name Cougars in 1922, that won the vaunted Stanley Cup in 1925 and reached the final the following year, the last non-NHL hockey team to contest that trophy.

The PCHA revolutionized the game of hockey. The Patricks' influence led to the creation of blue lines, penalty shots, numbered sweaters, assists on goals, playing three lines, forward passes, the development of a farm system to nurture future players, allowing the goaltender to leave his feet to make a save, and the changing of players on the fly. Quite a contribution for a league that lasted only until 1926 due to financial problems and the inability to compete for players with the new National Hockey League.

On September 25, 1926, the Cougars' roster was sold to a Detroit group who had just been granted an NHL franchise. The name was changed to the Falcons in 1930 and to the Red Wings in 1932. The rest is history!

Lester Patrick was not done with hockey yet. He took over the New York Rangers in 1927 and led them to three Stanley Cup triumphs – in 1928, 1933, and 1940. He is perhaps best known for an incident in the 1928 final against the Montreal Maroons. When goalie Lorne Chabot suffered an eye injury, Patrick, aged 44, donned the pads and led his team to a 2-1 overtime win. In those days, teams did not carry as many backup players as they do today.

Lester Patrick's family continued the hockey tradition with his sons Lynn (born in Victoria February 13, 1912) and Muzz (born in Victoria June 28, 1916), both playing for and coaching the Rangers. His grandson Craig was a general manager with the Pittsburgh Penguins and another grandson Dick was president of the Washington Capitals.

The Lester Patrick trophy was created in 1966 to honour the executive or player who "helps expand the game in the United States." Lester Patrick died of a heart attack in Victoria on June 1, 1960.

Quite a legacy that had its humble start in a building on Cook Street in Victoria. You never know what you are going to find when you start digging!

1030 Cook Street – October Mansion: built for love

This article was published in the May/June 2008 issue of *Moss Rock Review*.

How often have you walked by the apartment block at the corner of Fort and Cook Streets and wondered about its history? The stately Edwardian building has been part of the Fairfield landscape for as long as most of us can remember. It was, in fact, built in 1910, and the story behind its construction is one of the most romantic tales in Victoria's history.

The land was purchased in 1909 by Alderman Albert Edward (Bert) Todd – Mayor of Victoria (1917–18), for the princely sum of $9,000. He was the third son of Jacob Hunter Todd of West Coast cannery fame and a sober businessman

1030 Cook Street, 2022

in his own right. He had met and fallen in love with a much younger woman, Ada Elvira Seabrook, the daughter of Bagster Seabrook, an inventor who managed the Victoria Machinery Depot.

Bert intended the land and the subsequent building as an engagement present for Ada. He was 32 years old; she was 19. The couple became engaged on October 19, 1909 – hence the name October Mansion. They were married March 16, 1910, and, by then, contractor George Mesher had measured and started the construction of the building. The total cost, including the land, was more than $48,000, or an average of $2,000 for each suite. The entrance staircase is made of marble, and the entrance lobby is still decorative. Some of the flooring is hardwood, and some of the doorways to the street have decorative windows. Through the large windows on the lower floor, you can still see the original mouldings. The exterior is somewhat clean, as befits its Edwardian style, but the use of patterns in the laying of the brick, and the parapet and corbelling add architectural interest to the structure. Rooms on the upper storeys have large windows, ensuring natural light in the suites.

Despite the difference in their ages, Bert and Ada were a devoted couple. Their honeymoon – a motoring tour of some 5,000 miles – was a true adventure. From Los Angeles, they went to Mexico and north again up the Pacific coast to Vancouver, driving mainly on normally untraveled roads. It is said that Ada became adept at putting air into flat tires. Bert promoted road projects and later became known as "Good Roads Todd." Both sent postcards home to their families in which they outlined the trip, he more sober and she with a lighter flare. However, all did not go well for the Todds. In 1927, Bert collapsed and was eventually examined by a Seattle physician who discovered he had a brain tumour. Bert died during surgery in Seattle in October 1928. Ada remarried, but her second husband died after a short marriage, and she married a third time. However, she remained in close contact with Rosanna Todd, Bert's mother, and still felt she was part of the family. The property remained in her name until her death in 1968, when it was passed to her two sons.

October Mansion stands as a perpetual reminder of the love of a man for his young bride, and the generations of tenants who have called it home have undoubtedly felt they were part of the story.

To learn about the history of their home, see 721 Linden Avenue in *The Heritage Detective, Volume Two.*

Fairfield Properties west of Cook Street

I undertook basic research on some of these properties in 2006 as part of a contract for the City of Victoria. I have done more in-depth research and enhanced the stories of those buildings. Other buildings I discovered while walking around the neighbourhood.

617 Vancouver Street

This building has always fascinated me. It is a commercial building set in what is essentially a residential area, so I decided to research its history.

The original building was purpose built as a service garage in 1911. The first operator was Henry Angus Davie, who lived at 1122 Johnson Street. He called his business Davie's Garage, and he sold used cars in addition to doing repairs, if the countless ads in the local newspaper are any indication.

When this building first arose, the Fairfield area was in the midst of a building boom. The draining of the marshlands in south Fairfield after the construction of the causeway on Government Street in 1904, meant the land could be developed. In 1908, James Douglas' grandsons began selling large parcels through the BC Land & Investment Agency Ltd., owned by Thomas Dixon Galpin, formerly of London, England. At one time the company owned or controlled half of the land in the Victoria area. Smaller parcels of the Douglas land were sold up to 1909. Most infrastructure was constructed during this period, with development along a strict rectilinear grid, similar to that in downtown Victoria. In 1890, the City of Victoria added Fairfield to its municipal boundaries and constructed Fairfield Road to connect the community to the downtown core. As the streetcar lines were extended into Fairfield, development took place along their routes. Much of the neighbourhood was subdivided in a residential building boom that ended in 1913 with the collapse of the world lumber market. Streetcars ran along wide roadways that were designed for vehicle traffic and bicycles; modern buses travel the same routes. In addition, automobiles were becoming more popular and needed to be maintained. A service station in this location made good business sense.

617 Vancouver Street, 1972 M06856, COURTESY OF CITY OF VICTORIA ARCHIVES

Henry Davie was born in Durham, England in 1868 and came to Canada in 1910 and settled in Victoria in 1911.[130] His long-time home in Victoria was at 231 St. Andrews Street. He operated this business until the early 1920s although he also managed a garage at 860 Yates Street. City Directories are not particularly useful for this address for some reason.

Mr. Davie died April 27, 1923 of complications after surgery. The news was even carried in the *Vancouver Province* where he was noted as "one of the best-known automobile men in Victoria." His funeral was held at St. John's Church, and he was buried at Ross Bay Cemetery.[131]

The second owner of the garage was David William Atkinson. He was born March 26, 1876 in County Armagh, Northern Ireland. He married Margaret Eleanor Bainbridge June 21, 1899 at St. Columba's, Southwick, Durham, England and their first three children: Dynes (1900), Thomas (1902), and Elizabeth Jane (1907) were all born in England. The family came to Canada in 1911, departing from Liverpool and arriving in Quebéc City July 21, 1911. Their son Ernest was born in Canada in 1917.

The family lived for many years at 1001 Richardson Street, blocks away from the business. When David Atkinson died September 31, 1931, his son Thomas took over the business. Thomas had married Hilda Betts May 10, 1922 at Christ Church Cathedral; the couple had two children. The family lived briefly on the Gorge, for a few years in Oak Bay at two different addresses on Victoria Avenue, and then settled in Esquimalt, where they lived at 300 Fraser Street. Thomas continued to operate the business until his death December 8, 1978.[132]

The business became Lou's Auto Repair and operated until about 2019, specializing in the repair of Volkswagens. It was extensively renovated in 2020 including new lighting, new floors, and fencing. The property was offered for sale in 2021 with a notation that it could be rezoned for other commercial use.[133] The attractive building now sits vacant. What is its future?

617 Vancouver Street, 2022

700-block Vancouver Street and the Vancouver Street Cluster

These houses, located at 725, 731, 737, and 743 Vancouver Street, 1011 McClure Street, and 1012 Richardson Street, are six extant examples of eight houses built at the end of the nineteenth century for British investor Hedley Chapman. The BC Land & Investment Agency acted as agents and arranged for the construction of the houses by contractors Bishop and Sherborne in 1894. Two years later, the Agency advised Chapman to sell due to a decline in property values. Mrs. Gertrude Cunningham purchased all lots and houses as an investment and held title until 1908, when she subdivided the property into six lots, moved two houses further down Vancouver Street to 435 and 441 Vancouver Street, and sold the remaining six. The houses that were moved made a second move to James Bay and were later demolished. This cluster clearly illustrates the early speculative rental market, a trend that began in Victoria's early building boom.

Gertrude Jeffree was born September 6, 1859, in Manchester, England, to William Joseph Jeffree and Caroline Jones. William came to North America in 1862, where he engaged in gold mining in California and the Cariboo before settling in Victoria. Here he established his business as a merchant, specializing in clothing and men's furnishings, trunks, and valises with premises at 40 Yates Street. His company was originally called W. J. Jeffree Clothing Store. The name was later changed to the Golden Rule Clothing Store. His wife and daughter came to Victoria after he had settled here. Caroline left England by ship July 20, 1868, with her nine-year-old daughter, Gertrude, arriving at Esquimalt.

William had an interest in a soap factory in Victoria with his nephew, W.J. Pendray. He brought the first telephone to Victoria in 1880. He and Gertrude went to San Francisco, California, to purchase the phones which were installed between the clothing store and Pendray's soap factory. He also owned a grocery store at Mosquito Creek, a very prosperous mining area near Barkerville, which he and a Mr. Mills owned and sold in 1870. William also owned land in Royal Oak in Saanich, which his wife Caroline's attorney sold after William's death. William and Caroline owned a house on Fort Street east of Cook Street, then called Cadboro Bay Road, away from the dust and noise of the town. In the 1970s, the home, near the Royal Bank at Fort and Cook Streets, with the address now 1116 Fort Street, was an antique store with the name Murdoch Bartholomew Antiques. William was a member of the Victoria City Council in 1877, being very interested in public affairs. He died suddenly March 18, 1885,[134] from a cold that settled in his bowels. His son, William Joseph Tresyhair Jeffree, born October 21, 1870, in Victoria, took over the clothing store after his father died. Gertrude married gold miner Robert Andrew Cunningham in

Victoria November 20, 1881. They had two children. Robert died March 17, 1935, in Oak Bay, and Gertrude died there December 2, 1945.

All the houses are identical in size and layout but have subtle differences in architectural embellishments. The Italianate styling reflects the architectural tastes of the late 19th century with these examples more modest expressions of the villas owned by more affluent owners. The occupations of early residents reflect the growth of the middle class. They are excellent examples of modest domestic architecture by architect John Teague, better known for larger, institutional commissions in Victoria such as City Hall, the Church of Our Lord, and the Masonic Temple. That he was most comfortable with the Italianate idiom in residential architecture is evident both in these examples and his larger commissions for Victoria's elite.

725 Vancouver Street

FORMERLY 47 VANCOUVER STREET

The first occupant of this house was Mrs. Ellen C. Bourchier, born on the Isle of Wight in about 1837. She lived here in 1894 and 1895 and died at Royal Jubilee Hospital January 18, 1910. Miss Julia Devereaux moved into this house in 1898 and lived here until 1902. She was born September 3, 1846, in Bermondsey, Surrey, England, to Charles John Devereaux and Sophia Tate. She was a schoolteacher who had previously lived at 55 Vancouver Street, where she operated the English Academy, a school for young women. She then taught at Angela College and worked as an employment agent. Julia died in Victoria March 9, 1920 and is buried at Ross Bay Cemetery.[135]

After two years, when the house was run as a boarding house, Mrs. Clara Amy King moved in. Born in Valparaiso, Chile, June 30, 1855, to John Allen and Susannah Jane Gardiner, she came to Canada in 1858, settling in Victoria by 1863. She married Alfred Nelson Codrington King, an accountant and a former British naval officer,[136] in Victoria, December 21, 1887. They moved to the mainland, where they had four children. Alfred died December 24, 1899, in Vancouver. She called the home "St. Bernard's" and lived here until 1911. Clara died in Victoria March 5, 1943, at age 86, having outlived three of her children.[137]

Plumber Richard Tanner lived here until 1914. Born June 11, 1874, at Clevedon, Somerset, England, to Richard Tanner and Annie Willcox, he married Flora Anne Hammond December 28, 1901, in Thetford, Norfolk, England. Their son, Richard, was born in 1906, and the family came to Victoria in 1910. He worked as a plumber when they lived here until 1914. He was living at the Bell Apartments on Cook Street when he signed Attestation Papers on January 25, 1917. He served with the Forestry Battalion.[138] Richard died in Victoria

September 25, 1955, and Flora died February 23, 1961. Carpenter John Deane Corke lived here in 1917. Born in Yorkshire, England, he lived in Victoria for ten years before moving to New Westminster, where he died October 30, 1923.[139]

Percy Stoddart lived here from 1918 to 1923. Born August 20, 1874, in Montreal, he came to Victoria in 1890. He married Barbara Elizabeth Shirley, served in World War I, then returned to Victoria, where he worked as a jeweller until his retirement in 1936 as the owner of the Watchbench at 1114 Broad Street. He died in Victoria May 20, 1950, living then at 618 Blanshard Street.[140] Walter Hichens-Smith, born in Seattle, Washington, December 10, 1893, to Walter Hichens-Smith and Fannie Margaret Weston, worked as a marine engineer. He lived here with his wife, Helen, from 1924 to 1928. Walter died in North Vancouver on September 12, 1980, of pneumonia.

725 Vancouver Street, 2022

About 1931, Thomas Charles Smith and his wife, Linda, bought this house. He was born September 27, 1881, in Bufferland, Pembrokeshire, Wales, to Thomas Edward Smith and Mary Lewis. He was a veteran of the Boer War, serving with the Durham Light Infantry. He then joined the British Army on June 10, 1907 and was discharged December 12, 1907. He came to Canada in about 1910, living in Fernie, where he married Linda Hugall July 13, 1914. He signed up for service in World War I on May 13, 1916 and was sent overseas with the 13th Canadian Field Ambulance. He was discharged at William Head as a Lance Corporal, Special Guard, Canadian Military Police Corps, April 14, 1920. His normal trade was a coal miner, and he also worked as a steward at the Royal Canadian Legion. By the time he lived here, he was retired. The Smiths rented a room to Ethel K. Gray, an agent for Sun Life, for some years in the 1940s. Thomas died August 7, 1955, in Saanich.[141]

Allan Alexander Fidler and his wife, Martha, moved into the house in 1953. He was born June 15, 1897, in St. Clements, Manitoba, to William Charles Fidler and Sophia Spence. He saw service during World War I with the 2nd Battalion Canadian Army Machine Gun Corps and moved to Victoria in 1928. He married Martha Stewart Geater, from Merritt, BC, in Seattle, Washington, November 6, 1933.[142] He worked as a launchman at HMC Dockyard and died January 31, 1958, living at this address.[143]

731 Vancouver Street

FORMERLY 49 VANCOUVER STREET

The first occupant of this residence was Helen Scholefield. Born Helen Ann Coleman Gilbert in 1845 in St. Leonard's, Sussex, England, to Henry Gilbert, MD, and Anna Maria Coleman, she married Stuart Clement Scholefield October 13, 1865, in Blofield, Norfolk, England. Stuart attended Oxford University, graduating with a BA and MA in 1868.[144] He then trained for the ministry. He was ordained deacon in 1868 and priest by 1870. He worked at Chard, Swanmore, Facecombe, and Stoke Poges in England, and then in New Westminster and Kamloops in British Columbia. The family, with their twelve children, came to Victoria in 1887. He then became rector of St. James' Church in Victoria and, in 1891, accepted the rectorship of St. Paul's, Esquimalt. He resigned his position in June 1894 due to ill health. Rev. Scholefield was visiting friends in Lytton and had gone to Kamloops for treatment from which he did not survive, dying on August 8, 1904.[145] Helen lived here until 1898, then moved back to England, where she was living by 1911. She died April 4, 1931, at Foulsham Rectory, Guist, Norfolk, England. Their son, Ethelbert Olaf Stuart Scholefield, born May 31, 1875, on the Isle of Wight, came to BC with the rest of the family and married Lillie May Corbould in New Westminster in 1907. He worked as the Provincial Librarian for 20 years and was a Fellow of the Royal Geographical Society, a Fellow of the Royal Colonial Institute, president of the British Columbia Library Association, a member of the council of the American Library Association, and honorary president of the BC Soldiers and Sailors Help Society. He was an expert on the history of BC and co-authored *British Columbia from the Earliest Times to the Present* with Frederic William Howay in 1913. He died December 25, 1921, after a year of illness.[146]

731 Vancouver Street, 2022

The next resident is listed as Mary McNaughton-Jones. She is shown as the widow of William McNaughton-Jones, physician. However, his wife's name was Annie, and there are no listings for a Mary McNaughton-Jones, so it is likely a misprint in two city directories. All other entries show her name as "Mrs. McNaughton-Jones." The correct spelling of her surname was Macnaughton-Jones.

As noted in the article on 1114 Rockland Avenue in Volume Two, Dr. Macnaughton-Jones served as the superintendent of the Dominion Quarantine Centre at William Head from its construction in 1893 until his death May 3, 1896.[147] There are obviously questions that must be asked when full access to assessment documents is once again available. In any event, Mrs. Macnaughton-Jones lived here from 1899 until 1903.

James Henry Greer and his family lived here in 1908. James was born November 17, 1865, in London, Ontario, to James Henry Greer and Maria Amelia Grant. He married Emily Pender Cudlip in New Westminster on April 12, 1888. The family lived briefly in Washington State, beginning in 1889 but was back in Victoria by 1901. James worked for years as a shipping and commission agent and died July 11, 1939, in Vancouver, Emily having predeceased him December 6, 1930.[148] Their son, Thomas Edward, born May 16, 1891, in Yakima, Washington, and known as Edward, was in partnership with Newton in the Newton-Greer Paint Co. He eventually moved to the United States and died March 9, 1950, in San Francisco.

Miss Elizabeth Harriet Jones and her sister, Sarah Hannah Jones, lived here from 1915 to 1922. They were born in Manchester, England, to Henry Jones and Mary Frances Bolas; Elizabeth on April 13, 1861, and Sarah in 1870. Elizabeth received her nurses' training at St. Mary's Hospital, receiving the silver medal for general proficiency. She came to Canada in 1893 and became a charter member of the Graduate Nurses Association and was president during World War I, when the younger nurses were overseas. Together with Sarah, she operated a nursing home on Blanshard Street and later at this address, where she died August 9, 1922.[149] Sarah closed the nursing home after Elizabeth died. She herself died in Victoria May 5, 1948.

In 1926, William Alexander Lorimer and his family lived here. He was born in Victoria, September 15, 1872, to William Lorimer, a well-known pioneer contractor, and Lily Main. He married Elsie Mae Arthur in Victoria April 20, 1905. The couple had four children. He worked for the City Treasury office for nearly twenty years. A member of the Native Sons of British Columbia, he was chairman of the committee in charge of the restoration of the old Craigflower School. In his youth, he had been a keen soccer player and had recently been active with the James Bay junior team. William died in Victoria March 8, 1929.[150]
Elizabeth Magilton moved into the house in 1929. Born June 21, 1880, in Church Ballee, County Down, Ireland, to Hugh Magilton and Sarah Jane West, she came to Canada in 1916. She worked as a saleswoman for the Hudson's Bay Company. She died in Vancouver August 10, 1946.[151]

Violet Emeline McPhee lived here in the early 1930s. She was born July 18, 1873, in New Windsor, Berkshire, England, to Robert William Coatsworth and Elizabeth Fudge, and came to Canada in 1896. She married Donald Bertram

McPhee and came to British Columbia around 1905. Donald was the lighthouse keeper at Lennard Island when he died September 3, 1929.[152] Violet died in St. Joseph's Hospital December 23, 1961, survived by her son, Percy, lighthouse keeper at Albert Head, and a daughter, Violet, who was living in Victoria.[153]

By 1939, Annie Elizabeth Cleaver had moved in with her family. Born May 2, 1861, in Belton, Leicestershire, England, to Joseph Draper and Eliza Warren, she married Charles William Cleaver in the Caistor District, Lancashire, in September 1884. Their children were all born in Croydon, Surrey, England. Charles died there May 19, 1903. Annie and her daughter, Marion, came to Canada in 1918, living in North Battleford, Saskatchewan, before they moved to Victoria in 1920. Her son, Arthur, and his wife Winifred bought this home in 1941 after moving from Saskatchewan and lived here until about 1960. Annie died May 2, 1861, then living with her daughter Marion at 1034 Sutlej Street.[154]

737 Vancouver Street

FORMERLY 53 VANCOUVER STREET

The first residents of this house were Nathan C. Mayo, a contractor; Miss Inglis, principal of a ladies' boarding school; and Dr. J.E. Steers, a physician with an office in the Doane Block on Douglas Street. Commercial merchant Henry Marymont lived here in 1895. He worked for the New York Clothing and Furnishing House at 89 Government Street. He was born in 1860 in Poland and married Anne Goldstein, an immigrant from Russia, and they had three children. By 1901, the family was living in Oakland, California, where Henry sold millinery.[155] He died November 10, 1917. Anne lived until November 4, 1957.

737 Vancouver Street, 2022

Harold Edwin Bruce Robertson, a barrister, lived here in 1898. He was born in Victoria February 26, 1875, to Alexander Rocke Robertson, Chief Justice of the BC Supreme Court, and Margaret Bruce Eberts. He was educated in Victoria, studied at the University of Toronto and Osgoode Hall, and was called to the Ontario bar in 1897. He married Helen McGregor Rogers June 2, 1903, in Peterborough, Ontario. He practiced in Victoria until 1925, when he moved to Vancouver with the law firm of Robertson, Douglas & Symes. In 1933, he was appointed to the bench of the BC Supreme Court and, ten years later, elevated to the Court of Appeal. He retired in 1955 and died in Vancouver

June 7, 1961. At the time of his death, one of his sons, Alexander Bruce Robertson, was barrister and senior vice-president of BC Electric; another son, Alan McGregor Robertson, was the president of the BC Sugar Refining Co. Limited; and a third son, Dr. Harold Rocke Robertson, was an outstanding surgeon, former acting dean of the faculty of medicine at the University of BC, and current chairman of the department of surgery at McGill University.[156]

Francis Victor Austin, who worked as a music teacher with a studio at 60 Government Street, resided at this address in 1899 and 1900. He was born in 1895 in Elma, Washington, to William Henry Austin and Lulu Elizabeth Kellerman. On November 17, 1923, he married stenographer Helen Scott in Vancouver. The couple returned to Seattle, where they spent the rest of their lives. Francis died October 4, 1979[157] and it is unknown when Helen died.

Harry Walshe Windle and his family lived here in 1900. Born in Calcutta, India, March 24, 1868, to Joseph Allen Windle and Anna Mary Walshe, he was educated in England and came to Vancouver Island in 1886, where he joined the staff of the Bank of BC in Vancouver. In 1892, he married Elene Austin in San Francisco, California. In 1896, he left the employ of the bank to search for gold in the Klondike. On his return, he lived in Victoria and then relocated to the Comox Valley, where he died May 17, 1932. Elene moved back to Victoria and died here July 27, 1953.

Clara Amy King lived here until 1904. Born June 30, 1855, in Valparaiso, Chile, to Captain John Allen Gardiner and Susannah Jane George, she moved to Victoria with her parents in 1858. On December 21, 1887, she married accountant Alfred Nelson Codrington King, who had been born in 1841 in England. They moved to North Vancouver, where their four children were born. Alfred died in Vancouver December 24, 1899, and Clara moved to Victoria in 1901, where she lived at 55 Vancouver Street, which at that time would have been next door to her new home. It was one of the houses that was moved further down the street. Amy died March 4, 1943, living on Balmoral Road.[158]

Edward Ernest Greenshaw and his family lived here in 1908. Born January 21, 1868, in Thixendale, Yorkshire, England, to Robert and Charlotte Greenshaw, he came to Canada with his brother Charles Henry in 1882. Ernest set up a hardware business in Shoal Lake, Manitoba. Harry, his brother, was at one time in Shoal Lake but soon moved to Hamiota and set up a hardware and lumber business there. Ernest married Edith Emily Castell in Shoal Lake January 15, 1896; their seven children were all born there. By 1908, the family had moved to Victoria, where Ernest set up the BC Hardware Company. Two sons, Arthur and Charles, both enlisted in World War I. Charles was killed in action September 2, 1918, and his brother, Arthur, who had just received his military medal, died of wounds September 9, 1918. They are buried in different cemeteries in France.[159] Edward died in Vancouver November 23, 1920, while Edith lived until July 16, 1947. Both are buried in Mountain View Cemetery in Vancouver.

Alexander McCallum lived here in 1911. He was born June 10, 1893, in Roland, Manitoba, to Angus Charles McCallum and Sarah Hughes. He came to Victoria in 1911 and married Constance Emma Farmer here June 4, 1917. By 1921, they were living in the Skeena region of BC but returned to Victoria, where Alexander worked as a sales manager for Union Oil. He died at St. Joseph's Hospital February 19, 1968. He was a Past Master of Mount Newton Lodge, AF & AM, BCR, and a life member of the Lake Hill Bowling Club.[160] Constance died February 22, 1974.

Emma Holmes, born about 1888 in Church, Lancashire, to John Holmes and Margaret Ellen Gudgeon, came to Victoria in 1910. She ran a boarding house in 1912.

Ewart Sidney Birt, a carpenter and real estate salesman, lived here from 1913 to 1920. He was born June 23, 1881, in Painswick, Gloucestershire, England. He was living in Victoria by August 17, 1912, when he married Hilda Heard. After she died, he married Florence Margaret Callow. Ewart died in Victoria April 15, 1946.[161] For some of the time the Birts lived here, Kate Hayman rented a room from them.

Mary Emily Philion lived here from 1921 to 1927. She was born in March 1880 in Yorkshire, England, to William Kirkby and Emma Jackson, she came to Canada in 1896. She married John Jean Guillaume Philion, a retired government clerk, about 1900; they lived in Prince Albert, Saskatchewan, and Winnipeg. They then moved to Victoria, where Mary worked for Spencer's as a sales clerk. Her husband died April 10, 1925,[162] and Mary continued to live here, leaving briefly to live in Vancouver, where she married Charles Thomas Ward. He died in Vancouver October 22, 1949, and she returned to Victoria, where she died August 26, 1971. Mary's son, John Eugene Philion, born April 25, 1911, bought the house in 1933 and lived here until 1946. He worked for the *Victoria Daily Times* newspaper, and on August 24, 1934, he married Evelyn Gertrude Cox.

Harold S. Holben, who operated Sidney Roofing, lived here from 1950 to 1952. After that, the building was operated as rooms to rent.

743 Vancouver Street

FORMERLY 57 VANCOUVER STREET

This house was empty until 1895, when Patrick Thomas Patton moved in. He worked as a bookkeeper. Frederick Hammet Worlock and H.A. Macaulay, a clerk at Spratt and Macaulay, commission and insurance agents, lived here in 1897. Frederick was born in Bristol, England, in 1848. His obituary tells us, "He came to Victoria in 1888 to join his brother-in-law, Alexander R. Green, in the banking business of Garesché-Green, which afterwards became Green Warlock & Company. Upon the closure of the firm during the 1918 flu pandemic,

Mr. Warlock went to Dawson in connection with the Canadian Development Company and was associated in this firm with Mr. Maitland Kersey for many years. Owing to his health he returned to Victoria and was for a short time interested in the salmon canning industry. Later, he joined the Victoria-Phoenix brewery in the business of which he was connected for the last 22 years."[163] He died July 30, 1926.

William Christie, the manager of the CPR Telegraph Office, lived here in 1899 and 1900. Born February 5, 1863, in Pictou, Nova Scotia, to James and Isabel Christie, he came to Victoria, where he married Christie Annie Sinclair Holmes, born in Springville, Nova Scotia, April 11, 1898.[164] He died May 23, 1922, in Onehunga, New Zealand.

743 Vancouver Street, 2022

James Jones Sargison and his wife, Laurella, lived here between 1901 and 1904. He was born in 1856 in Québec and was in Victoria by 1877. He married Laurella Silverthorn July 12, 1894. James worked as an accountant for Lenz & Leiser, wholesale dry goods. He died in Victoria May 11, 1936.

The house then sat vacant until Ellen Testar, widow of Henry, operated it as a rooming house in 1908. Linotype operator, Frank L. Mimmack, lived here in 1909. By 1911, Asa Bancroft Steele and his family were living here. He was born August 26, 1868, in Cassburn, Prescott County, Ontario, to Robert Steele and Angeline Maria Bancroft. He was a farmer for many years. On September 13, 1888, he married Sarah Priscilla Davidson. They had seven children in Ontario and then moved to West Derby, Vermont, where two more children were born. The family then came west, spending eight months in Winnipeg, before settling in Victoria in 1910. He was well-known in the city as a real estate agent. Before his death January 7, 1918, he had suffered from cancer for two years. He was survived by his wife, three daughters at home, and six sons. Two of his sons were on active service: Evan George with the ammunition column and Arthur W. with the Canadian Railway troops. William R. went with the 88th Battalion and was returned in November as being underage.[165] Son Robert Wesley Steele played professional baseball for the St. Louis Cardinals, Pittsburgh Pirates, and New York Giants between 1916 and 1919.[166] Sarah lived to age 100 and died April 19, 1965. She was survived by six children, 19 grandchildren, 49 great-grandchildren, and 16 great-great-grandchildren.[167]

Lillian McDougall, the widow of James, lived here in 1912. William Wood, who worked for the Strathcona Hotel, resided here in 1913. Edward Judson Tate and his wife, Ethel, were here in 1914. Born August 15, 1888, in Washington, DC, to Levi Lambert Tate and Ruth Foster Judson, he married Ethel McCumber April 2, 1912, in Prince Rupert. He worked here as the manager of Aldous & Murray Ltd., real estate, with offices at 305 Jones Building on Fort Street.

Agnes Hamilton Kenway lived here between 1915 and 1917 when her husband, Douglas Maitland Kenway, was serving overseas. He was born in 1855 in Glamorgan, Wales, to John Seymour Kenway and Janet Maitland. He worked as a chemist's assistant in England before being qualified as a chemist (the term used today is pharmacist). He married Agnes Hamilton Hedley April 29, 1879. They immigrated to Canada in April 1910 on the *Empress of Britain* and made their way to the west coast. When he returned from military service, they lived at 1146 Rockland Avenue before retiring to Colwood. Agnes died January 14, 1928[168] and Douglas lived until May 14, 1932.[169]

Thomas Mercer, a gardener, and his wife, Ethel, who was a clerk for John Stewart, lived here for one year, as did Mrs. C.M. Blackley. Widow Isabel Parkyn, who worked for Barnard, Robertson, Heisterman, & Tait, was here in 1921 with her daughter Isabel, while William and Catherine McDonagh lived here in 1923. He was a physical instructor, and she was a music teacher.

Miss Beatrice A. Finlinson lived here between 1925 and 1927. She was born in 1878 in Bedfordshire, England, to Wilkinson Finlinson and Ann Jane Cousier. She married retired rancher Frederick William Godsal in Victoria on July 1, 1928. Their honeymoon took them to Vancouver and Banff, where they intended to join the Canadian Alpine Club's annual camp at the Lake of the Hanging Glaciers.[170] He died October 13, 1935.[171] On May 1, 1936, it was announced in the local press that Beatrice would receive $125 a month from now on from the estate of her husband. She had petitioned the court under the Testators' Family Maintenance Act to review the provision that had been made for her by her husband. "I am of the opinion that the testator did not make adequate provision for the proper maintenance and support of his wife," said the judge today, "all the beneficiaries under the will are willing that she should have the whole estate. I could only give it to her if I find it necessary to do so to make provision for her which is 'adequate, just, and equitable'."[172] It is unknown when Beatrice died.

In 1929, the house was converted to two suites with a variety of tenants. One family who lived here for many years was Frank Mortimer Kelley and his wife, Helen. He was born March 21, 1875, on Cape Breton Island, Nova Scotia, to George Peter Kelly and Mary Simpson. By 1888, the family was living in Victoria. On September 19, 1913, Frank married Helen Aimee Grogan at Saint Mary's Church, Oak Bay. In 1891, he launched himself into a widely varied career by rounding up other teenagers and putting on plays in a coach house at the corner of Vancouver and Johnson Streets. He spent a year in Seattle and San Francisco working on newspapers, then spent 15 years in the woods of Vancouver Island. The result of his travels was a geological map of the area covered. During World War I, he was engaged in personnel in public relations work for shipyards in Victoria, Seattle, and Portland. At one time, he managed the Victoria lacrosse team that won the Mann Cup. When the players gave him a cigarette case bearing his name spelled "KELLEY" instead of the "KELLY" he was born with, he preferred the new spelling and retained it. He went to Anyox for nine years to entertain copper miners and turned down a Hollywood offer to join the *Colonist* newspaper. He served as a marine editor of *The Daily Colonist* from 1929 to his retirement in 1946 but continued to contribute right up to his death July 19, 1958.[173] Helen died May 27, 1982, at age 88.[174]

John Cameron Stillman lived here from 1941 with his wife, Jean, and purchased it in 1949. He was born August 19, 1891, in Seymour, Ontario, to Andrew Stillman and Jane Cameron. He married Ethel Mitchell February 24, 1915, in Peterborough, Ontario. He then moved to Campbellford, Ontario, where he worked as an electrician. By June 5, 1917, he was working as a brakeman in Detroit, Michigan. He married Jean Carruthers in Cleveland, Ohio, January 9, 1930. In June 1937, he became a naturalized American citizen, working as a railroader. By 1941, he was back in British Columbia and was licensed to train and race horses in California, Arizona, Mexico, and Cuba. John died June 10, 1975, in Victoria of heart failure. He is buried at Royal Oak Burial Park.[175]

1012 Richardson Street

The first person to live here was William Spencer Hampson. Born in 1859 in Preston, Lancashire, England, to William Hampson and Margaret Spencer, he moved to New Zealand, where he married Emma Louisa Heywood on March 22, 1883. Three children were born there. The family immigrated to Victoria in 1887, and two children were born here. William was a drygoods and millinery merchant with his store, Stanley House, at 55–59 Douglas Street. He was here in 1894, then moved his family back to New Zealand. He died in Nelson, New Zealand, in February 1920. After Gertrude Cunningham purchased the buildings in 1895, she lived briefly here with her husband, Robert, and son, Jeffrey.

Katherine Eliza Stewart Wallace, known as "Kate," was in this house from 1898 to 1908. Born October 13, 1819, in Halifax, Nova Scotia, to William James Raymur and Mary Ann Ortt, she married Captain Marshall Wallace there on September 26, 1850. She came to Victoria in 1869 after her husband died (date unknown), with her two children. Her daughter Cecelia Isabella Wallace, born in February 1852, married William Henry Tyrwhitt Drake on July 15, 1882. She died on May 23, 1889, and William died on April 13, 1898. Kate then became the guardian of her grandchildren, and they lived with her. She died in Victoria on December 12, 1909.[176] Her brother, James Arnold Raymur, born in 1823 in Halifax, was noted as a sea captain. Qualified as a Master Mariner, he was the Master of vessels in the West Indies trade. He served in the Liverpool firm of Anderson, Anderson and made several voyages for tea between Hong Kong and London. The first cargo of tea which was landed in Halifax from Hong Kong, was on a vessel he commanded. The company owned timber interests on the Alberni Canal region of Vancouver Island. On April 15, 1867, he was appointed as Pilotage Commissioner in Victoria. In Vancouver, he was the resident magistrate at Burrard Inlet, BC. He worked for Captain Edward Stamp in the Stamp's Mill and was appointed as manager when Dickson, Dewolf and Company took over. In 1879, he was appointed as a Marine pilot in the Vancouver Pilotage District and was the first chairman of the New Westminster Pilotage Authority. He retired in 1881 and died in Victoria on July 31, 1882.[177] [178]

1012 Richardson Street, 2022

The house had several short-term residents after Kate Wallace moved to 1116 Fort Street. In 1926, William Bigelow bought the property and moved in with his family. Born May 24, 1863, in Pine Hill, Argenteuil, Québec, to Miles Bigelow and Elizabeth Warwick, he married Rose Ann Hutchin on December 25, 1885. They had nine children. The family was living in Victoria by 1925. William worked as a labourer and farmer. The family lived in this house until the 1940s, when they moved to Florence Lake. William died on July 11, 1945,[179] and Rose followed him on June 21, 1957.

George Wilson Steele, a fish buyer, and his wife, Margaret, moved into the house in 1944, living here for three years. He was born March 17, 1907, in Nanaimo, to William Wilson Steele and Henrietta Gibson Bell and married Margaret Blaine Barr in Victoria February 18, 1929. He died in Victoria March 6, 1985,[180] and Margaret died March 8, 1997. Gordon Roy Slater and his wife, Laura, lived here from 1944 to 1946. Born December 23, 1923, to Thomas Henry Slater and Dora Kate Collins, he married Laura Josephine Whitehouse in Victoria November 9, 1946.[181] Gordon served in the RCAF during World War II, after which he was employed in men's clothing. He first sold at Les Palmer, then spent 36 years at the Hudson Bay Company. He died in Victoria October

22, 2010,[182] and Laura died in 2017. Boilermaker J. Louis Bowman and his wife, Edna, lived here in the early 1950s. The house was then operated as a rooming house.

In 1979, owner Bill Murphy won an award from the Hallmark Society for his detailed restoration of the home.

1011 McClure Street

This is the only house of the cluster that has not been restored. It is covered with stucco, but the "bones" of the original structure are still there, including the original double-hung windows with horns.

The first resident of this house was John Cameron, who was a horse and cattle dealer. He lived here until 1900, but nothing is known about his life. In 1902, Captain Joseph Gosse moved in and stayed here for two years. He was born about 1853 in Newfoundland and became a master mariner. He came to Victoria in 1887 and was the captain of the *Princess May*[183] but left that position to become the Pilot in Nanaimo.[184]

Accountant Thomas Mulligan lived at this address in 1905 and 1906. He was born about 1844 in England and came to Victoria in 1901. He died here on January 28, 1920.[185] William B. Grant, a chemist, lived here in 1909, after which W.G. Davidson operated the property as a boarding house until 1914. James Hamilton, the foreman for the City of Victoria street cleaning department, lived here from 1915 until his death on September 19, 1932. He was born in County Armagh, Ireland, and came to Victoria in 1867. His widow continued in their home until 1935 when the building was vacant. Mrs. Mary Taylor, a widow, lived here in 1938, followed by Miss S.E. Lemon, who was here for two years.

1011 McClure Street, 2022

In 1941, Melvin Woods operated the building as a rooming house. He was born in Kitchener, Ontario, on January 15, 1884, to John C. Woods and Rebecca Perrin. He moved to Alberta in 1901, where he married Hazel Rosalia Hubbard on the grounds of her family's Ghost Pine Ranch. In 1910, he married Ina May Hobson, and they had three children. In 1930, he married Nellie

Bassett in Calgary, and they moved to Victoria, where he worked as a hospital orderly at Royal Jubilee Hospital. He died in Victoria April 23, 1963, and Nellie died July 22, 1989.[186]

The Stevenson family bought the property in 1946 and ran it for many years. Elijah Michael Stevenson was born February 2, 1886, in Doncaster, Yorkshire, England, to Elijah Michael Stevenson and Mary Jane Butterfield. A mechanical engineer by trade, he was drafted under the Military Service Act, 1917, on October 27, 1917. He arrived in England on the SS *Melita* on April 3, 1918, and was assigned to the 38th Battalion, which saw action in France. He was wounded with a gunshot in his leg October 18, 1918, and invalided to the Mill Road Hospital in Liverpool, England, where he was placed on the seriously ill list. By January 28, 1919, he had been removed from the seriously ill list, was returned to Canada June 10, 1919, and demobilized at Kingston, Ontario, August 21, 1919. He married Violet Elizabeth Edwards in Welland, Ontario, June 11, 1925, and their daughter, Claire, was born in Ottawa February 9, 1935. The family later moved to Victoria. They retired to Kelowna, where they both died of pneumonia, Elijah, August 3, 1978, and Violet, August 25, 1978.

The house has been operated as a rooming house ever since.

1002 Vancouver Street

This article was first published in the January/February 2008 issue of *Moss Rock Review.*

As I walk the streets of Victoria, I often wonder about the history of the buildings I pass. In the case of Mount Edwards Care Home, I had a personal reason for my curiosity. My father was a resident in the home for the months that preceded his death in 2007. I had also had a co-worker many years ago who had lived in the building when it was apartments. What was the history? Why was it built? Who was the architect? These were questions I needed to find answers to.

The neo-classical Mount Edwards Apartment House containing 30 private suites was built in 1911 for Fred and Celia Reade. Frederick Murray Reade was born in 1849 in Henley on Thames, Oxfordshire, England. His father was William Barrington Reade, noted county magistrate. Frederick was privately educated and came to Canada sometime before 1882, as he is shown as a Manitoba farmer on his marriage certificate to Marianne Cecelia Colman in Toronto July 18, 1882.[187] After the ceremony, the couple must have returned to England, as their daughter, Edith Madeline, was born there August 26, 1884. Records for their son, Wilford Murray Colman Reade, show him born in Oregon on May 6, 1886, although this cannot be confirmed.

By 1900 the couple had moved to Victoria, where Fred worked for the Balmoral Hotel on Douglas Street. At some point, the couple must have acquired substantial funds to be able to purchase the lots at the corner of Vancouver and Coutts (now Rockland Avenue). The architect, William D'Oyly Rochfort, designed a three-storey brick structure with a heavy tin cornice and columned entranceway.

William D'Oyly Rochfort was born in 1884, the son of Captain D'Oyly T. and Constance Rochfort. He came to BC in 1904 and began his work as an architect. In 1910, he married Eiglenna E. "Glen" Switzer, the daughter of John William and Margaret Katherine (née Wilson) Switzer. In 1912 William and Glen had a son Pat. Throughout this period, Glen worked as an actress on the local stage. About 1923, the couple moved to England, and in 1937, they divorced. William died in 1943, and Glen in 1975 in London, England. William was known for his Edwardian designs, and many of his residential commissions remain today, including 1528 Cold Harbour Road (1914), 1009 Cook Street (1908), 1063 Davie Street (1908–09), 1077 Davie Street (1908), 1385 Rockland Avenue (1911), and 516 Trutch Street, (1910). He also designed the clubhouse for the Royal Victoria Yacht Club (1913). One of his most impressive terra cotta and brick designs is the Royal Theatre, in which he was assisted by E.W. Sankey, architect (Victoria), William Kingsley, architect (Seattle), and Henry Britman, Engineer (Seattle). The theatre was restored a few years ago and received many awards.

The Reades moved into The Mount Edwards Apartment House in 1912; they would live there and manage the suites until his death August 11, 1933. Cecelia Reade then moved to 1558 Beach Drive, where several of her relatives lived with her over the years, although she continued to manage the apartment building until around 1941, which is likely when she sold it. About 1948, Cecilia moved her household to 2720 Somass Drive, where she died May 10, 1950.

The Mount Edwards Apartment House was converted to 32 suites and five light housekeeping units in 1950. It continued as a multi-unit housing structure until June 25, 1979, when a building permit was given for its conversion to a

1002 Vancouver Street, 2022

care home facility, including an extension to the rear of the building. Tenants were moved out, the building gutted, and the rear excavated. Work ceased in the fall of 1979 as a result of a foreclosure. By the spring of 1980, the work re-commenced with new ownership. The building subsequently opened as Mount Edwards Care Home, owned and operated by the Baptist Housing Care Society. In late 2014, the society built a new facility, The Heights at Mt. View, and moved the residents of Mount Edwards there. The building sat empty until February 2016, when the BC Ministry of Housing purchased the building to provide traditional housing and support services. On February 23, 2016, Victoria's Cool Aid Society started operating the facility to provide supportive housing services for 38 people. Floors that had been closed by the former operators have been renovated and are now operational, increasing the facility's capacity. The building is staffed round the clock, creating a safe environment for both residents and neighbours.

1003 Vancouver Street

I often admired this home when I was visiting my father at the Mount Edwards Care Home across the street. I was pleased to discover links between this property and others I had written about.

This home is a two-and-one-half-storey wood frame picturesque Italianate villa located in Victoria's Fairfield neighbourhood. The Italianate styling reflects the architectural tastes of the late nineteenth century, with this example an expression of the taste of the emerging business class. The corner location allows additional decorative elements on the south elevation. The home was built in 1885 by architect John Teague, better known for larger institutional commissions such as Victoria City Hall, the Church of Our Lord, and the Masonic Temple. That he was most comfortable with the Italianate idiom in residential architecture is evident both in this example and his larger commissions for Victoria's elite.

The original owner of the home was Charles Hayward. Arriving in Victoria in 1862, the year the City of Victoria was incorporated, Charles Hayward began his working career as a carpenter. He secured the contract to construct the Church of Our Lord for his good friend Bishop Cridge, then went into the coffin business, forming the funeral company that bears his name to this day. He entered municipal politics in 1873, serving on the school board for twenty-five years (ten years as chair) and Mayor from 1900 to 1902. His son Reginald was also Mayor (1922–24), the only father and son Mayors in Victoria's history. He also served on the boards of the Royal Jubilee Hospital and the BC Protestant Orphanage. Like many of his contemporaries, mostly of British extraction, Hayward took his social obligations seriously. Isolated in a far-flung corner of the

British Empire, this group pulled together to ensure the physical and mental well-being of the less fortunate by endowing and serving on the boards of charitable organizations.

Charles married Sarah McChesney at All Saints Church in London, March 14, 1862, and left three days later for the New World, leaving Sarah behind until he was settled in his new home and could send for her. The couple had nine children, of which two died in infancy; their daughter Florence was the sole survivor of a set of triplets born in 1873. Only four children lived to adulthood. Sarah died July 31, 1901, while Charles died July 8, 1919, and is buried at Ross Bay Cemetery.

1003 Vancouver Street, 2022

Florence, who was educated at St. Ann's Academy, married Walter Stanhope Fraser October 23, 1901[188] and they were living with her father by 1914. With his brother, Gilbert, he owned and operated Walter S. Fraser & Co. Hardware, with offices at 1129 Wharf Street. The couple continued to live here even after Walter retired. He died in 1930, and Florence moved from this home soon afterwards.

From 1935 to 1940, the building was the home to St. Christopher's College, an Anglican Training School. Miss Barbara Carlisle was in charge of the school, which, in addition to courses for educators, offered public lectures of interest to "parents, school masters, school mistresses and others engaged in the upbringing of children and young people." An official opening was held on August 31, 1935, at 8:30 pm, at which the Bishop-Coadjutor spoke on the aims of the school. Over the next week, the lectures included "The Training of Boys," "Girls," "Some Problems of Boyhood: Leisure, Behaviour, Sex, Religion," "Some Aspects of Successful Leadership: Enthusiasm; Honesty; Discipline; Sympathy," and "Religion and Life."[189] Miss Carlisle gave numerous reports over the ensuing years showing how the young men and women trained at the facility were having a positive impact on the greater church community.[190, 191] Barbara M. Carlisle was born in London, England, in 1890 and came to Canada in about 1930.

After the demise of the college, Miss Violet Bridgewater, born in 1874, operated the home as rental rooms. Little is known about her life; she died in Victoria February 13, 1955. The following year, piano tuner Alexander Cameron Criab and his wife, Lydia, operated the rooming house. He was born March

18, 1890, in Inson, Aberdeenshire, Scotland and married Lydia Ellen Mason in Ontario April 18, 1933. It was a second marriage for both of them.[192]

After the home was vacant for a year, Louise Leotta Hayward, widow of Ernest Chesney Hayward, moved into the house. Ernest was born November 5, 1876. He had a brilliant scholastic career, having been educated in public school in Victoria then, after matriculating at the age of fourteen, he attended Stanford University, graduating in 1895 with the degrees of Master of Arts and Bachelor of Science. He taught there as a relief teacher. Then, between 1898 and 1905, he was a professor of electrical engineering at Oregon State University at Corvallis. On returning to Victoria, he formed the firm of Hawkins & Hayward with former Alderman T.W.C. Hawkins.[193] He married Leone Leotta Louis, and they had three children. Ernest entered municipal politics in Oak Bay in 1916, when he was elected a school trustee, remaining in that position for two years. In 1922, he was elected as a councillor for 1922 and 1923. After being defeated in 1924, he was re-elected to council, topping the polls. He served again in 1925 and 1927. In 1928, he was elected Reeve and held that office until the close of 1932.[194] Louise lived here for five years, with Mrs. Ada Barner, Matron of the BC Protestant Orphans Home (started by Ernest's father), living there as well.

In the 1940s, the house was converted to nine suites and retains that use today. It is well maintained and is still a local landmark. It serves as a reminder of the prominent Victorian who built it and whose family owned the property for decades.

1004 Fairfield Road

1004 Fairfield is a rare surviving example of a small Victorian cottage. It was one of a group of four built c. 1892–1896 in this location, including 611 Vancouver Street. It was the duplicate of the house at 1002 Fairfield Road (now altered); the fourth house is now gone. It has value as an example of residences built for those in the working class along the main transportation link of its day.

It is difficult to determine who built the house because it did not appear in City Directories until 1894, when it was listed as vacant. Miner Charles Ross McDougall and his wife, Jane McKenzie, lived here with their eight children in 1901–1902. Charles was born in Whycocomagh, Nova Scotia, in 1863, and Jane was also born in Nova Scotia in 1869. They married in Port Hawkesbury, Nova Scotia, October 31, 1884, and were living in Victoria by the late 1890s. Benjamin O. Taylor was here in 1903. He was born February 12, 1876, in Glasgow, Scotland, and married Lillian Fleming McEwan there. The family was in Victoria by 1901. He worked as a coachman and later drove a taxicab and provided sightseeing services. He died in Victoria June 11, 1963.

The property was again vacant until John Henderson moved in around 1908, living here for two years. He worked as a waiter at the Driard Hotel. He saw service overseas during World War I, signing up April 11, 1916, and sailing to Europe February 17, 1917. Alfred Gibson, a real estate agent, was here in 1910–1911 while foreman George A. Foden called this address home in 1912.

1004 Fairfield Road, 2022

After some years of vacancy, the house was purchased in 1917 by the Frith family. Fenwick William Frith was born February 18, 1864, at Saint John, New Brunswick, to Frederick C.K. Frith and Charlotte Robinson Arnold. The family moved to Calgary, Alberta, by 1891. Fenwick married Jane McAllister, a native of Glasgow, Scotland, October 19, 1899, in Nelson, BC. Their two daughters, Georgina Alice (August 30, 1900) and Mary (1903), were born in Cranbrook. Frederick worked for years as a hotel clerk, moving locations from time to time. They moved to Victoria in 1907 and bought this house in 1917. Fenwick died August 14, 1946,[195] and Jane, December 29, 1952. The daughters continued to live in the house after their parents died.

Owners Laurie Edmundson, Melinda Seyler, and Mikal Williams won both a local and national award in 2002, for the rescue of the house after years of neglect. When they took possession, the building had been the scene of various drug activities, and they had to remove 56 bags of trash and garbage as well as three truckloads of miscellaneous rubbish. In addition, they had to remedy years of poor alterations and the effects of a "grow-op" in the house. The house had had a very hard life, particularly in the last fifteen years, necessitating the removal of almost all interior wall finishes. Anaglypta was installed in the front hallway and stairwell. The bathroom walls were tiled. In keeping with their theory that people do not wish to live in beige boxes, bold colours suitable to the age and character of the home were used throughout. The same ceiling and trim colours are used throughout to unify the rooms.

Despite its small size, the cottage has several distinctive features that were enhanced during the restoration, and it now sits proudly as a testament to dedication and hard work.

913 Burdett Avenue

913 Burdett Avenue is a wood frame two-and-one-half-storey English cottage style residence located in Victoria's Fairfield neighbourhood. With the hipped roof, it presents an illusion of lowered height. The building serves as a transition from the modern residential block on its west to Mount St. Angela to the east, a significant brick Anglican School constructed in 1865.

913 Burdett Avenue, 1959–1964
M03313, COURTESY OF CITY OF VICTORIA ARCHIVES

The house, built in 1904, a particularly well-executed example of the work of architect Samuel Maclure, represents a transition from earlier designs that were influenced by American architects to the Tudor Revival style for which he is most famous. It enhances the scale and character of the Cathedral Hill precinct.

The original owner, Major Cecil Morton Roberts, was born January 30, 1866, to Colin Russell Roberts and Jane Flintoff, in London, England. He served as an engineer cadet in the Royal Navy before coming to Victoria in 1888 to work in the Dominion public works department. Two years later, he became Chief Draftsman with the Provincial Surveyor-General. He served as a Private in the Boer War and remained in the reserves here on his return. Cecil married Georgina Penelope Storey at Christ Church Cathedral November 19, 1902.[196] He resigned from his government position in 1911 to enter private practice as a land surveyor with Ryan-McIntosh Timber Ltd. In 1914, Roberts joined up and served with the 30th Battalion. By 1916, he had attained the rank of Major and became aide-de-camp to Sir Arthur Currie, who later became commander of the Canadian forces in 1916–1917. After the war, he returned to his work as a land surveyor and commissioned Hubert Savage to make additions to the home; he and his wife lived there until 1950. Georgina died in Victoria on November 19, 1960, residing at The Royal Anne Apartments, 853 Burdett Avenue, half a block from her former home. Major Roberts died on April 10, 1961, having lived at the Faircliff Nursing Home for two months. His obituary noted that he had been an athlete in his youth. He was the "last survivor of the Victoria representative rugby team of 1887–88, which included Lindley Crease, QC, W.H. Langley, Senator G.H. Barnard, and Major-General H.E. Burstall, among others."[197]

The house was later acquired by the Sisters of St Ann for use as a home for retired nuns. In 1976, they wanted to have it either demolished or moved to make space for an expansion of their adjacent property Mount St. Angela. However, moving the house would have involved cutting down a rare silver maple. The Heritage Tree Society was strongly opposed to this plan and was successful in stopping it. Despite the issuance of a demolition permit, City Council listened to activists and prevented the destruction of this significant part of the Burdett Avenue streetscape. The house was designated heritage in 1977. It will be retained in its present location as part of a proposed redevelopment of the Mount St. Angela lands.

913 Burdett Avenue, 2022

929 Burdett Avenue

I decided to research the history of this home as it will likely be demolished when the adjacent lands are redeveloped.

This modest residence was built in 1908 for John and Ada Stevenson. Ada Jane Bruce Skinner was born at Esquimalt, February 6, 1856, to Thomas James Skinner and his wife, Mary Lowdham Goode. Her parents had arrived in Victoria January 16, 1853, on the *Norman Morison*, travelling as cabin passengers; they had five young children with them.[198] Daughter Constance Langford Skinner was born just over a month after the family arrived. Work was promptly commenced on the Constance Cove Farm. The house was built on a sunny, southern slope overlooking the little bay in Esquimalt Harbour, later known as Skinner's Cove. The giant oak trees, still to be seen scattered over the parklike slope where the old house stood, suggested the name that the Skinners gave to their new home, "Oaklands."

929 Burdett Avenue, 2022

By 1881, the family was living in Quesnel Mouth, where Ada married trader Joseph B. Mason on April 19, 1882. The couple had five children by the time Joseph died December 2, 1890, at Barkerville. Ada, left with children to raise, then married John Stevenson at Cowichan March 11, 1899. One of the few pioneers who came into the Cariboo in the early 1860s, he first engaged in mining but was appointed assessor and collector for the Barkerville assessment district, a position that he held until his death. He also served as sheriff. His name appears in the 1908 city directory as a resident of 929 Burdett Avenue, but there is no other evidence linking him to this address. Subsequent directories showed the resident as Mrs. Stevenson. John died in Barkerville of heart failure, induced by Bright's disease, December 3, 1918. His obituary notes that "Mrs. Stevenson, who lives in Victoria, arrived in town on Tuesday, accompanied by her daughter, Miss Mason, and was at the bedside when the end came."[199] Ada continued to live at 929 Burdett Avenue until just before her death July 24, 1924.[200] She is buried at St. Peter's Anglican, Quamichan, Duncan, near the graves of her parents.

The next resident of the house was Mary Anne Wigley. Born July 2, 1875, at Brampton, Ontario, to Arthur Benjamin Wigley and Anna Lynch,[201] she moved to Victoria in 1898. For many years, she was the accountant at Robertson, Heisterman & Tait, Barristers & Solicitors. She lived at 929 Burdett until about 1930 when she moved down the road to 857 Burdett. She died January 2, 1936. Her funeral was attended by representatives of many of the organizations she was actively involved with. These included the Victoria Business & Professional Women's Club, the International, Vancouver, and Washington State Business & Professional Women's Clubs, the Women's Workroom, the Lady Douglas Company of Girl Guides, Gonzales Chapter, IODE, the Canadian Red Cross Society, the Victorian Order of Nurses, the Catholic Women's League, and the Local Council of Women. Victoria City Council, service clubs, and various veterans' societies were also in attendance.[202] Mayor Leeming said of her, "She was indefatigable in her work of caring for under-privileged women, and her service to the community will be greatly missed."[203]

Reginald Francis Osborn Pulteney was the subsequent resident. Born September 30, 1882, in London, England, to Francis Basil Pulteney and Harriet Jane Osborn, he was educated at Cambridge University, completing his BA in 1906. He came to Canada in 1928. He married Helen Wiseman Sutcliffe and lived in Calgary for many years. The family was living in Victoria, where their daughter lived by 1929. His family lived in this house for two years before moving to 1137 Rockland Avenue. At the time of his death May 19, 1934, he was living on Linden Avenue.[204]

Dorothy Gertrude Robinson lived here in the early 1930s. Born June 17, 1911, in Victoria, to Charles John Campbell and Winifred Emma Cox, she married Edwin Ainsley Robinson September 10, 1936.[205] She died November 20, 1884 and is buried at Royal Oak Burial Park.

In the mid-1930s, Duncan Douglas McTavish moved into the home with his wife, Emily. He was born June 13, 1882, in North Saanich, to pioneer stock. His father, George McTavish, owned a 630-acre farm in North Saanich and his mother, Catherine Amelia Helmcken, was the eldest daughter of Dr. John Sebastian Helmcken. In 1889, the family established the Intertavish Nursery gardens, a successful floral and seed business that operated until the record snowfall of 1916 demolished their greenhouses. At that time, the McTavish home was converted to a boarding house, and the property was subdivided. Amy, who had been abandoned by her husband in the late 1880s, moved to Victoria, living at 912 Heywood Avenue. She died November 1, 1922.[206] Educated in Victoria, Duncan joined the staff of Molson's Bank in 1897, then worked for E.G, Prior & Co. as a young man. He lived and worked in Spokane, then Prince Rupert, where he married Emily Lysle Craig September 28, 1911. Duncan joined his brother John in Victoria in late 1911, and they took over Leeming Brothers as customs brokering and shipping agents. In 1939, he went into real estate and insurance and became a notary public. Duncan served as a member of Victoria City Council for 14 years. He was one of three local businesspeople who promoted the beautification of Beacon Hill Park in the 1930s. In his later years, he moved to View Royal, where he lived on land which he inherited from his grandfather. He served there as police commissioner, then View Royal fire protection district trustee. He was an avid gardener and held memberships in the Victoria Horticultural Society and the American Rose Society. He was a life member of the American Poultry Association and president of the BC Agricultural Society. Duncan died February 9, 1967.[207] [208]

After the McTavishes moved out in 1937, the home at 929 Burdett was divided into two suites. Among the residents who lived here during that time was Emeretta Meredith Smith, the widow of Benjamin Albert Smith, and Thomas Fowler Singleton, a machinist at Yarrows.

By 1948, only one family was living here. Joseph John Baptiste Lagacé and his wife lived here for many years. He was born December 16, 1883, in St. Boniface, Manitoba, to Amable Lagacé and Philomena Rioux and married Mary Ann Elizabeth Byers in Victoria September 19, 1916. Joseph worked as an engineer at Mount St. Mary Hospital, directly next door to the east of his home. He died at the home March 15, 1962[209] and his wife followed him just over three months later, on July 3, 1962.

Unfortunately, this home, with its rich history, will likely be demolished as part of the redevelopment of the Mount St. Angela lands.[210]

1016 McClure Street

FORMERLY 1011 BURDETT AVENUE

This house is a wood frame two-storey Carpenter Vernacular style residence located in Victoria's Fairfield neighbourhood. It is a rare example of a Carpenter Vernacular cottage and is representative of the type of housing built by the emerging middle class in the late Victorian period, often builders' interpretations of the architect-designed homes in more affluent neighbourhoods.

The building appeared in public records in 1912, but its design indicates an earlier construction date, so it is highly likely that it was moved from elsewhere. The original owner was Edward Mainwaring Johnson, a government official who also ventured into real estate. Like many others in the pre-World War I building boom, he sought to make money as land prices rose. With the collapse of the world lumber market in 1913, the bottom fell out of the housing market, and he resumed his career with the government. Edward was born in New Zealand July 16, 1843. He worked as a real estate broker and agent. On October 10, 1868, he married Louisa Helen Davies at Christchurch, Canterbury. The couple had seven children. The following year, he applied for a patent for "improvements in machinery for gold-saving purposes;" he received the patent in 1870. In 1875, he was charged with helping another man fraudulently obtain a certificate of title under the Land Title Act.[211] He was found guilty and sentenced to one year of imprisonment. A petition for clemency and commutation of his sentence was denied.[212] Edward responded to his treatment by selling his possessions July 19, 1876. He moved first to San Francisco, and after spending two years there and in Oregon, moved to Victoria, arriving in March 1978 where he joined the firm, Lowenburg & Company. He then opened his own business as a notary public and conveyancer.[213] After a somewhat colourful life in Victoria, Edward died February 18, 1920, and is buried at Ross Bay Cemetery.[214]

1011 Burdett Avenue, 2022

James Fowler Walker was the first resident of this property. He was born November 25, 1872, in New Brunswick, to David Walker and Elizabeth Dixon, and lived briefly in Spokane, Washington, where he married Olive Marie Calhoun September 14, 1899. The couple came to British Columbia, where James worked as a miner and later as a carpenter. He died in Vancouver February 22, 1957 and is buried at Forest Lawn Memorial Park. Andros Taylor, the widow of Edward, lived here in 1917 and 1918. Nothing is known about her.

By 1920, Charles Augustus Manuel deMacedo and his wife, Emma, were living here. He was born in December 1887 in Scarcroft, Yorkshire, England, to Joaquim Antonio deMacedo. He came to Canada with his family in 1912, settling in Victoria. On June 23, 1919, he married Emma Rosaline Southall, who was also born in England.[215] George Hurst, who worked as a waiter at the Poodle Dog Café, resided here in 1923.

Painter John William Knight lived here with his wife, Selina, and his family until 1928. He was born September 24, 1868, in Bath, England, to John Knight and Rosina Parfitt. On March 14, 1903, he married Selina Lawrence at Bath; the couple came to Canada in 1905, settling in Ontario. By 1913, they were living in Saskatchewan and were in Victoria by 1921. The couple had eight children. John died September 15, 1944[216] and Selina died on March 8, 1963, leaving behind six children, 12 grandchildren, and nine great-grandchildren.[217]

The next resident was Francis Joseph Henry deMacedo, the older brother of Charles who had lived here earlier. Born April 2, 1884, in Leeds, England, he was 28 when his family moved to Victoria in 1912. On May 23, 1914, he married Elise Josephine Ratcliff. Frank served with the Royal Air Force of Canada in World War I but never went overseas.[218] He worked as a clerk for year and became foreman at Speedy Waste Paper service. The couple divorced in 1938, and she married Herbert Scrase. Frank continued to live at 1011 Burdett, and their son, John Bernard Joseph, worked as a janitor. John went overseas during World War II and was killed in a training accident October 3, 1943.[219]

1016 McClure (formerly 1011 Burdett), 2022

The house sat vacant in 1941, and then John Cameron Stillman and his wife, Jean, lived here until 1945, renting rooms to tenants. They also operated rooms at 1219 Pandora Avenue. He began his working life as a tinsmith at a hardware store, then became an electrician. After retiring, he operated race horses, travelling around the west coast of North America to racetracks. He died June 10, 1975.

Nicholas and Caroline Chomoway lived here for two years. They had been married in Bruno, Saskatchewan, November 16, 1935. In 1941, they left their farm and moved to British Columbia. He was the operator of Victoria Gas, and she worked as a waitress at the Topper Restaurant and later Stevenson's Café & Chocolate Shop. He died January 29, 2007, and she died in 2011. Widower Elliott Robertson lived here until 1951 when Don Peterson and his wife, Shirley, moved in. He worked at Sidney Roofing. Alden Victor Romkey and his wife, Elsie, were the residents from 1953. Born in Eastern Passage, Nova Scotia, April 28, 1885, to John Alexander Romkey and Janet McDonald Leslie, he moved to Saskatchewan by 1906. He married Elsie, and they moved to Victoria after he retired. She died January 31, 1968, and he joined her October 30, 1975. They are buried at Royal Oak Burial Park.[220]

It is significant that this house has survived. As these small structures built for the middle class were once so common, they were not valued in the past and were demolished and replaced by concrete apartment blocks in the 1970s and 1980s. This building is a rare survivor of this trend and is thus more valuable.

In 2013, the house was lifted and relocated to 1016 McClure Street as part of a larger development on Burdett Avenue. The house was restored, and it now looks much like it did years ago. It is a perfect example of how a vintage building can be re-used as part of a development that adds much-needed housing to the city.

1060 and 1054 Burdett Avenue

I decided to research these buildings as one of my brother's elementary school friends had lived in one of them.

1060 Burdett is a wood frame two-storey-plus-basement example of the Edwardian villa in the Fairfield neighbourhood. It has a strong street presence in collaboration with its twin neighbour, 1054 Burdett Avenue, to the west. The house is typical of the type of homes built by the emerging middle-class in Fairfield during the early 20th century and is an important component of the urban streetscape. The property was originally owned by William and Francis Press, who sold the property to Elijah Howe Anderson. Anderson sold 1060 Burdett Avenue back to William Press soon after its construction, retaining 1054 Burdett Avenue for his own use.

1054 and 1960 Burdett Avenue, 2022

Born in England March 1, 1841, Elijah came to Victoria in 1862, the year the city was incorporated, on the *Tynemouth*, the first sail and steam packet to come to the port. He was among those who went to the Cariboo in search of riches in the gold rush. He also owned a large tract of land near Cadboro Bay that he named "Twin Oak Farm." In 1923 and 1924, he ran for the city school board but never won public office. Although he died at age 87, he was fond of walking, particularly in the Cook Street neighbourhood. His long-time residence in the neighbourhood represents a link to the colonial past and the pioneer spirit of many early citizens of Victoria.

He built two homes on one parcel of land, seeking to take advantage of the rising market. Victoria had its most significant population increase and land value escalation from 1908 until 1913, when the world lumber market collapsed. The histories of the two houses are intertwined.

William Press was born April 4, 1873, in Nottingham, England, to William Press and Betsy Clark. He came to Canada in 1889, settling in Brandon, Manitoba. He married Frances Elizabeth Giles April 16, 1900, in Portage la Prairie, Manitoba and the family was in Victoria by 1911.[221] When they moved into this house, William was working as an accountant for Green & Burdick. By the time he signed Attestation Papers September 11, 1915, he had three children. He sailed from Halifax on the SS *Southland* February 17, 1917, arriving in England ten days later. He served as an acting pay sergeant with different battalions. He was hospitalized with influenza July 12, 1918, during the height of the Spanish Flu pandemic, and was discharged 12 days later. He was demobilized at Halifax July 9, 1919 and made his way back to his family in Victoria.[222] He worked as an accountant for the Soldier's Settlement Board on his return and then for the Begg Motor Company. William died November 17, 1958, and the family moved from the house soon after. When Frances Elizabeth died August 30, 1967, she was living at 1400 Beach Drive in Oak Bay. Both are remembered at the Christ Church Cathedral Columbarium.[223] The building was designated a heritage site in 1997.

1054 Burdett Avenue is a wood frame two-storey-plus-basement example of an Edwardian villa in the Fairfield neighbourhood. Built in 1910, it has a strong street presence in collaboration with its twin neighbour, 1060 Burdett Avenue.

Elijah Anderson sold 1060 Burdett Avenue back to William Press soon after its construction, retaining 1054 Burdett Avenue for his own use. He married Charlotte Anna Alderton, and the couple had two sons. He lived at this address until his death at age 87, July 10, 1928.[224] Charlotte moved to Vancouver and died there August 10, 1936.

The next owner was Frederick Allan Carter. Born in England, October 15, 1882, to Robert Carter and Mary Ann Apps, his family came to Canada in 1904 and lived in Saskatoon before settling in Victoria around 1910. He married Alice Bertha Sarah Miller at the home of his parents in Victoria, March 9, 1912; they had two daughters. He worked for years as a mechanic at Begg Motor Co., the same firm that employed his next-door neighbour, William Press. In his later years, he worked as an electrician at McLeod-Lumsden Motors. He was a past president of the Liberal Association. At the time of his death June 29, 1952, he was living at 1920 Stanley Avenue.[225] Alice lived until July 19, 1964.[226]

The subsequent resident was William Sherman Fawcett. Born in Peterborough,

Ontario, December 12, 1893, to James Henry Fawcett and Rachel Ellen Fletcher,[227] he lived in Saskatchewan by 1906. He came to British Columbia the following year. He enlisted for military service with the 1st Depot Battalion at Vancouver October 22, 1918 and was demobilized February 3, 1919. He then returned to Victoria, where he lived with his mother. He worked as a building contractor for his entire career. At the time of his death July 12, 1960, he was living at 490 Fraser Street in Esquimalt.

The homes are well maintained and remain twin local landmarks.

916 Southgate Street

FORMERLY 916 HEYWOOD AVENUE

I became intrigued by this intact cottage while walking in the area and decided I should discover its history.

This delightful cottage was built in 1926 for Thomas Forbes Baxter. He was born January 11, 1895 in Regina, to Samuel Baxter and his wife, Alice Jane Barton. The couple immigrated to Canada around 1890 with their daughter, Mina, and moved to Victoria in 1899, with their two children. He was an engineer on the SS *City of Nanaimo* and lived first on Rithet Street. In 1902, Samuel became Provincial Boiler Inspector and moved to 65 Superior Street, and later moved with the family to 631 Superior Street. When Samuel died January 14, 1924, Alice Jane remained in her home until 1932, when she moved to 678 Dallas Road.

916 Southgate Street, 1959–1964
M05273, COURTESY OF CITY OF VICTORIA ARCHIVES

Son Thomas signed Attestation Papers at Esquimalt November 11, 1915 and was assigned to the 5th Regiment, C.G.A. Movable Armament with the rank of Corporal. He went overseas on the SS *Missanabie,* arriving in England December 27, 1915. He embarked for France in March 1916 and was gassed in action November 3, 1917. He returned to England on November 9, and was a patient in Fuse Hill Hospital, Carlisle. Thomas was discharged February 4, 1919 and returned to Canada.

On November 7, 1925, Thomas, at that time a clerk with the provincial government, married Nora May Morrow, a schoolteacher, at Matsqui, BC. Shortly after that, they moved into their new house on Heywood Avenue.[228] By 1937, Alice Jane Baxter was living with her son and daughter-in-law and remained there until her death July 12, 1938.

Thomas became a draughtsman with the provincial government[229] and retained that position until his retirement. Nora May died on December 9, 1974, but Thomas lived at this house until his death April 6, 1984.

With the reconfiguration of the streets in this area, the name of the street was changed to Southgate Street as it is today.

The home is remarkably intact with its adjacent garage, indicating the importance of the automobile in the early twentieth century. The wire fence in front of the property appears to be original.

916 Southgate Street, 2022

This residence is representative of small homes that were built for middle-class workers who lived in them for decades. How it escaped the demolition of similar houses in the area is a miracle, but it stands as a testament to the housing of its era.

1023 Oliphant Avenue

1023 Oliphant Avenue, constructed in 1912, is a heritage-designated wood frame Edwardian Arts and Crafts residence located near the Cook Street Village in the southwestern quadrant of Victoria's Fairfield neighbourhood. The designation also includes the front yard fence and interior features. It is exceptionally well detailed and has been well maintained. It represents the type of housing built in the Fairfield neighbourhood after the construction of the Government Street causeway and the draining of the underground waterway made the development of the low marshy areas of south Fairfield possible.

The house was built by William Oliphant, for whom the street is named. He was born in Peterhead, Scotland, July 22, 1850, to William Oliphant and Helen Gray. In 1871 he was a seaman aboard the ship *Windward*, a sailing whale ship plying the waters of Davis Strait and the east coast of Greenland. He acquired both captain's and engineer's papers. He married Helen Shaw, from Maybole, Scotland, in Calton, Lanarkshire, June 25, 1875. The first of 11 children, daughter Helen, arrived in 1877, followed by a son in 1879. By 1881, they were living in New Jersey, where William worked as a consulting engineer in the silk manufacturing industry. The next five of their children were born there.

They returned to Scotland, but in 1905, they emigrated to Victoria, and he became a speculative house builder and land developer. This occupation soon involved him in several court cases revolving around surveying and flooding of his land. His property consisted of land from Vancouver to Cook and Oliphant to Park Boulevard. Likely to prevent charges of conflict of interest when William was on Council, a number of the lots in this area of Vancouver Street and Park Boulevard were in Helen Oliphant's name while others were in the name of her daughter Elizabeth. In 1916, William became involved with the coal business in Edmonton.[230] He is credited as the founder of the Victoria Lawn Bowling Club in 1909. In 1920, the family moved to Los Angeles, where William ran a silk mill. In 1926, when Helen died, he was Managing Director of the *Los Angeles Times*, founded by Cornelius Vanderbilt, and which William had saved from bankruptcy. He then moved back to Canada, living in Mill Bay and then Victoria, where he died June 10, 1929.

1023 Oliphant Street, 2022

The first occupants of the home were Alvah Ernest and Josephine Foreman. Born December 28, 1878, in Haldimand County, Ontario, to Christopher F. Foreman and Elizabeth Ann Lamb, he moved to Vancouver with his family in 1891. In 1899, he attended McGill University and took a four-year course in engineering. He had a brilliant career there, being a gold medalist and leading his class every year. During his time at McGill, he won 34 first prizes and was vice president of his graduating class. He was an outstanding athlete, prominent in baseball and lacrosse, and was a member of the Vancouver team which went back in 1901 to contest the Minto Cup. In 1903, he graduated with a BSc., and that year, he was chosen by Dr. R. Tait McKenzie as a model for his statue of "Modern College Athlete." After graduating, he travelled for a year, getting a business education in Toronto between 1904 and 1907. He then returned to British Columbia as secretary and manager of the Concrete, Engineering & Construction Company. He married Josephine Birdella Geneva McDonald Pugsley in York, Ontario, September 19, 1908, and returned to Vancouver, where their son, Ralph, was born in 1909. From 1909, he was a member of the firm of Dutcher & Foreman, consulting engineers in Vancouver. He was the resident engineer in charge of the construction of the concrete power dam at Revelstoke in 1910 and was the supervisory engineer of the Dallas Road seawall in Victoria, and then became construction engineer at Smith Hill Reservoir. He began working as the Assistant City Engineer Foreman in 1912. During his time in this position, he organized a cost data system, which was described in two technical journals, "brought order out of chaos in the management of many public works and notably in the northwest sewer construction, saved on the estimates." In the outfall at Macaulay Point and the sewer crossing of Selkirk water, he employed methods new to the profession. He resigned from his position with the city of Victoria on October 31, 1916.[231] In 1917, he was made chief engineer of the provincial works department, a post he occupied until 1920. From 1920 to 1930, he was British Columbia manager for the Portland Cement Association of Chicago and then was in business for himself. He died in North Vancouver February 19, 1944.[232] Scores of pioneers attended his funeral, and the Kiwanis choir, of which he was a member, led the singing. Many of the principal figures in engineering in the province were present, as were two past presidents of the Vancouver Pioneers' Association, J.H. Cocking and Judge Forin.[233]

John and Mary Collins and their eight children were living at this address by 1918. He was born in Cork, Ireland, June 9, 1869, and married Mary Murphy there. The family came to Canada in 1904. John was a member of the military and signed up as an officer at West Sandling Camp, noting he had spent 21 years in the Imperial Army Corps. He was appointed Lieutenant of the 10th Battalion September 9, 1914 and sailed for England aboard SS *Scandinavia* on October 3, 1914. He qualified for the rank of Captain January 22, 1915 and proceeded to France on February 12. He returned from France December 18, 1915 and transferred to the PPCLI RCR Depot in April 1916. He was struck off strength of the Canadian Expeditionary Force, having resigned his commission for the purpose of returning to his previous status of sergeant major and was appointed cadet company officer at the Canadian training school in March 1917 and took additional courses to commander cadet company in November 1917. He returned to France for duty with the Canadian corps school November 20, 1917 and was returned to England January 31, 1918. He was again Struck Off Strength of the Canadian Expeditionary Force, having resigned his commission for the purpose of reverting to his permanent force status of Sergeant Major Instructor, in the Royal Canadian Regiment, March 31, 1920. The family lived on Oliphant Street until 1924, after which nothing further is known about them.

Eva Davidson, the widow of William J. Davidson, moved into the house in 1927. She was born in the United States and had been married before to a man with the surname Nichol. She came to Canada in 1920. Nothing is known about the family after 1921.

Benjamin Cannon Wright and his wife Jessica lived here from 1930. He was born in Great Hormead, Hertfordshire, England, in January 1869 to Charles Wright and Mary Warren. He married Jessica Bretton in 1893 and came to Canada in 1911, settling in Salmon Arm, where he was a farmer. The family moved to Victoria in 1929 when he retired. Jessica died December 26, 1943, and Benjamin lived to the age of 92, dying August 1, 1961.[234]

This house is located in the middle of the 1000-block of Oliphant Avenue, one of the few blocks in the area that has not been converted to apartment buildings. Its designation as a municipal heritage site in 2001 contributes to maintaining the character of the neighbourhood.

1029–1031 Pakington Street

Constructed in 1890, this home is a wood frame two-storey early Italianate style residence in the heart of Victoria's Fairfield neighbourhood. It features fish scale shingles in the string course. The Italianate styling reflects the architectural tastes of the late 19th century, with this example an expression of the taste of the emerging business class. It is a landmark building on the street, sited on a hill overlooking the lands to the south. Tenders for the construction of the building in *The Colonist* of May 2, 1890, by architect Thomas B. Norgate, described the house as "New Gothique a la Japanaise style."[235]

Thomas Burroughes Norgate was born in Clifton, Gloucestershire, England, in the second quarter of 1864, to Frank Burroughes Norgate and Anne Maria Evans.[236] He is listed in the England and Wales census records for 1871 and 1881, but by 1891, he appears in the Canada Census. His listing in the 1891 City Directory shows him as "T. Burroughes Norgate, Architect, Mechanical Engineer & Patent Solicitor" with an office at 76 Yates Street and his residence as 151 Cook Street. He worked in British Columbia in the 1890s and, in 1894, was part of the first "The Province Exploring Expedition of Vancouver Island." The expedition, sponsored by the *Province* newspaper, was led by the Rev. William W. Bolton and explored Vancouver Island from Cape Commerell to Woss Lake in the summer of 1894. Regular reports appeared in the newspaper, including an introduction of the participants, in which Norgate is described as "being well known in Victoria where he has exercised his profession as draughtsman and architect for several years."[237] The BC Archives has 77 black and white photographs, ten watercolours, and three maps produced by Norgate while on the expedition. He used this publicity to place an ad offering his services for several months in 1894. Thomas died at the Flower Hospital, New York City, March 16, 1906, and is buried in the St. Mary's Churchyard, Bristol, England. In addition to the house on Pakington, he also designed St. Saviour's Anglican Church, 310 Henry Street.

The original owner, Thomas Stephen Futcher, was born in Salisbury, Wiltshire,

England, May 1, 1847, to Robert Futcher and Martha Jane Lewis. He married Emily Florence Bell March 17, 1875, at Saint Thomas, Marleybone, London, England. He was active in politics in his hometown, serving on its council and then becoming mayor. He came to Canada in 1890 with his wife and children. He was the owner of the Japanese Bazaar, specializing in imported goods from Japan, with headquarters at 41 Fort Street. In 1905, he was appointed by the provincial government as judge of the Court of Revision and held courts at Victoria, Duncan, Nanaimo, Alberni, Cumberland, and Salt Spring Island. According to his obituary, he was an ardent philatelist and had an unusually fine collection of unused stamps from all over the world. Mr. Futcher sold the property in 1902 to Andrew and Isabella Keating but continued to live in the home until 1912 when plumber Andrew Sheret paid the taxes. He was living at 1899 Foul Bay Road when he died November 18, 1928.[238]

1029–1031 Pakington Street, 2022

In 1914, Charles and Jane Dunsford moved into the home. He was born in Ontario in 1845 to Hartley Dunford and Catherine Mary Rubidge. He married Jane McDermot September 6, 1871, in Goderich, Ontario, and they moved to Winnipeg, where Charles worked as a banker. They retired to Victoria and lived in this house until their deaths. Charles died on May 6, 1928[239] and Jane continued to live here until she died on June 23, 1934. Their son, Charles Rubidge Dunsford, Jr., lived here until his marriage to Florence Mildred Frampton May 5, 1923. In 1925 or 1926, there was a fire that damaged the upper storey and the roof. In 1928, after her husband's death, Jane converted the house to a duplex with an outside staircase on the east side; the upstairs was given the address, 1031 Pakington Street. The first resident of this new suite was Donald MacIver Campbell, who had married Catherine May Dunsford, the daughter of Charles and Jane, in Fort William, Ontario, September 24, 1907. Don was the secretary of the BC Government's PGE Railway.

William Bennet Chester Pepper and his wife, Jane, bought the house in 1935. Born in Tipperary, Ireland, April 25, 1884, to Edward Pepper and Emily Leal, he came to Canada in 1908. He married Jane Gertrude Martin in Winnipeg, Manitoba, November 28, 1929.[240] They moved to Victoria, where he worked as an accountant at the Royal Jubilee Hospital. In 1936, they divided the upper storey into three small suites and rented them to primarily single women who worked as stenographers. In the 1950s, they sold off the garden lot and moved elsewhere in 1955. William died June 28, 1958, living at 1069 Southgate Street, and Jane died January 12, 1971.

By the 1970s, the house was ten units with a caretaker in the basement. In the 1980s, it was returned to a duplex, this time side-by-side with a front door for each on the porch and has been carefully maintained ever since.

522 Quadra Street

Built in 1897, 522 Quadra Street is a wood frame two-and-one-half storey residence, backing onto St. Ann's Academy, a National Historic Site. It is a good example of the Queen Anne Revival style popular in the late Victorian period. It reflects the type of house built by the emerging middle class. and its rich embellishment reflects the excesses of the period. The British Columbia form of the style served as a bridge between the early wood frames of the pioneer families and the West Coast bungalow so prevalent in the 1920s. This building serves as a reminder of the large mansions that once lined the street, now replaced with apartment blocks and other buildings. Alexander Charles Ewart drew and signed the plumbing plan in 1897, so it is likely he was the architect.

522 Quadra Street, 1903
M00578, COURTESY OF CITY OF VICTORIA ARCHIVES

The original owner was Anton Christian Henderson. Born in Denmark December 15, 1853, to Henry James and Elizabeth Henderson, he came to Victoria via the USA in 1880. He worked for the CPR and several transport companies in Victoria and the gold fields. He married Ellen Orr December 30, 1882. That year, he joined the Victoria Transfer Company, soon becoming superintendent and took wagons and supplies to the Klondike by 1898. He operated a warehouse in Skagway and later in Nome. Henderson, who helped form the Victoria Tourist Association, founded the Tally-Ho service in 1903, a tourist transportation amenity that continues today. Henderson served as Alderman for the City of Victoria in 1893 and 1907–1909 but was unsuccessful in his bid for Mayor. He held high offices in both the Oddfellows Lodge and the Masonic

Order. For years, he was a familiar site on Victoria streets, being the driver of an old Model-T car. The Hendersons lived here until 1911, and their son, Henry James Henderson, a dentist born in 1888, lived here in 1912. Ellen died in 1943, and Anton died January 25, 1950.

Samuel Boond moved into the house in 1914 and stayed for two years. Born in 1873 in Liverpool, England, he married Margaret Alice Hayes in Prescot, Lancashire, England, on August 23, 1897. They had four children, one of which died young. The family came to Victoria in 1913, where Samuel worked for the provincial government and his daughter, Doris, was a cashier at Spencer's Stores. February 16, 1915, Samuel signed Attestation Papers listing his occupation as an electrical engineer. He served overseas, returning in 1920. Sometime before 1926, he divorced Margaret. On October 7, 1930, he married Maria Carlotta Coy (née de Almeida Portugal). They moved to Comox, where Samuel worked as a fishery inspector for the provincial government. He died February 24, 1950, at Quathiaski Cove. Carlotta died January 25, 1952, at sea on a trip from Brazil to England. Margaret Evans, about whom nothing is known, lived here in 1917, followed by Arthur Rinman, who worked on a ship.

Ivor Napier Austin, a carpenter, lived here in 1920 and 1921. He was born in Hackney, Middlesex, England, October 20, 1881, to Charles Napier Austin and Lucy Lindley. The family immigrated to Canada in 1903 and lived in Victoria. August 11, 1923, he married Edith Sellers. She died October 8, 1955, and he died April 27, 1957. John William Bond and his wife, Annie, purchased the house in the early 1920s and lived here until their deaths. He was born about 1876 in England, and moved to Australia, where he married Annie Mulhall in about 1900. Their son, Victor, was born November 4, 1902, in Woollahra, New South Wales, Australia. The family then moved to Edmonton, where Alethia was born November 11, 1903. By 1921, they were in Victoria, where John worked as a builder. Annie died September 21, 1943, and John died August 20, 1946.

Arthur Green, a shipwright, and his wife, Gertrude, bought the house by 1940 and lived here for a year. Timothy and Jane Heiberg and their son were in the house between 1950 and 1952. They immigrated from Norway in 1947. The approval documents note, "These proposed immigrants are citizens of Norway, presently residing in that country, who are desirous of coming to Canada for permanent residence accompanied by their five-year-old son, born in England. Timothy is a former member of the Norwegian Air Force who while temporarily stationed in Canada met his present wife, who is Canadian born. They were married in England in 1942. It is stated that Timothy's father in Norway who has been in the shipping business for a great number of years, will assist his son in becoming established in Canada. The settlement arrangements appear to be satisfactory for the reception of this couple and their child."[241] Timothy worked at Yarrow's.

522 Quadra Street, 2022

In 1986, owners Clifford Whitehead and Marjorie Parsons won an award from the Hallmark Society for the restoration of the house.

Of interest is the continued evolution of the property. Built as a private residence, it was converted to apartments in 1958, suffered a disastrous fire in 1966 and was restored as a Bed and Breakfast inn in 1984. Its location close to downtown and tourist transportation links and its position as one of several such establishments in the area reflects the changing use of that portion of the Fairfield neighbourhood from solely residential to commercial.

906 Fairfield Road

FORMERLY 637 QUADRA STREET

This home is a modest one-and-one-half-storey vernacular cottage designed to fit an irregular lot at the corner of Fairfield Road and Quadra Street. This parcel has always been irregular due to minor differences between the grid of lots in the downtown core and those in Fairfield. The angle at which Fairfield Road runs across the grids contributes to the unusual lot configuration. Despite its small size, the building is rich in ornamentation, with many features found more often only in larger homes. Due to changes in the street configuration, the house is now set very close to the sidewalk. It backs onto an important cluster of heritage properties on Collinson Street. The address was originally 12 Beechy, then was changed to 522 Rupert Street in 1907. The address was changed again to the current one when the roads in this area were reconfigured. When this house was new, it was located adjacent to a busy industrial area.

The house was built in 1889. The first family to live there were the Farrells. Patrick, born in Ireland in 1831, came to Canada in 1863. Hannah (Annie) Tinian arrived in 1864. Their first child, Cecelia, was born October 14, 1866. The 1881 Canada census lists the family with three more children; Patrick Gerald, born June 20, 1870; John Dominick, born November 16, 1875; and Michael Joseph, born May 19, 1879. Patrick worked as a constable, a nightwatchman, a "convict guard, Victoria Gaol," and finally, as a brass finisher at Albion Iron Works. Patrick Gerald was an apprentice at Albion Iron Works and eventually became a machinist. John Dominick worked at the Victoria Post Office. Michael Joseph was a bartender at the Kings Head Saloon. Patrick died March 26,

1906, at Royal Jubilee Hospital,[242] and Hannah died August 19, 1911.[243] Tracing this family was interesting as their names were spelled at least four different ways on different documents.

In 1906, the building was connected to the sewer system, and the owner was the BC Land & Investment Agency. The property was subdivided with two lots created on the north side where 903 and 911 Collinson Street were built. George and Hannah Kearsley lived here for one year. He was born November 3, 1875, in England and was married to Hannah Wiley. George was a marine engineer on a cargo ship. Hannah died in Mission, BC, January 24, 1940, and George died in Vancouver July 8, 1949.

Harry Nesbitt, an employee of the *Colonist* newspaper, was here in 1909, and widow Mary Walker, her daughters, Evaline, a nurse, and Alice, a clerk with the *Times* newspaper, lived here in 1911 and 1912. Charles W. Adams, a constable for the CPR coast service, called this address home for two years, followed by Thomas Patterson.

Victor Banister lived here in 1920 but became the Proprietor of the Jordan River, Sooke & Otter Point Stage the following year and moved to 2519 Scott Street. In 1924, widow Sophie M. Harris purchased the home and lived here with her daughter, Marion, who worked as a stenographer with Dunlop & Foot. In 1926, Mary Ella Depew moved in. She was born in Hamilton, Ontario, June 5, 1872, to Theadore Fortman and Mary Eliza Lannin. January 13, 1892, she married John Abbington Depew, born November 18, 1873. Their son, John, was born October 17, 1892. By 1901, they were living in Vancouver and by 1911, they were in Victoria. John worked as a butcher and then as the foreman of J.A. Sayward's Alderley Farm. He enlisted in the Canadian Expeditionary Force January 18, 1916, showing his address as Royal Oak, BC, and arrived in England on the SS *Olympic* June 8, 1916. He was sent to France on August 27, 1916, and suffered multiple gunshot wounds October 11, 1916, at the Battle of the Somme, for which he was hospitalized. June 5, 1918, he was discharged as unfit for active service and returned to Canada, where his address was shown as 854 Broughton Street, where Mary had been living for years. He died March 26, 1950 and is buried in the Veterans Cemetery in Esquimalt. Mary bought this house in 1926 and lived and worked as a

906 Fairfield Road, formerly 637 Quadra Street

dressmaker here until 1947. She died October 25, 1955, living at 606 Douglas Street (The Glenshiel).[244]

Francis Wilbur Moore and his wife, Doris, lived here in 1949 and 1950. He worked as a taxi driver and also a bus driver for Gray Line.

The house was designated a municipal heritage site in 2010 and the address was changed again – to 906 Fairfield Road.

730 Quadra Street – Rose Manor

I had a personal reason to write about this building as my mother lived her last few years in one of their suites. She enjoyed her time there immensely and took full advantage of the many activities that the staff planned for the residents.

"HOME FOR AGED AND INFIRM WOMEN EVOLVES INTO A MODERN FACILITY"

In the 1890s, a group of Victoria women, spurred by the plight of hungry, homeless women, banded together to establish a safe haven for them. Undaunted by the poor response they had received from City officials, the Victoria Friendly Help Society (as the group became known) continued the battle, with Mrs. Lauretta Gould informing Council that "it would be kinder to have these poor old female sufferers dumped from the wharf into the water of the Outer Harbour, rather than leave them penniless out on the sidewalk at nightfall." She and her friends would not accept "no" for an answer and eventually received permission to renovate the old French Benevolent Society Hospital on McClure Street and reopen it as a home for aged females. Derived from Italian Renaissance models, this style reflects a restrained Classical expression whose traditions were deeply rooted in the ancient architectures of the Western world. Classical styles experienced widespread popularity in North America after they were used

Rose Manor, 2022

to great effect for the buildings of the Chicago World's Fair of 1893. Structural details often refer to Classical temples and civic architecture. Buildings were symmetrically massed, lacking applied surface ornamentation while retaining traditional Classical features.

Mrs. Gould, the wife of sealing captain Isaac Archibald Gould, had arrived in Victoria in 1891. Isaac was born December 19, 1846, in Hants County, Nova Scotia, to Matthew J. Gould and Ann O'Brien and married Lauretta Bernard, October 14, 1880, in Malpeque, Prince Edward Island. He sailed the Atlantic coast in various capacities until 1891, when he first came to Victoria. For many years, he skippered the small sailing ships on their voyages to the Bering Sea and across the Pacific to Japan. He found his first berth on the schooner *Ariel* and two years later was master of the *Katherine*; later, he had command of the *E L Marvin*. When the sealing industry ended, Captain Gould was named to the Marine staff at the William Head quarantine station. He had charge of the tenders that met the incoming freighters and passenger liners. From William Head, he went to the old drydock at Esquimalt and, for nearly 20 years, was dockmaster there. When the new drydock was opened across the harbour, Captain Gould retired on pension.[245]

Lauretta was born in Prince Edward Island, on February 5, 1856, to James Bernard and Catherine Champion. She died in Victoria May 9, 1936.[246] With the support of her husband, she worked with other women to help the less fortunate. Her first glimpse of the premises was not very promising with dirt everywhere and dog remains on a moldering mattress. Nevertheless, she and her hardy group worked together and, in April 1898, opened the doors to women. In 1901, Florence Nightingale Clay, wife of William Leslie Clay, minister of St. Andrew's Presbyterian Church in Victoria, was named to the board and 17 years later, was appointed president, a position she held for 27 years until she died in 1945.

Dr. William Leslie Clay was born November 14, 1863, in Bedeque, Prince Edward Island, to John Clay and Jane Townsend Cousins. In 1884, he went to Montreal indentured McGill, graduating three years later with his BA. During these college years, he demonstrated an aptitude for philosophical study, winning the Prince of Wales gold medal in mental and moral philosophy, a foundation dating from 1860. It was also during his years at McGill that he definitely decided to enter the ministry, and so from there he went to the Presbyterian College of Montreal. He graduated from there in 1890, again distinguishing himself by winning another prize, the gold medal and the McKay scholarship for general proficiency. Although at that time it was valued for the acknowledgement it made for the winner's academic prowess, the scholarship today has direct material benefits entitling the holder to travel abroad. History records that Dr. Clay was valedictorian of his class in the year when he left the Presbyterian College.

He began his career in Moose Jaw, Saskatchewan, in 1890 and was the minister of St. Andrews Church in Victoria from 1894 until his death. He was also the moderator of the Presbyterian Church in Canada. He was on his second visit to Eastern churches when he was stricken with a heart attack and was removed from a train to a hospital in Winnipeg. He died there on February 2, 1928.

He married Florence Nightingale Leitch on July 3, 1890, in Stanhope, Prince Edward Island. They had six children, one of which died in infancy. Their eldest daughter, Margaret Jean, born in Moose Jaw, Saskatchewan, September 30, 1891, came to Victoria with her parents as a child. She ran the Victoria Public Library from 1924 to 1952, when she retired. She joined the library as a clerk in 1913, leaving the following year to study at the Carnegie Institute of Technology in Pittsburgh. On her return to Victoria, she became the children's librarian. She served on the provincial public library commission,[247] the Canadian and American Library Associations, and was a past president of the Business & Professional Women's Association of Canada. She received an honorary Doctor of Laws from the University of Victoria in recognition of her contributions. She was a friend of noted Canadian artist Emily Carr and one of Carr's paintings, given to her as a gift, hung in the family living room. It was sold at auction after Margaret's passing on April 17, 1982.

Both Lauretta Gould and Florence Clay reflected the social consciousness of the early twenty-century residents in Victoria. Like many of their contemporaries, mostly of British extraction, the women and their husbands took their social obligations seriously. Isolated in a far-flung corner of the British Empire, this group pulled together to ensure the physical and mental well-being of the less fortunate by endowing and serving on the boards of charitable organizations.

Prominent Victoria architects Thomas Hooper and C. Elwood Watkins designed the earliest section of the current building in 1908 – named "Home for Aged and Infirm Women" on the plans – linking it stylistically to other buildings in the area for which Hooper did design work – St. Ann's Academy and the former St. Joseph's Hospital, both on Humboldt Street. Among Hooper's other commissions were E.A. Morris Tobacconists on Government Street, Centennial Methodist Church on Gorge Road, the Roman Catholic Bishop's Palace on View Street, and Rogers' Chocolates on Government Street. Interior stained glass skylights were a hallmark of Hooper's buildings. A magnificent example, hidden for years, came to light during earthquake-proofing and interior renovations in 1995. It was subsequently restored and became the first heritage-designated interior in Victoria. The skylight is clearly seen through clear glass that complies with fire regulations yet allows visibility of the stunning colours. The octagonal skylight is eight feet across and has eight sections, in the centre of which is a painted flower. The glass is red, green, and gold, with gold as the predominant colour.

Additions to the main building have been made over the years, but it retains the character of its original design and has evolved into an assisted living facility for ladies and gentlemen. Operations were initially carried out by women exclusively for women, and it was not until 1979 that males were admitted as residents. The current name of the facility, Rose Manor, pays homage to the magnificent rose gardens on the grounds. In 1958, then Victoria Mayor Percy Scurrah toured the facility, and his favourable comments on the gardens gave rise to the new name. Once threatened with closure, the complex is now on a secure financial footing and will serve as a home for the elderly for many years to come.

In keeping with the name, the walls inside are wallpapered in rose patterns, reflecting not only the feminine history of the home but also the grounds. This is a building where the heritage significance is not exclusively in the architecture, although it is important in its own right. Rather it is the social history and its connection with women's history that make this a very important historic site in Fairfield.

911 Quadra Street

Christ Church Cathedral and its Precinct

The Cathedral is an imposing stone Gothic Revival Anglican Cathedral located on the corner of Quadra Street and Rockland Avenue adjacent to Pioneer Square Cemetery in Victoria's Fairfield neighbourhood. It is one of four historic buildings on the city block bounded by Quadra Street, Rockland Avenue, Vancouver Street, and Burdett Avenue.

Christ Church Cathedral, 2022

Construction began in 1926 and was essentially complete by 1954. It is an outstanding example of Gothic Revival ecclesiastical architecture. The style, which originated in mid-18th century England, grew in popularity in the nineteenth century, reviving mediaeval forms in distinction to the classical styles that were prevalent at that time. The movement had significant influence throughout the western world, with perhaps more Gothic architecture built in the 19th and 20th centuries than in the past.

This cathedral, the third with the same name, was designed by John Charles Malcolm Keith, who won an architectural competition in 1891. It was a blend of Durham Cathedral in England and Grace Episcopal Cathedral in San Francisco. Funds for construction were woefully inadequate, so it was not until August 1926 that the Bishop of London laid the foundation stone. Keith moved his architectural practice from England to supervise construction, designing several local landmarks while waiting for this project to begin. The Cathedral is sited atop Cathedral Hill, across the street from the location of the two previous cathedrals, for symbolic reasons, as a beacon for the loyal congregation of Anglicans in this remote outpost of the British Empire. Its hilltop and street-head location ensures that it is an eye-catching building, visible from some distance. Only the nave was initially completed and was consecrated in 1929. Further construction was delayed by the Great Depression, then World War II. The western towers were completed in the 1950s, and reconstruction of the East End, completed and consecrated in 1991, renders the Cathedral one of Canada's largest churches.

The exterior is faced with native sandstone from Newcastle Island, foundations and steps are granite from Nelson Island, with slates for the roof from Jervis Inlet, and native woods for interior finishing. Tracery windows are formed from camus (cast) stone. There is historic value in the bells that hang in the northern tower. Installed in 1936, with two additional bells added in 1983, they are modelled on the bells at Westminster Abbey. The bell ringers are one of a few groups left in Canada that regularly ring the changes.

The church sits amid spacious grounds that include lawns, a brick meditation circle, mature trees, annual plantings, and perennials. These continue the green space found in Pioneer Square Cemetery to the north and provide an oasis of calm close to Victoria's urban core.

Memorial Hall, 2022

The second building in the precinct is the Christ Church Cathedral Memorial Hall, a two-storey stone Gothic Revival structure located to the east of the Cathedral on the corner of Vancouver Street and Rockland Avenue. Built in 1923, it is an example of Gothic Revival ecclesiastical architecture. The Memorial Hall was designed to complement the Cathedral on the west of the complex and to continue the logical evolution of the medieval church as part of a master plan.

Designed by John Charles Malcolm Keith, the architect for the adjoining Cathedral, which was, in fact, not started until after this building was completed, the building was intended for use as a church hall, including an auditorium, classrooms for Sunday School, a workroom, guild room, recreation hall, and synod office for the church. Originally designed to connect to the Cathedral via a small structure on the west end (never built), the Hall was designated a memorial to those who had fallen in World War I, with the auditorium intended as a memorial to Bishop Hill, the first Anglican Bishop of British Columbia. Ground was broken in 1923, and although plans called for facing in Newcastle Island stone to match the Cathedral, considerable funds were saved by using rubble stone instead.

The Hall was the home of the Christ Church Cathedral pre-school until it was converted into an independent religious school.

The third building on the site is the Deanery, a two-storey wood frame English Arts and Crafts residence located on the grounds of Christ Church Cathedral, facing Burdett Avenue.

Deanery, 2022

Designed in 1938 by prolific Victoria architect Percy Leonard James, the Deanery is valued as an example of English Arts and Crafts architecture. The English Arts and Crafts movement, which originated in the mid-nineteenth century, was an approach to architectural design rather than a true style. English architects revived vernacular domestic designs (stone, brick, and stucco cottages) to nationalistic ends and to promote the ideology of the family home and hearth. The setting was integral to the overall design. The style, as interpreted in North America, was essentially a re-creation of "England." Use of the style by the Anglican Church, also known as the Church of England, was a logical continuation of the development of the Cathedral complex. The building is set on the south of the building site, high atop Cathedral Hill, providing view corridors to the south. To finance its construction, the Cathedral sold the original church site to the west of the current location in 1937 and set aside funds to replace the outdated original (1858) Dean's house.

There is value in the connection of the building with Church function. Known as the Deanery, it served as the home to the Dean of the Cathedral for many years. The first resident was the Reverend Spencer Hayward Elliott, who served the Cathedral from 1939 to 1948. The house was the social and entertaining centre of the parish, but the Dean no longer lives on site. Thus, the building is now home to the Cathedral administrative offices that moved out of the Memorial Hall when the Cathedral School was established.

The fourth building on the site is the Yarrow Chapel, a small one-storey structure with a rounded apse on the east side. Built in 1938, it is an excellent example of a French Romanesque Basilica. The design is in direct contrast with the Gothic styling of neighbouring Christ Church Cathedral and the Memorial Hall. Romanesque architecture features round-headed windows, barrel vaulted stone ceilings, and stuccoed exterior walls. Derived from the buildings of the Roman Empire, it was prevalent in Europe in the 11th–13th century. Examples in North America are rare and, consequently, of more significance.

Yarrow Chapel, 2022

The Chapel was the only ecclesiastical commission for prolific local architect Percy Leonard James. It was funded by Norman Yarrow, son of noted Scottish shipbuilder Sir Alfred Yarrow (who also owned Yarrow Shipyards in Esquimalt). The Chapel was built in memory of Norman Yarrow's son John who was killed in a motor accident in England in 1938. It was intended for the use of the first Bishop of Victoria, Harold Sexton, and is associated with the history of Christ Church Cathedral. The chapel adjoined Bishop Sexton's residence, which was demolished in the 1960s. It was used as a private prayer chapel, and for small christenings and weddings. After a period of abandonment, it was renovated in 1980 by early conservation architect Nicholas Bawlf to house the Christ Church Cathedral Archives.

850 Humboldt Street

I have a personal interest in this building as it is where my siblings and I were born.

St. Joseph's Hospital is a four-and-one-half storey plus basement stone neo-Classical Edwardian structure located across the street from St. Ann's Academy. Built in 1876 with additions in 1888, 1897, and 1908, it is valued for its association with the Sisters of St. Ann.

St Joseph's Hospital postcard, c. 1910

Founded in Quebéc in 1848, the Sisters of St. Ann represent the strong presence of French-Canadian missionaries in British Columbia's formative history. From the Pacific Northwest headquarters of the order at St. Ann's Academy, directly across Humboldt Street from this building, they adapted and evolved their missionary work in Victoria to include a school, convent, a novitiate program, and nursing services to better serve the educational, medical, and spiritual needs of the population for over a century.

Architecturally, this historic place was designed and built in stages, but it is the 1908 addition by Thomas Hooper and C. Elwood Watkins that is most prominent in today's configuration. The first phase of St. Joseph's Hospital was built on Collinson Street (now renamed Fairfield Road) in 1876 under the leadership of Sister Mary Providence and Dr. John Sebastian Helmcken. In 1888, an additional 48 beds were added, and in 1897, another 67, bringing the total to 150. The 1908 addition was designed to face Humboldt Street. With its Edwardian solidity and strong classical features, it serves as a foil to the Hooper wing at St. Ann's Academy and further reinforces the significance of the Order in Victoria's development. The opening ceremonies on October 3, 1908, were attended by BC Premier Sir Richard McBride, Dr. John Sebastian Helmcken, Dr. James D. Helmcken, and the Mother-General of the Order of St. Ann, the Very Reverend Sister Mary Anastasia, who came from Montreal for the ceremony. Many speakers applauded the Sisters for their outstanding care of the patients under their care.[248]

In 1949, the hospital was greatly enlarged, and the original 1876 building was demolished. In the late 1960s, the Sisters of St. Ann transferred ownership

850 Humboldt Street, 2022

of the property to the province of BC, and it was renamed Victoria General Hospital. When a new, larger Victoria General Hospital was built in View Royal in the mid-1980s, this facility was renamed the Fairfield Health Centre for geriatric care. However, members of the public could use their laboratory facilities, and I took my new-born daughter there for blood tests in 1987. In 2000, the 1908 building was given heritage designation, including the historic chapel on the northeast of the structure and other interior features. It was, therefore, not demolished when the new Mount St. Mary Nursing Home was built on the site.

In 2001, this building was sold to a developer who planned a boutique-style hotel. Fortunately, this did not happen, and the building has been rehabilitated for use as rental accommodation, known as the St. Joseph Apartments.

The building sits amid a large expanse of manicured lawns with mature plantings that give a park-like setting. When coupled with the St. Ann's Academy grounds and Beacon Hill Park just to the south, it provides a counterpoint to the hard urban landscape of the City core. 850 Humboldt Street remains a local landmark and will continue to do so for the foreseeable future.

998 Humboldt Street

This article was published in the February 2007 issue of *Moss Rock Review.*

What did you get for wedding presents – toasters, sheets, fondue pots?? Well, if you were the daughter of a wealthy businessman in early Victoria, you got a house! Did you ever wonder about the history of what is now The Beaconsfield Inn? It all goes back to a love story and an adored only daughter.

Robert Paterson Rithet was one of Victoria's most successful businessmen. He arrived from Scotland in 1862, the year the City of Victoria was incorporated. Rather than follow the lure of the gold fields, he went into business, eventually forming R.P. Rithet and Co., importers and agents for liquor and groceries. He also established the Victoria Wharf and Warehouse Company that built the Outer Docks in James Bay in the 1890s, enabling the CPR Empress ships and other deep-sea vessels to dock in Victoria. He also maintained sizable farms in Delta and Victoria. He owned what is now Rithet's Bog and the surrounding property and raised thoroughbreds on the farm. His most famous was "Broadmead," a name that is continued in the name of the subdivision that arose on part of his former holdings.

Rithet believed in public service, as did others of the tiny British community prominent in Victoria in the early days of the City's development. He was a president of the Board of Trade, Mayor in 1885–1886, and an MLA from 1894 to 1898. His family was very prominent socially. His home on Humboldt Street was named Hollybank. It comprised an estate including tennis courts, formal gardens, and stables.

When his daughter Gertrude announced her intention to marry Lawrence Arthur Genge, Robert decided that only the best was good enough for his beloved daughter. So he commissioned prominent architect Samuel Maclure to design a mansion on land adjoining the family home. Building the home close to Hollybank meant that mother and daughter could continue to ride together there or across the countryside to Beacon Hill Park and beyond. It also ensured that Gertrude would have a home that matched the standard of the one in which she had been raised. The gifting of a home was not a new idea, however.

998 Humboldt before restoration HALLMARK HERITAGE SOCIETY ARCHIVES

When Robert Rithet married Elizabeth Munro, her father had made them the gift of Hollybank. Although Hollybank was demolished after Elizabeth Rithet died in 1952, the Genge home has entered a new phase of its life – as a luxury Edwardian Inn.

How it got there is another story. A demolition permit was requested by the new owners March 5, 1982 after the building had been used as a nursing home and a rooming house. One Saturday, they were holding an unofficial "demo sale" – totally without authorization – were caught in the act by diligent neighbours and forced to stop. Through the efforts of local heritage preservationists, the building was saved and acquired by a sympathetic owner. Within two years, he had painstakingly restored the mansion to a Bed and Breakfast Inn, named the Beaconsfield after a posh London hotel frequented by King Edward VII during his reign in pre–World War I in England. The name further solidifies the "Englishness" of both the building and its style.

998 Humboldt Street, 2022

The structure is an outstanding example of an Edwardian Tudor Revival mansion. Revivals of previous architectural styles were prominent in the early twentieth century as property owners sought to bring back the stability and glory of a former age. In Victoria, this style can be seen on residential buildings ranging from small cottages to large opulent houses. Characterized by prominent half-timbering, strong masonry foundations, and tall ornate chimneys, The Tudor Revival is closely associated with the Victorian, Edwardian, and Arts & Crafts styles. The half-timbering found on this type of house is derived from Elizabethan England, where heavy timber structural frames were infilled with stucco panels. This building type became popular in Vancouver and Victoria between

1900 and the 1930s, particularly because of political and cultural ties to Britain.

The building is a particularly well-executed example of the work of Samuel Maclure. Born in New Westminster, he became the foremost domestic architect in British Columbia from 1890 to 1920 and established a building style that gave Victoria and parts of Vancouver a distinctive Canadian West Coast flavour. His works, a very personal interpretation of the shingle style and half-timber façade treatment, influenced a generation of British Columbia architects throughout the province. Maclure's influence on B. C. building design was so pervasive that into the 1940s, government buildings and schools throughout the province still emulated his early half-timbered commissions. This historic place is a particularly well executed example.

The building still sits on the hillside and serves as a link to Victoria's past and a reminder of a well-loved daughter and her father's generosity. It is also a landmark to the perseverance of the heritage movement.

895 Academy Close

The Athlone Apartments is a two-storey apartment block in the Streamline Moderne style located one block to the south of St. Ann's Academy and to the north of Beacon Hill Park in Victoria's Fairfield neighbourhood.

Constructed in 1940, it has been called one of the most sophisticated pieces of Streamline Moderne design in Victoria. Built in three sections, it represents a change in thinking from classical designs and illustrates the new alliance between art and technology that was characteristic of modernist architecture. Designs in Art Deco and Streamline Moderne were popular in Europe after the *L'Exposition Internationale des Arts Decoratifs et Industriels Modernes* in Paris in 1925. The style made its way to North America in the 1930s, where its sleek lines soon rose above major American cities. There are two-storey-high leaded-glass feature

895 Academy Close, 2022

windows in each of the three curved stair towers on the north façade. Each stair tower gives access to four suites. There were originally 12 suites with the caretaker's suite in the basement. Solomon Ezra "Sidney" Levy was the original owner, and E. J. Hunter was the contractor.

Of historic value is the adjacent garage, built at the same time as the apartment block. Given the association of the Streamline Moderne style with speed and the technological advances of the time – ocean liners, aircraft, automobiles – it is logical that the automobile would be accommodated in a structure as elegant as this residence. The two structures work together as a definitive statement of the modernist ethos.

It is an excellent example of the work of Studley Patrick Birley, a prolific local early modernist architect, whose Victoria commissions include the Sussex Hotel, the Salvation Army Citadel, and several residences. He was born March 17, 1904, in Birmingham, England, and educated at Trinity College, Cambridge. He came to Victoria in 1930, taught at Brentwood Grammar School for three years, and was then articled to the architectural firm of Spurgin and Johnson in Victoria. He practiced under his own name after 1936, designing the Sussex Apartment Hotel in 1938. After serving with the Royal Canadian Navy during World War II, he formed a partnership with a former navy acquaintance, John Wade. They later added a former provincial government architect, Bill Stockdale. Their firm executed a number of important post-war buildings in Victoria designed in a progressive, modernist style.[249] In June 1952, their firm was dissolved, and Birley continued to practise in a new partnership with Ian Simpson from 1955. At the time of his death July 29, 1962, he was head of the firm, Birley and Wagg. One of his last projects was the re-building of St. John's Anglican Church within the walls of the old church, which had been gutted by fire in December 1960. He served as an Oak Bay Councillor and contested the Reeve's seat in 1958 but was defeated by a narrow margin. His widow, Patience, was an accomplished photographer and artist.[250]

This building retains its fine original features including suite numbers and fretwork. It remains a landmark in the St. Ann's Academy precinct.

900 Park Boulevard

Tweedsmuir Mansions is a three-and-one-half-storey stucco-faced, flat-roofed apartment building in the Streamline Moderne style located to the north and east of Beacon Hill Park.

Built in 1936, Tweedsmuir Mansions is valued as a seminal example of Streamline Moderne design in Victoria. Designs in Art Deco and Streamline Moderne were popular in Europe after the *L'Exposition Internationale des Arts Decoratifs et Industriels Modernes* in Paris in 1925. The style made its way to

900 Park Boulevard, 2022

North America in the 1930s, where its sleek lines soon rose above major American cities. Billed at the time of construction as "the last word in apartment house design and construction," the building represents a change in thinking from classical designs and illustrates the new alliance between art and technology that was characteristic of modernist architecture. New technologies such as refrigerators, electric ranges and clocks, washing machines, and extensive soundproofing were heavily advertised. It was Victoria's first building with a penthouse suite.

It is valued as an example of the work of architect William Jacobus Semeyn. Born in Holland, he began his career in Canada in the Victoria office of Samuel Maclure but was a sole practitioner for much of his career. Semeyn experimented with several different building styles but is noted for his modernist forms. He also designed the Rainbow Mansion apartments (805–811 Academy Close) on the north side of Beacon Hill Park in a more muted form of the Art Deco style.

The original owners were Colin Murray and Florence Forrest. Colin was born December 16, 1886, at Hampstead, London, England, to William Forrest and Katherine Murray. An accountant by trade, he moved to China where he was associated with the firm of Butterfield and Swire, a branch of the London shipping firm of John Swire and Son Ltd., remaining there for thirty years. He married Florence Mary Valentine, born in Shanghai, China, April 17, 1893, to James Valentine and Edith Eliza Sharp, there September 4, 1920. Three children were born there. The family arrived in Victoria from Shanghai in August 1935. That they were willing to invest considerable funds, no expense was spared, demonstrates their faith in the future of Victoria's economy even in the midst of the Great Depression. Permission to use the name "Tweedsmuir" was obtained from the Governor-General. The Forrests also built the modernistic Cathay Apartment Hotel at 855 Douglas Street as well as the Royal Oak Inn (now renovated as the Fireside Grill) at 4509 West Saanich Road. He sold the Cathay and the Royal Oak Inn in about 1940. He had served in World War I and was badly gassed. Colin died of an apparent heart attack in Vancouver February 26, 1941, while on a business trip there.[251] Florence continued as the owner of this property until 1944. She then married chartered accountant Leo Grogan October 16, 1945, and moved to North Cowichan, where she died May 7, 1979.

Social value is evident in the community's desire to protect this building from unsympathetic redevelopment. On two occasions, in 1988 and 1991, citizens resisted extensive changes and made strong cases to City administration. The 1988 proposal to add eight new apartments was unanimously defeated by Council, and the 1991 changes were modified to be more in keeping with the original style. The building continues to be a landmark in the community. The building was converted from rental to strata suites in 1995 with upgrading at that time. A third storey on the west side provided space for two of the suites.

The site's location has heritage value. Considered "the most desirable from all points of view," in a 1936 *Daily Colonist* article, on the west and south, it faces Beacon Hill Park, overlooking the lawn bowling and cricket pitches and beyond them to the Olympic Mountains. The park's walking paths, cultivated areas, and natural areas provide amenities to residents.

902–906 McClure Street

This building has always fascinated me because of its design, but it became of more interest when my research identified the original owner as a distant relative of my husband.

Abigail's Inn is a three-and-one-half-storey Edwardian Tudor Revival stucco hotel located in the northwestern quadrant of Victoria's Fairfield neighbourhood. Built in 1930, it is an excellent example of a Tudor Revival apartment block. This style, popular in Canada because of the country's political and

902–906 McClure Street, 2022

cultural ties to Britain, is characterized by prominent half-timbering, a strong masonry foundation, and tall ornate chimneys. The half-timbering is derived from Elizabethan England, where heavy timber structural frames were infilled with stucco panels. Among other hallmarks of the style are jettying (elements on the upper storeys projecting over lower levels), tall narrow windows in groups of three or more, and verticality.

Mrs. Maude Mary Hutchinson built her first apartment building at what was then the corner of Quadra and McClure Streets in 1928. Born in Clarence, Ontario, February 22, 1870, to George Edwards and Harriet Louise Whitcomb, she was educated at Moulton College, Toronto and later at the kindergarten training school in Ottawa. She journeyed to the Yukon in 1900 when her father, a civil engineer who had gone to the Klondike in 1898 to survey a number of the earliest claims, found that mining camp fare in the far north was anything but wholesome. So he sent an SOS to his daughter to come and cook for him. Not only did she cook for her father, but she organized schooling for kindergarten and primary students in the far north. She stayed in Dawson City for five years, marrying Edward McKay Hutchinson there in 1902. The couple moved to Seattle in 1908 and by 1910 were living with her brother Arthur. They resided in Nanaimo by 1911 but moved back to Seattle eight years later, where they lived in a boarding house. Edward died May 13, 1920, and Maude moved back to Canada.

Faced with the need to support herself, she built the two-storey, eight-unit Willingdon Apartments at 902 McClure Street to provide a comfortable home for herself and her tenants. Furnishings and fittings were of top quality, including Sarouk carpets, French cretonne window hangings, embossed linoleum on kitchen floors, and coloured pottery to match.[252] Maude lived in the building and managed it for several years.

In 1930, she built the two-storey, six apartment Bessborough Apartments at 906 McClure. It was named for Vere Brabazon Ponsonby, ninth Earl of Bessborough, Governor-General of Canada from 1931–1936. It represented the latest in luxury suites with dining rooms, dens, and fireplaces on a street of similar homes. This building was designed by Percy Fox. Born in England, he came to Canada in 1911. He worked briefly in Thomas Hooper's office, then went into private practice. He worked in partnership with Ralph Berrill but returned to a sole practice in 1921. He designed in several styles, including Craftsman, Tudor Revival, and English cottage. By 1934, Maude had moved to the Douglas Hotel and subsequently to Rockland Avenue. As she aged, she moved to the Aged Women's Home at 857 McClure Street and died on May 9, 1952, living then at 332 Douglas Street.[253]

The two buildings continued to be marketed as prestigious dwelling places with apartments in high demand. However, The Willingdon was demolished when the City redesigned the intersection and extended Quadra Street.

The award-winning conversion of the building to a bed and breakfast establishment in 1985 is an excellent example in the City of adaptive re-use. A two-storey "coach house" was added on the west side in 1998, and there were further renovations in 2005. In 2022, a new building is being constructed on the east side of the old building that will expand the capacity of what is now called Abigail's Hotel.

903–905 McClure/725–727 Quadra Street

Erected in 1938, this building is a concrete fourplex in the Streamline Moderne style located on the corner of Quadra and McClure Streets, on the western edge of Victoria's Fairfield neighbourhood. When it was built, this part of Quadra Street was named Rupert. Buildings in this style represent a change in thinking from classical designs and illustrate the new alliance between art and technology that was characteristic of modernist architecture. Designs in Art Deco and Streamline Moderne were popular in Europe after the *L'Exposition Internationale des Arts Decoratifs et Industriels Modernes* in Paris in 1925. The style made its way to North America in the 1930s, where its sleek lines soon rose above major American cities. This building is a modest example that indicates acceptance of the idiom for rental accommodation. While the decoration on this building is more restrained than that of more sophisticated designs, it nonetheless celebrates the age of the machine and new technology.

The Victoria Bungalow Building Co. Ltd. constructed the fourplex. It is an early example of purpose-built rental accommodation. The term "bungalow" was more generally connected with the building boom of 1908–1913 when companies like this built houses on speculation for young working-class and lower middle-class families to buy on the "installment plan" with the company

903–905 McClure, 2022

providing the financing. In this case, the building was operated for years as a rental with a limited turnover of tenants. I have decided to showcase some of the families who lived here for longer terms.

Albert Rudolph Ascah and his wife Olive lived in 903 McClure from 1940 to 1944. He was born October 4, 1900, to Alpheus-Charles Ascah and Alice-Caroline Coffin, in Gaspé-Est, Québec and joined the RCMP, marine division. During the mid-1930s, he was in command of the RCMP cruiser *Adversus* on the Pacific Coast. He married Olive Kate Lownds, born in Winnipeg in 1912, at Halifax October 11, 1938.[254] During the time they lived here, he was on active service. He died in 1988, and Olive died in 2002; both are buried at Fairview Lawn Cemetery in Halifax.

Frederick Dawson Lionel Wormald and his wife Una lived at 905 McClure Street from 1940 to 1942. Born December 30, 1904, in Liverpool, England, to Charles Wormald and Susan O'Reilly, he came to Canada in 1912. On June 17, 1935, he married Una May Bevan at 1133 Rockland Avenue in Victoria.[255] During his time here, he worked at VMD. He died March 1, 1952, and was survived by his second wife, Nany Lenora Shute.

John Garmansway Temple and family lived at 725 Rupert (now Quadra) Street from 1941 to 1945. He was born December 11, 1915, in Vancouver, to Charles John Garmansway Temple and Elsie Blanche Davis. He married Dorothy Evelyn Campbell at Dawson City, Yukon, worked in Victoria as a salesman for W.H. Malkin, and was on active service from 1944. He died December 21, 2008, at Halfmoon Bay, BC, and Dorothy died there May 8, 1990.[256]

Percy Angus Macfarlane married Margaret Muriel Shaw February 15, 1941, in Vancouver, and they moved into 727 Rupert (now Quadra) Street shortly afterward. He was born February 20, 1907, at Lillooet, BC, to Samuel Angus Macfarlane and Elizabeth Ann Taylor, and she was born in Vancouver about

725–727 Quadra Street, 2022

1912. Percy worked as a salesman for the National Cash Register company; they lived here for three years.

Alfred Ernest Gingell and his wife Dorothy resided at 905 McClure Street from 1943 to 1952. Born December 2, 1901, in Brentwood, England, he married Dorothy Grace Smith July 8, 1940, in St. Paul's Church, Vancouver. While in Victoria, Alfred worked as the manager of American News. He died September 15, 1998, at age 97,[257] and Dorothy followed him on July 27, 2007, at age 93. Both are buried at Royal Oak Burial Park.

In 1946, Albert Bruce and Emily Attwood moved into 903 McClure. Born January 16, 1874, in Riceville, Pennsylvania, to James Attwood and Sera Bruner, Albert worked for the CPR in various prairie cities before coming to British Columbia. He married Emily Elizabeth Van in Medicine Hat, Alberta, in 1908. Albert was with the E & N Railway at Ladysmith for 13 years before he moved to Victoria in 1932. By 1946, he was a confectioner and grocer at 3586 Quadra Street, a building currently being redeveloped. Albert died July 23, 1953.[258] Emily lived here until shortly before her death at Glenwarren Private Hospital February 24, 1968.[259]

The building remains virtually unchanged today and still provides much-needed housing for citizens.

924 McClure Street

Built in 1906, 924 McClure Street is a two-and-one-half-storey Arts and Crafts residence located in the Cathedral Hill area of Victoria's Fairfield neighbourhood. Buildings in this style featured pride in craftmanship and rejected the classical inspiration of Edwardian forms. This example has interesting touches, such as the decorative ends on the bargeboards and the vertical boarding in the gable ends.

Ernest Temple, the original owner, is of local significance. Born about 1868 in London, England, to Henry James Temple and Jane Gertrude Cook, he came to Canada in 1891. He married Eleanor Anne Toldervey Lee in Vancouver July 14, 1919. He was an accountant and later worked as the manager of Hickman Tye Hardware, one of Victoria's most important companies. In this location, he would be within walking distance of his place of employment.

Thomas Dufferin Pattullo lived here in 1911–1912 when he was manager of the real estate division of R.V. Winch & Co. Born January 19, 1873, in Woodstock, Ontario, to George Robson Pattullo and Mary Ann Rounds, he went into the newspaper industry and worked for the *Woodstock Sentinel* in the 1890s and became editor of the *Galt Reformer* in 1896. He then went to the Yukon in 1898 as secretary of the Yukon commission. He married Lillian Reidermeister there in 1899. In 1912, they moved to Prince Rupert, where he became Mayor

924 McClure Street, 2022

and was elected to the provincial legislature in 1916, serving as Minister of Lands. In 1928, he became Liberal Party Leader and Leader of the Opposition, and in the 1933 election, led the party back into government. He served as Premier from November 15, 1933, to December 9, 1941. During the Depression, he attempted to extend government services and relief to the unemployed. After an inconclusive 1941 election, he rejected a coalition with the Conservatives and quit the leadership of the Liberal Party and sat as an Independent. Defeated in 1945 in his old riding of Prince Rupert, he retired to Victoria. He returned to journalism and wrote a daily column during legislature sessions.[260] He died in Victoria March 29, 1956. The Pattullo Bridge that links New Westminster and Surrey is named for him, as is Prince Rupert's Pattullo Park, Mount Pattullo in North Tweedsmuir Provincial Park, and the Pattullo Glaciers in that range.[261]

Percy G. Forbes lived in this home from 1914 to 1917. He worked as a teller at the Imperial Bank, but little else is known about him. James Hamilton lived here from 1918 to 1929. Born January 19, 1869, at Ballyshield, County Armagh, Ireland, he came to Victoria in 1904. Percy was a valued employee of the City Maintenance Department for more than twenty-five years. He moved to 1011 McClure Street and died from there September 19, 1932.[262] [263]

Barrister Thomas Edward Clark lived here for one year. He was born in April 1869 in Bishop's Waltham, Hampshire, England, to Francis and Emily Clark. Thomas married Lucy Jeane Henen Edgelow at Spring Grove, London, England, February 23, 1910. They came to Canada in 1912, where Lucy ran a nursing home for twenty years.

By 1931, Edward Cornelius Burtt and his family lived here. Born in April 1878 at Middlesborough, Yorkshire, England, to Charles Henry Burtt and Mary White, he married Ellen Josephine Ramsey in July 1907 in Stokesley, Yorkshire, and came to Canada in 1908. He worked as an electrician and also the manager of the Willingdon Apartments at 902 McClure Street. His daughter, Kathleen, was a saleswoman at the Hudson Bay Company store. The family then moved to Vancouver, where Edward died October 7, 1949, and Ellen died April 28, 1968.

By 1938, Walter Engelhardt and his family lived in the house. Born March 26, 1876, in Victoria, to Julius Friedrich Emil Engelhardt and Sarah Matilda

Thain, he married nurse Elizabeth May Barkwell in Vancouver August 6, 1912. He was one of the survivors of the collapse of the Point Ellice Bridge on May 26, 1896 and told his story in an interview for the Sound Heritage Series of the Provincial Archives in 1962.[264] Walter worked at the City of Victoria from 1909 to his retirement in 1946. He was the water rates collector from 1920. His son, Lieutenant Norman T. Engelhardt, serving with the Royal Highland Regiment of Canada, was wounded twice by shell fragments during World War II. A graduate of Victoria High and Victoria College, he enlisted in 1942.[265] Walter was an enthusiastic stamp collector from his boyhood until shortly before his death and, in 1931, became one of the founding members of the Victoria Philatelic Society.[266] Elizabeth died in Victoria March 28, 1961, and Walter died in Victoria July 12, 1962. The family lived at this address until 1945.

Norman Isherwood and his family lived here from 1946 to the early 1950s. He was born in Manchester, Lancashire, England, July 10, 1898, to Joseph Isherwood and Eleanor Clayton. He came to Canada in 1911, living in Saskatoon, where he married Elizabeth Drysdale. The couple came to Victoria in 1943. He was the manager of the *Angela Hotel* at 923 Burdett Avenue. He also owned a farm in Saanich where he bred horses. He raised American saddle horses for a time but in the years before his death, he concentrated on thoroughbreds. Norman died in Victoria September 14, 1954,[267] and Elizabeth followed him on July 6, 1970.

This house will be moved to the east and restored under the redevelopment of the Mount St. Angela lands.

907 Collinson Street

This home is a one-and-one-half-storey, wood frame front-gabled example of the Edwardian Vernacular Arts and Crafts style located on the western edge of Victoria's Fairfield neighbourhood. As part of a remaining cluster of homes constructed over a period of 20 years beginning in the 1890s, it represents the type of housing built in this neighbourhood by those of modest means. Its architectural styling lacks the refinement of designs in more affluent areas but retains the key elements of its style.

It was built in 1908 for Lucy Gower Curtis, a single woman, as a rental property at a time when this was a socially acceptable means through which a female could support herself financially. She was born in December 1872 in Stroud, Gloucestershire, England, to Captain James Dillon Curtis and Emma Morley Saunders. Her father was well known in Victoria for his naval career; he likely provided the funds to have the house built. Born July 15, 1825, at King's Lynn, England, to Commander Thomas Curtis, RN, and Jane Taylor Raven, James was educated at the Blue Coat School, London, and, on completing his studies in July 1841, had his first experience of life at sea. He joined the Royal Navy as an officer cadet in 1842, serving in HMS *Queen,* the flagship of Vice-Admiral William Campbell Rich Owen. He participated in the suppression of the slave trade off the west coast of Africa while in HMS *Harlequin* and HMS *Waterglitch.* In 1842, he was part of the Xanthian Expedition. The Elgin marbles, which are part of the collection of the British Museum, came to England as a result of this expedition. During the Crimean War, he served as First Lieutenant of HMS *Royal Albert* and saw service in the Black Sea, Sea of Asoff, and the fall of Sebastopol. On retiring from active service in 1867, he was appointed in command of the Coast Guard stations in the North of Ireland. In 1860, Captain Curtis married Emma Morley Saunders; eight children were the result of the marriage, two of whom died in infancy. In 1889, James visited his son Thomas in Canada and, in 1903, moved here with his family. He owned a shipping company in Vancouver and resided for many years with Lucy in Victoria. Captain Curtis died March 10, 1920, having moved to North Vancouver to live with his son, James Morley Curtis.[268] On September 8, 1909, Lucy married Charles Rowland Serjeantson, the contractor who is believed to have built the home at 907 Collinson. They had one son, Rowland William, born May 17, 1915. Lucy died in Victoria February 8, 1921,[269] and Rowland moved back to England, where he died May 3, 1946.[270]

907 Collinson Street, 1959–1964 MO3474, COURTESY OF CITY OF VICTORIA ARCHIVES

John Hart and his new wife Harriet were the first tenants. Born March 31, 1879, in Mohill, County Leitrim, Ireland, to Johannis Hart and Mary Reynolds, John came to Victoria in 1898.[271] He married Harriet Cotsford Mackay June 29, 1908 and lived in this house until 1911. John was an insurance agent but soon became a partner in Gillespie, Hart & Todd. He entered politics in the 1916 election and was elected to the provincial legislature as a Liberal member from Victoria City. He served as Minister of Finance from 1917 to 1924, and from 1933 to 1947, he led the province as Premier as well. Hart was one of the few BC premiers who left office neither defeated nor under a cloud. The 405 km John Hart Highway, between Prince George and Dawson Creek, is named for him, as is the John Hart Hydroelectric development at Campbell River and the

Hart Highlands neighbourhood of Prince George. John Hart died in Victoria April 7, 1957 and is buried at Royal Oak Burial Park.[272]

In 1912, Frederick Wood and his wife, Ethel May Lawrence, moved into the house. He was born January 17, 1874, in Luton, Bedfordshire, England, and she was born May 15, 1876, at Gateshead, Northumberland, England, to James Lawrence and Mary Ann Gibbs. The couple married at Luton in April 1898, and came to Canada in 1907, arriving in Victoria in 1911. Frederick worked as a contractor, and, together with Reginald Percy James Richards, as Wood and Richards, designed and built five of the Soldiers' Settlement houses in Victoria in 1920.[273] Later, Frederick partnered with engineer Kenneth Basil Foyster in Wood-Foyster Construction Co. Frederick died November 17, 1935[274] and Ethel died March 19, 1969. Both are buried at Royal Oak Burial Park.[275]

City Clerk Andrew Messer was the next resident. Born May 6, 1900, at Galashiels, Scotland, to Thomas Walter Messer and Margaret Romanis, he came to Canada in 1909. On December 20, 1923, he married Evelyn Mary Pritchard, who was born December 30, 1898, in Dublin, Ireland, to William John Pritchard and Elizabeth Watters Balmer, at Victoria. The family moved to the interior of British Columbia, where William died February 28, 1974; Evelyn died February 9, 1981.

Frederick L. Smith, a bartender at the Commercial Hotel, lived here in 1914–1915. The building was then vacant for several years until labourer Herbert Hunt moved in with his family. He was born June 13, 1873, at Walsall, England, and married Maude Elizabeth Cox there June 27, 1898. Unfortunately, she died a year later. On April 30, 1911, he married Maude Martha Simmons in Staffordshire, England. Their daughter, Rose Mary, was born July 27, 1913, their son, Douglas, in 1915, and their son, Albert, in 1916. The family immigrated to Canada in 1919, settling in Victoria. They lived in this house until 1929 when they moved to 923 Collinson Street. At the time of his death at St. Joseph's Hospital, March 16, 1944, the family was residing at 1031 Richardson Street.[276]

Then, seaman William Giles Drayton moved in with his family. He was born October 30, 1890, in Cornwall, England, to Augustus Drayton and Harriett Mary Giles, and joined the Royal Navy on June 11, 1908, serving first in HMS *Ganges.* Over the next 12 years, he served on nineteen different ships.[277] He married Harriett Counihan in 1913, and their son, William A., was born in 1919. William came to Canada, where he transferred to the Royal Canadian Navy. Harriett and their son then immigrated to Halifax, Nova Scotia, in 1921, with her reason for the trip "to join husband."[278] William died June 5, 1960, at New Westminster and Harriet died October 11, 1968, at Burnaby, BC.

After a year, the Draytons left, and carpenter Frederick Burke moved in with his family. Born in October 1874 in London, England, he married Emma Elizabeth Price on May 10, 1896.[279] They had five children when they moved to Regina, Saskatchewan; five more children were born there. Frederick joined the 152nd Battalion and served overseas during World War I.[280] They came to Victoria in 1924, where he worked as a carpenter. He died July 18, 1937, leaving his widow, three sons, and six daughters.[281] Emma followed him on April 20, 1959. Both are buried at Royal Oak Burial Park.

Mrs. Anna Haikala (née Maki) lived at 907 Collinson with her family from 1931 to 1939. She was born in Finland July 17, 1885, and married Eino Haikala. The family came to North America in 1910 and lived in Portland, Oregon, where their son, Elmer, was born that year. By 1911, they were living in Comox and later at Tofino where the rest of their children were born. Eino worked in the forest industry.[282] There is no record of him after 1918 when he completed Attestation Papers in Vancouver, but we know that Anna was living in Victoria by 1923. Also living with her during the 1930s were her children. Elmer worked as a chauffeur for Quarter Cab and later for the Pioneer & Empire Wood & Coal Co., Helma was a waitress at the Dominion Hotel, Ina Helna was a cashier at the Empress Hotel, and Harold was a student. Helma married sailor Kay Pedersen on July 9, 1934, but the marriage was dissolved March 1, 1944. Harold married music teacher Clarice Duckett November 11, 1935, and Elmer married Grace Boulton May 28, 1938. Alma died in Vancouver August 17, 1957 and is buried in Mountain View Cemetery.[283]

907 Collinson Street, 2022

Subsequently, Mrs. Zena Parr lived at this address from 1939 to 1941. Nothing is known about her except that she first appears in City Directories in 1935. During World War II, Mildred Evans lived here while her husband, Stanley William, was on active service. George Humber Harvey Gorse and his wife, Ruth, lived here until 1951. He was born January 18, 1909, at Walsall, Staffordshire, England, to Frederick George Gorse and Mary Jane Wilkes. His family came to British Columbia in 1913, settling in Burnaby. Stanley's father was well-known as a musician who played bassoon with the original Vancouver Symphony Orchestra and had founded the North Burnaby Boys' Band.[284] George married Ruth Braidwood at Victoria February 14, 1944. The couple had two children. He worked as a salesman for Spencers Store, and Ruth worked as a waitress at the Sussex Café. She died April 24, 1978, and George followed her on March 6, 1983.[285]

In 1952, Duncan MacColl and his wife Janet moved into 907 Collinson Street. He was born November 24, 1915, at Morin, Alberta, to Donald MacColl and Christina McIntyre. He married Janet Ferguson Owen, and the couple had five children. Duncan worked as a helper at Yarrow's in the 1950s, then for the provincial civil service. He died in Victoria August 21, 1982, and Janet died June 17, 2006.[286]

911 Collinson Street

This house, built in 1912, is a good example of the bungalow style with Arts and Crafts detailing. It further represents the further subdivision of lots in Fairfield. Before 1910, the lots between Collinson Street and Fairfield Road ran the width of the block. In 1910, the lots were divided into east and west parts; in 1912, they were further subdivided into even smaller lots.

It was built by David Herbert Bale, a prolific Victoria contractor/designer who built many variations of this style in the pre–World War I era. At the height of the boom, he was completing two houses a week and was reputed to have had hundreds of projects at one time. He advertised his services as "houses built on the installment plan – no money required." This would appeal to potential clients of modest means.

911 Collinson Street, 2022

The original owner was Alfred Edward Carter, who was a representative of the new class of homeowners. He was an electrician with Hinton Electric. No longer was home ownership reserved for the wealthy; with smaller lots, tradespeople of modest means could afford land and build homes for their families.

Alfred was born in Victoria July 15, 1889, to John William Carter and Elizabeth Alice Miles. When this house was built, he was living with his mother at

756 Courtney Street. On September 4, 1912, he married Irene Beatson Nason, who had been born August 10, 1890, to Ithiel Blake Nason and Mary Agnes Watson in the gold-rush town of Barkerville. After a honeymoon to Prince Rupert, the couple moved into the new house at 911 Collinson Street.[287] Their son, Alfred Edward Carter Jr., was born May 29, 1914. However, they did not live there long, moving in 1917 to live with John's mother at 910 Fairfield Road, directly behind their Collinson Street home. By this time, Alfred was working as an electrical engineer at the BCER Power House. The family moved to Los Angeles July 28, 1938, on the SS *San Francisco*.[288] They both died in Athens, Georgia: Alfred June 7, 1975, and Elizabeth January 11, 1976.

The next resident was Mary Ann McKittrick (née Fairbairn), born in 1885 in Wakefield, Quebéc, to William Fairbairn and Martha Jane Rogers. She married William McKittrick (also born in Wakefield, Quebéc) August 26, 1873, at Ottawa, Ontario. The couple had nine children, one of which died in infancy. By 1879, the family was living in Victoria, where William was a member of the firm of blacksmiths, McKittrick, Knight and McGregor. He died July 16, 1908, leaving his widow with a large family to support. By 1921, she was living in Victoria with her daughter Hazel and her husband, Harold Brad. Mary Ann died in Vancouver November 28, 1925, and is buried at Mountain View Cemetery.[289]

US Immigration Inspector Roy Clinton Matterson lived here until 1922. He was born October 16, 1886, in Round Prairie, Minnesota, to Joseph Jerome Matterson and Florence Lydia Hosmer. He married Hazel Daphine Jardine at Auburn, Washington, August 1, 1914,[290] and worked in Winnipeg by 1916.[291] The couple's son, Duane, was born in Seattle May 28, 1919. Roy continued to work for the US Immigration Service, primarily at SeaTac Airport.[292] He died in Seattle May 25, 1960,[293] and Hazel died November 5, 1980, in Pacific Grove, California.

Taxi driver William Ernest Copp moved into the house in 1923. He was born March 21, 1893, in Fremington, Devon, England, to William Henry Copp and Amelia Kidwell. On September 6, 1922, he married Bertha Nightingale; the couple had two sons. William spent the last twelve years of his life as a chauffeur at the Department of National Defence. He died in Esquimalt October 6, 1956[294] and Bertha followed him on June 26, 1976.[295]

Lawrence Lupton lived here for one year. He was born July 21, 1870, in Rosendale, Lancashire, England, to Lawrence Lupton and Elizabeth Baldwin. Lawrence married Mary Annette Holt about 1897; their son, Henry Clifford, was born November 8, 1899. The family came to Canada in 1910 and settled in Victoria. He worked for years as a mechanic and then became a manager of a brick works. Lawrence died in West Vancouver June 12, 1964.[296]

Frederick Kingdon Bailey lived in this home for six years. Born January 8, 1891, in Portsmouth, England, to Frederick James Bailey and Ada Clara Payne, he came to British Columbia in 1902. He married Alice Louisa Westwood; they had one daughter. Frederick, a marine engineer by trade, worked for Bullen's Marine Ways and joined the CPR in 1920. He was, for many years, the superintendent engineer of the BC Coastal Service, which served as British Columbia's marine highway.[297] He died March 4, 1958, three years after his retirement.

The home was vacant for a year before Joseph Orrico moved in for one year. Born Giuseppe Urrico in Carolei, Italy, March 19, 1907, he came to Canada in 1926 and was the proprietor of Joe and Dom Shoe Shine. He soon moved to the United States and married Josephine Bell DiStefano in Seattle, Washington, on October 6, 1930.[298] He legally changed his name April 25, 1940, when he applied for naturalization as a United States citizen.[299] Joseph died November 6, 1984, in Seattle, having owned a grocery store for many years.[300]

The subsequent resident was Mrs. Julia Attwood, the widow of Frank Attwood. Born in January 1885 at Faversham, Kent, England, to Edward Andrew Tindall and Emma Fasham Burnap, she married Frank Attwood in July 1908. The couple came to Canada in 1912, where he worked as a bricklayer. He signed Attestation Papers in Victoria February 28, 1916, left Halifax February 17, 1917, and arrived in England February 27, 1917, on the SS *Southland.* He was killed in action at Passchendaele November 2, 1917[301] and is buried at the New Irish Farm Cemetery in Belgium. Julia received a gratuity of $180 to compensate her for the loss of her husband.[302] She lived at 911 Collinson Street from 1934 to 1950.

Louis I. Smith and his wife Myrtle then moved into the home. Born April 3, 1905, in Essex, England, to Jack Smith and Jessie Goldbone, he married Myrtle Kathleen Sparrow and worked as a municipal sanitation worker. He lived in this house in his retirement years. At the time of his death October 9, 1984, he was living at 1147 Quadra Street.

938 Collinson Street

This building is an almost two-storey, wood frame Vernacular residence located on the western edge of Victoria's Fairfield neighbourhood. Built in 1890, it has value as a rare survivor of a building type and for what its construction says about changing middle class values. It is the only single-family dwelling remaining on the north side of this block of Collinson Street. It represents a once common type of residence that was built by local carpenter/builders for their own use or on speculation. George Maidment built this home with his son Charles. They also constructed three houses similar to this one in James Bay; 117 and 119 Oswego Street remain today. While these houses do not have the architectural significance of architect-designed mansions built for wealthy citizens, they are perhaps even more rare as they were demolished by the scores in the 1970s and 1980s when they were replaced by multiple-unit apartment blocks. That this house has survived relatively unscathed is unusual.

George Maidment was born in Dorset, England, in 1839 and married Mary, born in 1831 in Kent, England. The couple came to Canada in 1871. Arriving in Victoria in 1889, they purchased this lot in their daughter Fanny's name and built the house. Mary died June 30, 1903, and George moved to 428 Quebec Street, where he lived with Fanny, later residing at the St. George's Hotel at 765 Esquimalt Road, where his son, Charles, was the proprietor. He died at that location March 30, 1916.[303] The family lived here briefly in 1894.

938 Collinson Street, 2022

One of the longer-residing tenants was Willard Francis Hogan, a deckhand, later an engineer, who lived here from 1895 to 1900. He was born May 7, 1868, at Oriskany, New York, and came to Canada in 1890. He married Maria M. Hughes, and their daughter, Sara Margaret, was born in Victoria October 16, 1895.[304] Maria died November 6, 1911, living then at 1112 Bean Street. Willard died January 3, 1939.[305]

In 1900, the Maidments sold the property to their neighbour, Edith Cullum. She lived there in 1904 but rented it out in other years. Edith Flora Williams was born about 1852 in London, England, to Charles William and Caroline Steedman. She came to Canada c. 1895. She married Thomas Francis Cullum July 14, 1891, whose second wife had died earlier that year, leaving young children to be cared for. Thomas was a retired naval officer who had built a cottage at Vancouver and Collinson and opened a grocery store. After Thomas died November 1, 1895, Edith continued to operate the store. Another house was built on the lot in 1902 or 1903. Edith sold this house in 1907.

Salesman Fred Bradshaw, salesman Thomas Cowan, real estate agent Alfred Gilson, City labourer Robert Simmers, and bank clerk James Bates all lived at 938 Collinson Street for one year each.

Plumber Arthur Gosling and his wife, Helena, lived here for about six years. He worked for Colbert Plumbing and Heating Co. From 1921 to 1949, Mary E. O'Neill, widow of Dr. Kieran Joseph O'Neill, resided here. Kieran was born December 8, 1888, in Wellington, Ontario, to Cornelius O'Neill and Julia Lynes.

He graduated from the University of Toronto in the class of 1909. He moved to Victoria in 1910 and married Victoria native Mary Elizabeth Brahm in 1911. Their daughters, Sheila and Druscella, were born here in 1912 and 1913. The family lived in Seattle by 1915, and two more children, Gerald and Eileen, were born in Washington State. Kieran died in Coupeville, Washington, on October 23, 1918, just two months after the birth of his fifth child, Noreen.[306] His death was tragic as he contracted the Spanish influenza, which ultimately developed into pneumonia. According to his obituary, "It was originally planned to bury the remains in Victoria and arrangements were under way to transport the body for that purpose, but, owing to the epidemic and the unsatisfactory transportation facilities, it was finally decided to ship the remains to Everett, where the funeral service was conducted by Rev. Father O'Brien, and where he was laid to rest in the Catholic Cemetery."[307] With five young children to support, Mary returned to Victoria, where both her mother and mother-in-law lived. She died in Victoria April 17, 1962 and is buried at Hatley Memorial Gardens.[308]

The youngest child, Noreen, lived until 2019. Her obituary outlines her eventful life: "Sister Noreen died at Mount St. Mary Hospital on Friday, April 12, 2019, at the age of 100 years and 8 months. Born in Coupeville, WA she was the youngest of 5 children born to Mary and Dr. Kieran O'Neill. Noreen received her education at St. Ann's Academy, Victoria, B.C. She received her teacher's certificate (with honours) at the Provincial Normal School in Victoria in 1937. After a year of teaching in New Westminster, she entered The Congregation of the Sisters of Saint Ann in 1938, professing her vows in 1940. Her years of ministry were comprised of teaching: regular classes in both Catholic and Public Schools at the elementary, secondary and college level; tutoring sick children both home-bound and in hospital; and programmes for gifted students as well as those with special needs. She taught music and directed choirs. During her later years, she provided Pastoral Ministry in New Westminster visiting the elderly, working with immigrant single-parent families, and ministering in the L'Arche community."[309]

After Mary O'Neill moved to a new address, Ernest Howard Shepherd and his family moved in. He was born August 11, 1889, at Wootton Bridge, Isle of Wight, to Charles Sheppard and Mary Ann Saint. He joined the Royal Navy in August 1907 and, at the outbreak of hostilities, was posted to HMS *Kangaroo.* Over the next 12 years, he served as a stoker in 29 different ships, including time at the Navy base at Alexandria.[310] He married Ada Helena Cull in Wootton, England, in October 1915. The couple arrived in Montreal October 27, 1929. By 1945, they were living in Victoria, where he was a storekeeper for the Department of Transport. Ada died February 6, 1960, and Ernest followed her on November 13, 1966.[311]

The next residents were janitor Wilbert Arnold Paul and his wife, Julia. He was born on December 23, 1895, at Egremont, Ontario, to Duncan Paul and Grace Horsburg. The couple moved to Victoria in 1953. She died in 1972, and he, on May 15, 1976. He was a veteran of World War I.[312]

This modest house has a fascinating history and deserves to be recognized for merely surviving against all odds.

940 Heywood Avenue

This home is an outstanding example of a frame two-storey Edwardian Tudor Revival residence. This style takes its inspiration from early England; these buildings feature stone, ornate chimneys, half-timbering, thick walls, cedar shingles, and hipped rooflines. Set on a large lot across from Beacon Hill Park, the house has a monumental presence on a street that is now chiefly populated by large apartment blocks. It was designated a heritage structure in 2002, including the garage at the front of the property.

Henry Thompson, a carpenter, built a house on this site in 1888. The property was bought in 1906 by Major Harry Howlett Woolison. Born April 9, 1870, in Warwick, England, to Henry John Woolison and Mary Ann Glover, he married Jane Langley on July 18, 1896, in St Margaret Anfield, Walton-on-the-Hill, Lancashire, England. The couple came to Canada in 1898 and, by 1901, were living in Saanich. Beginning his working career here as a clerk, he became an example of the merchant class of the early twentieth century in Victoria as Secretary-Treasurer of John Leander Beckwith & Co. Ltd., manufacturers agents and importers, commission agents, real estate and insurance brokers. From 1916, he was the Canadian representative of a number of British manufacturers of pottery and chinaware. Harry was an active member of Christ Church Cathedral and a former church warden. He was also a Boy Scout leader and served with the old Fifth Regiment here for many years.[313]

940 Heywood Avenue, house and garage
HALLMARK HERITAGE SOCIETY ARCHIVES

The original house was demolished to build the new house, leaving a generous front yard. The builder was noted Victoria firm Luney Brothers. This home was among the first in the neighbourhood to have a separate garage built at the same time as the residence. The garage represented a social statement that the owner was embracing the modern age and needed a garage to house his new car. The siting at the front of the property speaks to the vehicle's status for this prominent businessman. Major Woolison died on May 28, 1936, leaving his widow and five children. Jane continued to live in the home after his death. She died October 8, 1949.

The house remained in the Woolison family until 2000, when it was purchased by their next-door neighbour, Graham Garman. He gutted the old kitchen and combined it with an old pantry. All the new cupboards were made from reclaimed wood. He also added a small bathroom on the main floor, refinished all the floors, insulated under the main floor, and designed a full suite in the basement, carefully matching woodwork and features to those in the main house. He also added storm windows and protective glass over the stained-glass windows. One of the challenges of the work was the discovery that a support post under the front verandah was rotten. It was carefully restored so that the structure was once again stable. The rehabilitation work won an Award of Merit from the Hallmark Heritage Society in 2013.

940 Heywood Avenue, 2022

Subsequent owners were visiting from Winnipeg and walked by the house, dreaming of being able to live there. A chance meeting with Graham led to a tour of the restored house and an offer that was accepted. This home will remain as a monument to the past while being enjoyed in the present and preserved for the future.

This house has a fascinating history and deserves to be recognized for merely surviving against all odds.

956 Heywood Avenue

I became interested in this charming little house when I walked by and saw it was soon to be redeveloped.

The house was built in 1909 by John Avery, a contractor who pioneered the use of concrete block in home construction. He made the concrete blocks himself with the tradename, Ideal concrete building blocks. For more information on John Avery, see the articles on 97 and 139 Cook Street. He lived here with his wife Ellen and daughter May for one year.

Thomas Hodges then moved in with his family. He was a driver for L.

Dickenson, grocer, and his son, Frederick William, worked there as well. Thomas was born about 1836 in England and married Mary Ann Burns in Darlington, Ontario, June 15, 1889. Two children were born in Ontario, while four were born in Victoria after the family moved here in 1864. In 1912, Thomas moved to 1166 Camosun Street, leaving Frederick in the home. He had been born in Victoria February 25, 1877. On January 16, 1911, Frederick married Elizabeth Grace Sketch, the widow of Arthur Russell, who had died in 1907, leaving her with four small children.[314] At the same time, Frederick partnered with Arthur B. King to purchase L. Dickenson, grocer, changing the name to Hodges & King. The grocery store was located at 1425 Douglas Street. Frederick's Attestation Paper showed him to be married with four children. There is no record of him serving overseas, although it was known that he worked for the Imperial Munitions Board and later for the Victoria Phoenix Brewery. Frederick died August 28, 1936.[315]

956 Heywood Avenue, 2001
HALLMARK HERITAGE SOCIETY ARCHIVES

The building sat empty for two years until agent George A. Jones moved in. He was the first in a series of short-term residents about whom little is known. Widow Mrs. A. Stephenson and Julius G. Martin also lived here for one year. John A. Davidson, a department manager for the Hudson's Bay Company, resided here in 1927. Walter Tyers Gale moved into 956 Heywood Avenue in 1928. He was born October 10, 1864, in Cheltenham, England, to Charles Francis Gale and Harriet Tyers, and married Marion Glassford Roberts December 7, 1897, at Cheltenham.[316] He came to Canada in 1913 after the death of his wife. On March 14, 1918, he married Eleanor Smythe at Victoria. From then on, he was associated with the provincial government and was an active member of the British Columbia Provincial Police from 1926. He had reached the rank of Sergeant by the time he lived in this house. Walter died in Victoria January 3, 1938.[317]

Louis Charles Erb, a pastry chef at the Empress Hotel, was here for one year. He was born June 30, 1905, at Ludwigstrassen, Germany, to Jakob Heinrich Erb and Louise Theresia Bieger. The family moved to Canada in August 1923, settling in Calgary, Alberta, where Louis married Doris Emma Baldwin in 1926. The family was living in Victoria by 1930. When his parents died in 1956 and 1957, the family was residing at 607 Cook Street. Louis died February 2, 1975, at Royal Jubilee Hospital.

Laura de Turyznonwicz then moved in with her family. Born Laura C. Blackwell on August 28, 1878, in St. Catherines, Ontario, she married Stanislaus Gozdawa de Turyznonwicz June 26, 1907, in Krakow, Poland. Three children were born in Poland. It is not known when the family moved to Canada or when Stanislaus died, but Laura was a widow when she lived on Heywood Avenue. Her son Paul was an architecture student with J.C.M. Keith, while Peter and Wanda were students. In July 1935, the family moved to Los Angeles[318] where Paul died January 1, 1946, and Laura on October 25, 1953.[319]

956 Heywood Avenue, 2022

Mona Elizabeth Rickaby, the secretary to the Provincial Secretary of the BC government, lived here in 1934. She was born in Victoria July 9, 1893, to John Benjamin Hamilton Rickaby and Elizabeth Karsey. She never married and died in Victoria July 20, 1958. Her obituary tells the story of her remarkable life:

> "Mona Rickaby, probably the best known secretary ever to work at the legislative buildings, died Saturday at St. Joseph's Hospital after a brief illness. She had marked her 75th birthday 11 days earlier. Burial will be in the family plot at Ross Bay Cemetery, where her mother, Elizabeth, was buried in 1910, and her father, John Benjamin, in 1925, but arrangements for the funeral services by Hayward's Chapel still remain incomplete. Miss Rickaby joined the civil service here the year after her mother died and during a period of 36 years became popular and widely known as a secretary for ministers including former premier T. D. Pattulo. In 1943 after a year with the Provincial Rehabilitation Council which toured all parts of BC, she suddenly cashed in abroad in 1947. She went to work as a machinist helper at Yarrow's shipyard. At wars's end, she resumed secretarial work in the Commandant's office at the Royal Roads Military College for a year. Miss Rickaby fulfilled a long-held ambition of going abroad in 1947. She went to Ottawa and scored 98% in a federal civil service exam and was sent to New York as secretary to General A. G. McNaughton while he was delegated to the Atomic Energy Commission. Following other postings in Washington, DC, she was transferred to the external affairs department and spent three years in New Zealand as secretary to the Canadian High Commissioner. Miss Rickaby returned to Victoria in 1951 and became partner with Nell Edwards in a tea room,

> the Blue Room, at 1303 Broad St., where the two friends continued to live after closing down the business several years ago."[320]

Maurice Wilkinson of the Victoria Police resided here with his family for five years. He was born August 25, 1898, at Burton upon Trent, Staffordshire, England, to Herbert Wilkinson and Mary Ann Felthouse. The family immigrated to Canada in 1903, settling in Saskatchewan.[321] He married Kathleen Makepeace in Vancouver November 20, 1917. In 1918, they moved to Victoria, where he joined the police department as a peace officer. He died in Victoria January 8, 1981, leaving his wife, four children, seven grandchildren, and eight great-grandchildren.[322]

During World War II, Fannie Worthington lived here while her husband, Zebulon, and son, Douglas, were on active service. Zebulon was born July 12, 1895, to Zebulon Worthington and Sarah Ann Hind, at Bolton, Lancashire, England. He saw service in World War I and emigrated to Canada. The family lived in Toronto, where their three children, Douglas (January 17, 1922), Alfred (August 29, 1923), and Margaret (March 21, 1925), were born. At the onset of war, Zebulon and Douglas signed up for service and went overseas. Fanny died in Victoria April 27, 1981, and Zebulon three years later, on April 4, 1984.

Harry Holdsworth's family resided here from 1942. He was born about 1882 in Birkenshaw, Yorkshire, England, to Joseph Holdsworth and Martha Ann Bentley. He married Ethel Hayes in Bradford, Yorkshire, England, April 22, 1905, and their three children were born there. In May 1921, the family immigrated to Canada, settling in Sedgwick, Alberta. They moved to Victoria in 1942, where Harry worked as a bookkeeper. He died at the residence February 11, 1944. At that time, son Herman was serving with the Royal Canadian Artillery at Halifax and son Leslie with the RCAF.[323] Ethel continued to live at the house with their daughter, Marjorie, who worked as a maid, until about 1948. She died November 17, 1959.

Retired CPR pipefitter William Saunders and his wife, Florence, lived here for many years. He was born October 6, 1877, in England to William Saunders and Sarah Bates. He came to Canada in 1905, where he worked for the CPR in Winnipeg. At some point, he married Florence Stokes, and they had three daughters and two sons. He retired to Victoria in 1943 and died here November 3, 1960, living at 1124 Dallas Road at that time.[324] Florence died June 15, 1974.

The property is now being redeveloped into "soft density" townhouses, and that will mean the end of this charming little cottage. The proposal is for six units facing onto Heywood Avenue with a wide street-facing entry garden. The plantings and entry garden will be inspired by the meadows of Beacon Hill Park, which are directly across the street. Proposals in 2019 and 2021 were rejected by the City of Victoria, and the project is currently being redesigned.

941 Meares Street

941 Meares Street is a one-and-one-half-storey chalet style cottage located in the Meares Street cluster on the north side of the street adjacent to Pioneer Square Cemetery in Victoria's Fairfield neighbourhood. Built in 1906, it has the low profile of the colonial bungalow, the half-timbering of the Tudor Revival, and the picturesque qualities of the Alpine chalet.

There is value in the ownership of this residence by the middle class. The first occupant was William C. Warburton, who was born June 6, 1859, in Spotland, Manchester, England. He was the bookkeeper of Windsor Grocery at 815–817 Government and later was a member of the post office staff. He lived here with his wife until 1909. When he died January 30, 1922, he left behind his widow, Annie Blinston, and three children.[325] He is buried in Ross Bay Cemetery.

941 Meares Street, 2009
HALLMARK HERITAGE SOCIETY ARCHIVES

The next family to live here were the Christies. William Crichton Christie was born February 5, 1863, in Pictou, Nova Scotia. He entered the telegraph service as a boy at Truro, Nova Scotia, and later went to Texas to join an uncle on a sheep farm. He arrived in Victoria January 10, 1885 and entered the service of the Dominion Government Telegraph and Signalling Services, eventually becoming manager of the Canadian Pacific Railway telegraph office in the city in 1894. He married fellow Nova Scotian Annie Sinclair Holmes April 11, 1898, and they had one child. She died July 24, 1904, while visiting family in Nova Scotia. He worked for, and later became a partner in, Ship Chandlers, an early Victoria business. He died May 21, 1922,[326] while on a business trip to New Zealand, where he also visited his sister, whose husband was the chief electrician of the Pacific Cable Board at Auckland. He is buried in Waikaraka Cemetery in Auckland.[327]

Jackson Hanby lived here in 1923, and David G. Andrews the following year. Gas engineer William McNicol Cathels resided in the house until 1926. He was born in Gravesend, England, to Edmond Sutherland Cathels and Elizabeth McNicol and came to Canada in 1876. He worked for many years in Montreal, where he married Emma Julia Parsons in 1878. The couple had three children. William came to Victoria on his retirement in 1919. He died October 15, 1940 and is buried at Ross Bay Cemetery.

The Landman family moved into the house in 1927 and lived here for decades. Harold Eric Landman was born June 21, 1879, in Yorkshire, England. He married Gertrude Gosey and came to Canada in about 1912. He was a sales representative for Brett & Kerr, Real Estate, General Insurance and Financial Agents and, by 1942, was the Department Superintendent of Brokers for the BC government. He worked as a clerk for Pemberton Holmes and then became a barrister with E.L. Tait (name later changed to Tait & Holmes). Gertrude died on January 30, 1956, and Harold left the house soon after.

941 Meares Street, 2022

In 1985, the house was restored by Tom Palfrey and Tom Putnam, with painstaking attention to detail both inside and out, for which they received a Hallmark Society award. The home has been well maintained by subsequent owners.

This house is a valuable part of a series of four houses of similar mass built on the Christ Church Trust adjacent to Pioneer Square Cemetery. Singly the houses have heritage merit, but their significance is enhanced by their positions in the unified heritage streetscape. That the four have survived in their original locations enhances their value.

943 Meares Street

This home is a wood frame modest Victorian residence located in the Meares Street cluster on the south side of the street adjacent to Pioneer Square Cemetery in Victoria's Fairfield neighbourhood. Built in 1893, it is one of a pair built by the Anglican Church on the lot at the same time. The styling reflects the architectural tastes of the late 19th century, with these examples more modest expressions of the mansions owned by more affluent owners. The occupations of early residents reflect the growth of the middle class. The traditional name, "the bell ringer's house," almost certainly speaks to the building's close association with the Cathedral.

George Thompson, the first renter, owned Thompson & King Commission Agents & Customs Brokers. By 1895, Harry Ablitt Howell was living here. He was born on the Isle of Wight April 18, 1865, to Alfred Howell and Jane Ablitt. He immigrated to Canada in 1883 and was living in Victoria by 1884. He married Ena Vera Wentworth Coswell September 6, 1889, and they had one daughter. He established Annesty & Howell, a firm of grocers at 81 Douglas Street, then worked for the Provincial Lands Department for many years. The family moved to James Bay, where Harry died on October 18, 1923, and Ena died February 14, 1935.

Frederick George Brock moved here in 1900. Born in England in 1864, he immigrated to the United States in 1880. He married Nettie May Cheney in Seattle September 22, 1893. One child was born there. By 1898, the family had moved to Victoria, where their second and third children were born. The family relocated to Idaho in 1913 and filed for American citizenship. They then moved to Oregon, where they were listed on the 1920 census. There is no further information on what happened to them after that.

943 Meares Street, 2022

Thomas Roff and his family lived here in 1903. Born in England in 1855, he and his wife Harriet had two children. He worked briefly for Rithet's, then moved to Otter Point, where he operated a farm for decades. He died April 4, 1921.[328] Next to move into the house were Thomas's daughter Harriet and her husband, Augustus Brown. Harriet Eleanor Roff was born in England on July 21, 1885, and married Augustus Frederick Harold Brown June 1, 1903. Augustus worked as an undertaker for his entire career. Harriet died about 1924, and Augustus moved to Washington State, where he married Annie Mahlia Scott, in Port Angeles, June 16, 1926. The family moved back to Canada, where Annie died February 25, 1955. Augustus followed her March 26, 1963.

Henry Fields lived here between 1910 and 1914. He was born about 1874 in Australia and arrived in Canada on November 16, 1908. He worked for the T. Heaney Company as a teamster. John Peter Geddes was in this house between 1921 and 1923. He was born about 1864 in Scotland and had arrived in Victoria with his wife, Mary, in 1890. He worked for the City of Victoria and died April 7, 1928,[329] and is buried in Ross Bay Cemetery.

Mrs. Ethel Robinson lived here from 1927 to 1934, but nothing is known about her. After the property sat empty for two years, John Thomas Thornton

Iverson and his wife, Olive, moved in. Born in Dover, Kent, England, January 27, 1882, to John Thomas Iverson and Mary Ann Thornton, he came to Canada in 1899, settling in Calgary. He married Olive Elizabeth Ferguson there in 1909. Their daughter, Marian May, was born there in 1913, and the family then moved to Victoria, where their son, Robert John, was born in 1918. John was the proprietor of Iverson Signs and later worked as a sign writer for Bayliss Sign Company. Their daughter died in Victoria in 1933, and Olive died here February 1, 1949. John then married Frances Ellen Akroyd. He died January 27, 1971, living then at 314 Dallas Road.[330]

Frederick Wells and his family lived here from 1939 to 1941. He was born July 5, 1905, in Nayburn, Yorkshire, England, to George Wells and Jane Asquith. He married Thelma Florence Luckovich on July 20, 1935, at the Bishop's Palace, 740 View Street. He worked in construction, and Thelma was a waitress. She died December 20, 1978, and Frederick died January 27, 1982. Their son, Don F. Wells, was noted in the community as a draughtsman and a heritage activist.

James Tuck lived here from 1944 to 1953. He was born in Oughrington, Cheshire, England, September 14, 1878, to James Tuck and Ellen Schofield. He married Millie Rose Jeffs and came to Canada in 1905, settling in North Battleford, Saskatchewan. Their two children were born there. The family moved to Victoria in 1928 when James retired from farming. At some point, they moved to North Vancouver, where Millie died November 20, 1963, and James died June 2, 1966.

Sidney Harry Walker and his wife, Ellen Agnes, moved into the house in 1955. He was born in London, England, in 1885 and married Ellen Agnes Foote in 1910. Sidney worked as a fireman for 21 years and retired to Victoria in 1946. They both died in 1961, Ellen on October 11, and Sidney on November 22, still living at this address.

The house was designed by Cecil Evers and John Charles Malcolm Keith. Evers was a Seattle-based architect who, together with Keith, submitted a design for the proposed Christ Church Cathedral in 1891. Constructed with others in the city while awaiting the start of the cathedral project, these two modest homes were a departure from their regular commissions and were likely awarded as a compensation for the delay. Evers left Victoria before the end of 1893 and played no further role in the development of the new Cathedral. Keith became official Synod architect, a position he would hold until his retirement in 1937.

This residence is part of the historic grouping of houses originally built on the Christ Church Cathedral Trust lands. The relationship of these houses to each other and to the street is an important aspect of the Meares Street streetscape. That the four have survived in their same locations is also valued.

947 Meares Street

947 Meares Street is a wood frame Victorian residence located in the Meares Street cluster on the north side of the street adjacent to Pioneer Square Cemetery in Victoria's Fairfield neighbourhood.

Built in 1893, it is valued as an example of a Victorian residence. It is one of a pair built by the Anglican Church on the lot at the same time. The styling reflects the architectural tastes of the late 19th century, with these examples more modest expressions of the mansions owned by more affluent owners. The occupations of early residents reflect the growth of the middle class.

Ernest A. Pauline, the first renter, was an accountant with Matthews Richard & Tye. He was born in Henley on Thomas, Oxfordshire, England, July 22, 1864, to Frederick Pauline and Mary Cutler. He married Emma Jane Jennings in Yardley, Worcestershire, England, March 9, 1886, and was in Victoria by October 26, 1886, when his daughter, Dorothy Mary, was born. He worked as an accountant and spent time in both Canada and England. He died in Victoria on November 20, 1912.

947 Meares Street, 2022

Between 1895 and 1897, the property was operated as a Kindergarten and Day School by Miss Powell. After being vacant, it returned to residential rental in 1899 when J.W. Murray moved in. George P. Kelly and his family moved into the house in 1900 and lived there until 1909. He was born October 25, 1845, in North Sydney, Nova Scotia, to James Lochman Kelly and Rachel Way. George worked for the old Victoria Telephone Company and afterwards for several years with the Dominion Marine Department. He died August 6, 1930.[331] The Stiles family moved into the house in 1910. Edward Stuart Stiles was born in Australia December 1, 1867. He married Sybel Stuart in Vancouver January 30, 1909, and moved to Victoria, where he worked as an upholsterer. He lived here for two years, and it is unknown where he died.

Brother and sister, Annie and George Bridger, lived in the house for two years. They were born to Dan Bridger and Maria Peacey in Surrey, England;

Annie in April 1868, and George in 1871. Annie worked as a clerk for A.W. Knight, and George was a teamster. She died in North Vancouver on January 4, 1948, and there is no further information on George; he may have returned to England. By 1918, Joseph W. Chambers was in the house. He was born in England January 29, 1873, to John Cameron and Pauline Green. He came to Canada in 1903. He married Isabella Staniforth, and they had four children. During World War I, he was a Corporal in the 54th Canadian Infantry Battalion, based in Kootenay, leaving Canada in 1915 and returning in 1919. He died February 17, 1928, with his death attributed to his overseas service. His funeral, with full military honours, was held on February 18, and he was buried at the Royal Oak Burial Park.[332]

From 1921 to 1929, members of the Moore family lived here. Eliza Moore (née Shaw), the widow of Randall Moore, was born in 1854 in Doncaster, Yorkshire, England, and married there about 1885. They had seven children. Their daughter, Eliza Constance Moore, born in 1887, lived here with her mother. She was a music teacher and died in 1971.

After two years of vacancy, the Linden family took up residence. Eric Linden was a miner and then a fisherman, but there are no details about his life. His wife, Jessie Fraser Wright, was born in Kincardineshire, Scotland, July 26, 1888, to Isaac Wright and Mary Ann Duncan. She died in Duncan on January 15, 1981. By 1948, Stanley William Norman Saunders and his wife Alice were living at this address. He was born in England in 1884, and she was born there August 12, 1879. They came to Canada about 1909, moving to British Columbia in 1919. He worked in the check room of Mac and Mac before retiring in 1949. Alice died February 4, 1953, living then at 1049 Burdett Avenue. Stanley died January 21, 1969.[333]

There is value in the design by Cecil Evers and John Charles Malcolm Keith. Evers was a Seattle-based architect who, together with Keith, submitted a design for the proposed Christ Church Cathedral in 1891. Constructed with others in the city while awaiting the start of the cathedral project, these two modest homes were a departure from their regular commissions and were likely awarded as a compensation for the delay. Evers left Victoria before the end of 1893 and played no further role in the development of the new Cathedral. Keith became official Synod architect, a position he would hold until his retirement in 1937.

This residence has significance as part of the historic grouping of houses originally built on the Christ Church Cathedral trust. The relationship of these houses to each other and to the street is an important aspect of the Meares Street streetscape. That four of them have survived in their same positions is historically important.

949 Meares Street

949 Meares Street, built in 1901, is a wood frame one-and-one-half-storey classical variation of a bungalow located in the Meares Street cluster on the north side of the street adjacent to Pioneer Square Cemetery in Victoria's Fairfield neighbourhood. The paired posts on the full verandah reflect classical influence, while the horizontality and the verandah itself reflect its bungalow antecedents. The mature landscaping enhances the street presence of the residence.

Built for George and Mary Mowat, the house illustrates the type of housing being built at the turn of the twentieth century for the growing merchant class. The family arrived here about 1901 and purchased the land from the Anglican diocese. George was a florist and later worked as a bank messenger. The family lived here until 1906 when they moved to 1114 Richardson Street. George died March 6, 1923.

949 Meares Street, 2022

The subsequent owners were Donald C. and Agnes McKinnon. Donald was born about 1844 in Guelph, Ontario, to Alexander and Sarah McKinnon. He married Agnes Card in Vaughan, Ontario, December 22, 1880. They moved to Victoria in 1906 and took over the Imperial Hotel, but Donald's failing health soon compelled him to leave this position. When he died August 14, 1908, after a six-month illness, they were living next door at 957 Meares, but Agnes moved into this house by 1912. Before she moved in, she rented the house to Frederick Arthur Johns and his wife, Violet. He was born December 13, 1874, in New Westminster, to Isaac Johns and Isabella McGregor. He married Violet Gerry December 8, 1900, and shortly after their marriage, they were living at the Presbyterian School. They had two children. Fred worked as a waiter with his last job at the historic Poodle Dog Café. He died in Victoria March 26, 1911,[334] and is buried at Ross Bay Cemetery.

In 1925, Thomas Griffith Arthur Young and his wife, Clara, made this address their home. He was born in Croydon, England, to Thomas Young and Mary Jane Twiddy, February 18, 1870. He married Clara Jane Munday in London in 1900, and they came to Victoria in 1905. Thomas was a provincial civil servant with the Public Works Department and retired in 1936. They moved to Balmoral Road in 1932, from where he died November 3, 1951. Clara died September 3, 1958[335] and both are buried in the family plot at Royal Oak Burial Park.

By 1937, the owners were Bert and Marguerite Aaronson. He was born in Victoria on January 21, 1889, to Andrew Alfred Aaronson and Rose Van Der Sluis. He married fellow Victorian Marguerite Victoria Wilson, and they had two children. One of Victoria's first pharmacists, he founded Aaronson's Drug Store at the corner of Cook and Fort Streets in 1910 and was active in the business until he became ill in August 1967, after which the business was managed by his son, Gordon. There were 12 drugstores in Victoria when he opened his, and his store is the only one now operating under its original name.

When the building in which the drug store was located was demolished and the site redeveloped, Bert moved across the street where he and Marguerite lived above the store until their deaths. Bert died September 20, 1968,[336] and Marguerite continued in the apartment until her tragic death January 29, 1976. She was crossing Fort Street and was hit by a bus, fracturing her skull.

From about 1938 to the present, the owners have been Sue Jun Duck and his wife Sue Yee Ho, and their descendants. They were married when they came to Victoria from China in 1903, but Mrs. Sue arrived slightly later than her husband. They ran a grocery and produce store on Fort St. At least three of their nine children were born above the shop when it was at 818 Fort, now the site of BC Vital Statistics. After World War II, the Sues leased acreage on San Juan Avenue in Saanich for a market garden and ran a truck farming business. Sue Jun Duck died in 1956 at 77. Daughters Pansee and Lily lived in this house with their mother until 1962. Their son Robert Sue (aka Hung Qun Sue) married Sarah Ngo, and they moved in to look after his mother. From 1967, this house became a rental property. Mrs. Sue died in 1972 at 85, and the house was inherited by sons George and Robert until George's death in 1994. As George had no children, it was inherited by Robert's daughter, Michelle Sue.[337] In 1998, Robert and restoration carpenter Davyd McMinn won the Hallmark Society's highest award, the Louis Award, for their restoration. Painstakingly restored both inside and out, the interior has been retained in virtually original condition. It was designated a municipal heritage site in 2004, and the designation includes several interior features, including the living room, dining room, woodwork, and hardware and fixtures. The metal fence on the street front of the property is also protected.

962–964 Fairfield Road

Built in 1908, this house is a wood frame two-and-one-half-storey Queen Anne residence located on the major arterial road at the centre of Victoria's Fairfield neighbourhood. The styling reflects the prevailing taste in the early years of the twentieth century and reflects the growth of the middle class, whose homes were often builders' interpretations of the homes of the wealthy. It is an early example of a home built along the main transportation link between downtown Victoria and the eastern suburbs and was constructed at the beginning of the Victoria building boom of 1908–1913.

New research has revealed that the earliest documented resident was James Rideout. Born in Newfoundland in 1863, he married Ada Mary LeMessurier there July 5, 1889. Five children were born in Newfoundland before the family arrived in Victoria in 1907. James worked for years as a clerk for Melrose Paint Co. The family lived in this modest home for four years. James died January 5, 1935[338]and Ada January 2, 1955, in Seattle, Washington, where she had moved after James' death.

Ernest Woodman Tribe, a steward at the Empress Hotel, lived here in 1915. Born January 29, 1888, in Petworth, Sussex, England, to Walter John Tribe and Anna Louise Merritt, he was educated in England and served with the 5th Regiment, R.C.G.A. as a gunner during World War I. It is unknown what happened to Sarah, but she was with the family when they lived in Calgary in 1921.[339] Ernest married Margaret Euphemia Brown in Montreal June 9, 1929. He then moved to Toronto, where he worked as the general manager of George Coles, Caterers. At the onset of World War II, he joined the RCAF and served overseas. Squadron Leader Ernest Tribe died March 23, 1946, in Shaughnessy Hospital, Vancouver, BC,[340] and is buried in Burnaby (Ocean View) Burial Park.[341]

962–964 Fairfield Road, 2022

Donald J. Owens, who worked as the manager of P. Burns & Co., was at this address in 1917 and 1918, followed by Pauline Wardrop in 1920. She was born in England about 1876 and came to Canada in 1911, where she worked as a nurse. Richard Henry Simmons was here for one year. Born about 1880 in Ireland, he came to Canada in 1907 and married Gladys Blanche Hill in Victoria November 25, 1911. She died April 3, 1944, and he followed her June 27, 1963. He worked as a draughtsman for the BC Department of Lands for his entire career.

George Chalmers Grant and his family were the subsequent residents. Born in Inverness, Scotland, March 3, 1869, to Peter Grant and Christine MacKenzie, he was associated with the Scottish Legal Life Insurance in Scotland and in Leicester, England, before coming to Victoria in 1912. Nothing is known about his first marriage, but he is noted as a widower on his marriage to Charlotte Hamilton Shegog, August 27, 1915, in Vancouver. He joined the business staff of *The Times* in 1915 and was circulation manager for some years. In his later career, he was in charge of credits. He was an enthusiastic member of the Burns Club, which he helped to found, and served on its executive for years. He regularly spent his summers at Brentwood Bay and was active in sports activities there.[342] His widow, Charlotte, lived in the house for decades after his death.

This modest home stands as a reminder of early Victoria when neighbourhoods grew up along streetcar lines.

Fort Street, site of previously untold stories. Read on …

Fort Street

I decided to present all buildings on Fort Street in one chapter as they are located in multiple neighbourhoods. It seemed ridiculous to split them up as they are best considered as a contiguous group.

801–813 Fort Street

This article was published in the May/June 2007 issue of *Moss Rock Review.*

The Heritage Detective finds it fascinating when work leads to another trail. While working on a recent contract, I stumbled across the fascinating story of the commercial block at the very fringe of Fairfield. The series of storefronts at the corner of Fort and Blanshard – 801–813 Fort Street – exemplify the evolution of a historic building through adaptive reuse. It represents a link from the early days of the City of Victoria to the modern era. The alley at the rear clearly shows the original brick construction. Built in 1914 during the most significant population increase and construction boom in Victoria's history, to replace a wood-frame structure, the storefronts were "modernized" in the 1920s with the addition of a stucco coating and a stepped, pedimented tower over the corner entrance. A more recent intervention has further updated the storefronts, increasing the number of retail stores.

The first wooden structure on the site arose in the early days of Victoria, around the late 1880s or early 1890s. From the very beginning, it has been home to a variety of businesses and has housed some strange tenants. In the early years, most tenants also lived on site, presumably at the rear of each retail outlet. Located just a block from Douglas Street, the complex has always been crucial to the retail health of the City. There has always been a restaurant or confectionery in some form on the corner. The corner location, now the home of Starbucks, was once the home of W.J. Dwyer, a grocer who sold his business to Julius Francis Rausch in 1901. The first storefront up Fort Street (originally 121 Fort) housed a series of different businesses, including John Moffat's restaurant; Frank Hobbs, furniture dealer; and Mrs. Schneider's Candy Store. In 1901, it

801–813 Fort Street, February 1960 M01441, COURTESY OF CITY OF VICTORIA ARCHIVES

appears this storefront was merged with the corner location for the grocery store.

Further up Fort Street (originally 123 Fort) was a second-hand furniture store, replaced by Farwig's upholstery, Bernardo & Sures fish and fruit merchants, Levy's cigar manufacturers, and the Pumfrey Brothers fur dressers. At 125 Fort were a fish and fruit dealer and William Eden's second-hand store. There was only one tenant at 127 Fort. George Jaques, a watchmaker and jeweller, operated his business from this location from the opening of the wooden building until the new brick building arose on the site. He retired at the same time as the original building.

An examination of early merchants in the new brick structure clearly indicates social change. One of the earliest tenants was Tokio Pressers, who were in business from 1914 until 1942 when the family was interned. They were replaced by ABC Electric, who operated from their Fort Street location until 1959, when they moved to Yates Street. This business is still in operation, now located on Quadra Street. 805 Fort Street was the home of Lou Poy & Co. grocers from 1915 to 1951, when the business was acquired by Alpine Food Market. This company, too, was still in operation in 1907, having moved around the corner to a new location on Blanshard Street just a few years ago. 803 Fort housed the Edinburgh Café for five years after it moved from the corner location, then was replaced by P.W. Tow Taxidermist. That must have been a profitable business as it lasted in this location until 1951, when Mrs. Irene Carroll opened a lingerie and corset shop.

801 Fort Street had perhaps the greatest variety of tenants. The first business was Reliable Messenger Co., replaced after six years by Dominion Rubber. After two years, Arthur Southall moved in with his stoves and ranges. He was the last retail tenant, being replaced in 1939 by the Lido Café. All the subsequent tenants were restaurants, from the Atholl Coffee Shop to the Burger House Restaurant, the Alpine Restaurant, and the Cultured Cow. The corner location housed the Edinburgh Café, a series of confectionery stores, and, in 1942, it became the home of Victoria Electric Motors.

801–813 Fort Street, 2022

By following the changes in tenants, you can trace the social history of the corner. It has always been the home to leading-edge businesses, many of which have long since disappeared.

I have lived here all my life and was able to relive many memories during my research into this block. Who could ever forget Chicken Delight? However, I had no clue that this location had also held a corset shop (did people still wear them in the 1950s?) and a taxidermist. As for fur dressers, they have long been out of favour.

You never know what you will find as a Heritage Detective, but the searching sure is fun.

Chicken Delight sign discovered during construction

2022 UPDATE

The Alpine Food Mart is no longer in business, having closed a few years ago. There have been changes to the tenants on Fort Street, but most of the current companies seem to be thriving. This is an area where tenant turnover is normal, and different stores bring different clients, to the benefit of all of them. The courtyard area behind the stores has been opened up with access off Blanshard Street. Named The Fort Common, it is a 3,000 square foot urban outdoor venue perfect for events large and small, including family reunions, weddings, corporate retreats, and meetings. This is an excellent use for a previously hidden space and brings it to life.

1121 Fort Street
House on the Move

A short article appeared in the Autumn 2010 issue of *Preserve*. Additional research was completed in 2022 and has resulted in a much larger article.

The evening of August 9, 2010 marked a new beginning for the residence at 1121 Fort Street. The house had a hard life after it was no longer used as a single-family dwelling.

A storefront was appended to the front of the residence to make it commercially viable. For many years, it was home to an electronics firm, served as an annex to the aesthetics school next door, and finally, the location of an antiques and collectibles business. A new building was soon to arise on the site, so the house was purchased by a new owner who moved it to a new location.

Over the next few weeks, the building was carefully deconstructed to facilitate the move. The roof was removed and discovered to be constructed with

2x4s, nowhere near the modern building codes. The front gable was loosened from its supports and folded back onto the main structure. This reduction in height meant that the house could be moved without necessitating a conflict with BC Hydro and other utility lines.

The house was then lifted from its foundation and heavy I-beams inserted. Around 11:30 pm, the large moving truck was backed up, and the beams were fastened to the main vehicle. Just after midnight, with a police escort and flashing lights on tow trucks, the house began its journey to its new home adjacent to 1702 Fernwood Road. As the slow move continued, intersections were blocked as needed. It was quite an experience watching a house make its way down the road – down Fort Street to Cook Street, along Cook Street to Pandora Avenue, and up Pandora Avenue to Fernwood Road. The house has since been restored in its new location and fits in very well with its neighbours.

1121 Fort Street: (upper) before move, 2010; (lower) during move, August 9, 2010

The history of the house begins in 1910, but the story of the Bantly family in this area goes back many years before that.

Marcus Bantly was born April 14, 1848, in Württenberg, Germany. He immigrated to the United States in 1870 with Maria Anna Grimm, settling in California. They married in Virginia City, Nevada, August 27, 1873. Of the six children they had in California, only three lived into adulthood. They were Simon Anton (Tony), Rosina Theresa (Rose), and Benedict. Marcus became involved in the cigar industry and when the family moved to Victoria in 1883, he established a cigar business here.[343] Anna earned some money with fancy embroidery work and was the representative for Mme. Griswold's Abdominal Corset, with an outlet on Johnson Street opposite Grimm's Carriage Factory.[344] In February 1892, Marcus awarded a contract to Thomas & Glover for a "two-storey brick building at the corner of Fort and Quadra Street, to be used as a cigar factory and residence."[345] He moved to his new facility at 155 Fort Street (later 851 Fort Street) in June of that year.[346]

Marcus Bantly was an accomplished musician, and his children inherited his talent and love of music. From 1896 to 1902, the Bantly Family Orchestra was known throughout the region. Marcus played the clarinet, Tony played the violin, Rosina played piano, and Benedict played violin and piano. The local newspapers are full of articles on their accomplishments with comments like "to the satisfaction of all," "well rendered," and "a good time may be expected." In 1902, Benedict studied at the Royal Conservatory of Music in Leipzig. He left in 1906 with the equivalent of a master's degree and his new wife, Johanna. He opened a studio for the teaching of violin, piano, and theory in music in the Garesché block at 732 Yates Street and imported a fine piano for his own use from Leipzig.[347] He also worked as the organist for St. Andrew's Cathedral.

1706 Fernwood Road, formerly 1121 Fort Street, 2022

The Bantly family home was located on a double lot at 1127 Fort Street. In 1910, Tony and Benedict subdivided the property. Each had a home built beside their widowed mother, Marcus having died October 24, 1906. Benedict and Johanna lived at 1125 Fort Street, and Simon and his wife Frances built this house at 1121 Fort Street.[348]

Bantly cigar shop, 1883
A-08980, COURTESY BC ARCHIVES

In August of 1922, Benedict and Johanna moved to California. In his first year there, he composed music for silent movies starring Mary Packford, Douglas Fairbanks Sr., and Mae Murray. Benedict appeared on screen as an orchestra leader in a silent film on the life of Abraham Lincoln. He worked as the director of music at La Puente Union High School for 21 years and also served as concertmaster of the San Gabriel Valley Symphony Orchestra.

Simon moved to 605 Trutch Street around 1913, and the house on Fort Street was rented to various tenants until his death November 20, 1923. Frances then moved back into the home at 1121 Fort Street and lived there until about 1946, when she moved to Southgate Street. She died July 22, 1959.

The loss of this house removed the grouping of three Bantly houses from the Fort Street streetscape, but fortunately, the buildings at 1125 and 1127 Fort Street remain today.

1124 Fort Street – Trebatha

The original article appeared in the July/August 2008 issue of *Moss Rock Review*.

One of the most interesting buildings on Fort Street is Trebatha at 1124 Fort Street, built in 1886 to a design attributed to architect Edward Mallandaine Jr., for dentist Thomas A. Jones and his wife, Susanna. The address at the time of construction was 248 Fort Street. The origin of the name, Trebatha, is unclear, although there is a Trebatha Hall in Cornwall, England. To date, no one has been able to link Dr. Jones' family to the English source. Its Second-Empire styling with the characteristic mansard roof makes it a neighbourhood landmark on the Fort Street hill, just past Cook Street. Dr. Jones was influential beyond his dental work. Born November 4, 1844, to Thomas Joseph Jones and Mary Conway in Toronto, he practiced dentistry in St. Catharines, Ontario, where he was a member of the city council. Dr. Jones moved to Victoria in 1884 and was influential in the first Dentistry Act in BC on April 3, 1886. By 1890, he had the largest dental practice in the city, and was the first President of the BC Dental Association. His association with the dental profession was profound as many of Victoria's leading dentists passed through his office during their earlier years.[349]

1124 Fort Street, 2022

Dr. Jones helped get the first electric streetcar system going in 1890. One of the routes went past Trebatha, and a few blocks north, past Regent's Park, the mansion of the streetcar company's first president D.W. Higgins. Dr. Jones was later on the board of directors of the BC Electric Railway Co. The family only lived in the house for fifteen years, moving in 1902 to a new Queen Anne style dwelling, Dundalk (named for his mother's home in County Louth, Ireland), at the corner of Linden Avenue and Rockland Avenue. He died January 21, 1924, at Dundalk,[350] and was buried in Ross Bay Cemetery on January 23, 1924.

In 1911, Trebatha became a boarding house owned by Elizabeth Webb, widow of William, about whom little is known, for about five years. Then for a time after World War I, it was an emergency hospital for influenza patients.

George Wild Walton, his wife Ruth, and their family moved into 1124 Fort

Street in 1921. George was born December 24, 1869, in Darlington, Durham, England, to Robert Walton and Hannah Burban. He came to Canada in 1893, and married Ruth Ellen Feldon at Victoria, July 16, 1898. George had worked as an engineer on the Victoria & Sidney Railway, later joining the CNR in the same capacity. The story of his untimely death was front-page news on January 7, 1924. According to the article, "Instantaneous death overtook George W. Walton, fifty-five, at 9 o'clock yesterday morning when an extension electric light cord he was carrying became suddenly charged with 2,200 volts from a break in the transmission line outside the residence at 1124 Fort Street. William Walton, a son, narrowly escaped death, when he knocked the live wire away from the body of his father, the fact that he stood upon dry wood averting a double tragedy."[351] The accident occurred when the high-power transmission line, part of the distribution system that lights the city, broke outside the home and somehow transmitted power to the basement where Mr. Walton was trying to repair a defective furnace. I can only imagine Ellen's horror when she went to call her husband and son for breakfast only to discover her husband dead and her son traumatized. At the inquest, blame was assigned to the older wiring on the street, but the jury concluded that not even modern wiring could have prevented the tragedy. The lines of the nearby Victoria City Dairy "became similarly charged, but in this case, the fuse blew out, and the current was cut off." The coroner's jury returned a verdict of "accidental death by electrocution by current from an unknown source."[352] At the time of his death, William was employed as a locomotive engineer at the Esquimalt drydock. Ellen Walton continued to live at the home until about 1940, when she moved to Esquimalt, with a break where it was rented as rooms. At the time of her death March 9, 1959, she was living at 1116 Craigflower Road. Both the Waltons are buried at Ross Bay Cemetery.

William H. Caton and his wife Louisa were the next residents. He was born on March 8, 1885, in Manchester, England, and came to Canada in 1907. He worked as a labourer and ran this rooming house. The couple left this address in the early 1950s.

In 1958, Trebatha underwent conversion to 14 housekeeping rooms. It had sat vacant for two years until architect John Keay and his partners acquired it in 1992 and began the lengthy process of returning it to useable form. The ugly grey asphalt shingles that had been nailed over the exterior ironically had the effect of preserving the original wood channel siding underneath. Once the shingles were removed – no small task – the house was revealed as a grubby yellow. Happily, that was changed with the application of a new coat of paint that closely matched the historical photos.[353] Inside, plaster arches and ceiling rosettes were uncovered, and much original detail was discovered under layers of paint. The building was successfully converted to business offices and continues with that use today.

After the 1992 work was completed, the project was nominated for a Hallmark Society award but was turned down because the front porch had not been reconstructed. As noted in a newspaper article of the day, "..the $300,000 budget doesn't allow for reconstructing an imposing front porch, but that can be added later, Keay says."

That imposing front porch was added over 15 years after the original rehabilitation. The rehabilitated and restored building bears a remarkable resemblance to the original photographs and is now more of a landmark than ever. It is one of a grouping of heritage houses in this area that have been converted to commercial use, often the only way to make restoration economically feasible. The grouping also serves as a buffer between the commercial core of downtown and the residential areas of Fairfield and Rockland.

John Keay and his partners were recognized in May 2008 by the Hallmark Society for their determination to restore this fine building to active use, and for their willingness to complete the project years after their prior work. Trebatha was returned to an attractive building with a historically accurate rebuilding of the front porch.[354] It is still an attractive building in 2022. Dr. Jones would be proud.

1248 Fort Street

I was intrigued by this building as I walked by and decided to discover its history.

In the early days of Victoria, this address was noted as 38 Cadboro Bay Road. This home was built about 1898 for Arthur W. More who lived there for three years. He was born in St. Andrews, Fifeshire, Scotland, about 1855 and came to Canada around 1889. He was employed by the Bank of British Columbia until it was taken over by the Canadian Bank of Commerce. When he left the bank, Arthur went into business for himself in real estate. After suffering setbacks, he lived in Seattle for a short time but returned to resume his property activities and was successful. He organized transferring the old Albion Iron Works site to the CPR for terminal purposes. He died, unmarried, at Victoria, February 18, 1908.[355]

The next resident of the older building was Dentist Dr. Arthur John Garesché. Born in Volcanoville, California, in prime gold rush country, October 24, 1860, he started his professional career in 1881 as an apprentice dentist in Portland and eventually graduated from the University of Pennsylvania Dental College in 1887. He was still practicing at age 87 and was reputed to be the dentist with the longest record of years in service in Canada, and most likely, in North America. In 1947, he was a delegate to the biennial convention of the Western Canada Dental Association and the annual convention of the British Columbia

Dental Association at the Banff Springs Hotel. He brought with him a collection of old dental equipment, the likes of which would shock today's patients.[356] He married Millicent Mary Trimen at Victoria on September 18, 1902. Dr. Garesché built a fine brick office building at 732 Yates Street and ran his dental practice from a suite there. In 1910, he erected an investment property at 727 Johnson. The west half was a three-storey stable. Dr. Garesché died at Victoria September 14, 1952, three months after closing down his dental practice.[357]

By 1912, George Alfred Shepherd was living there with his family. Born December 26, 1868, in England to Joseph Herbert Shepherd and Martha Isabella Curteis, he married Mary Helen Frances McGavin in 1891. The family came to Canada in 1910, where he worked in various occupations, including as clerk for the Consolidated Rubber Company and as a dairyman. The family lived at this address for about six years. The next resident was Sarah J. Green, about whom nothing is known except that she was the widow of David.

There was a series of residents until John Herbert Elford purchased the property May 23, 1924.[358] He was born in September 1878 to John Pitcairn Elford and Mary Hattie Robertson at Victoria. His father was a noted builder in early Victoria. Born in Adelaide, South Australia, in 1850, of English parentage, he was only a few days old when his family sailed for the California goldfields. The vessel put in to Pitcairn Island where he was christened, and there he received the second of his given names, "Pitcairn," of which he was very proud. After a few years in California, his parents brought him to Victoria, where he was educated. In Victoria, John Elford lived at 1228 Fort Street, demolished years ago and replaced by an apartment block. He is best known for founding the Queen City Brick Co., later the Victoria Brick & Tile Co., in 1886. He built many of Victoria's landmarks, including the now-demolished North Ward School, Royal Jubilee Hospital, and two fine homes at 1190 and 1192 Fort Street. He also financed the sealing industry at a time when it needed financial support. In 1902 and 1904, he was elected to Victoria City Council. He died June 16, 1917, in Essondale and is buried at Ross Bay Cemetery.[359] Elford Street in Fernwood is named after him.

1248 Fort Street, 2022

During the Elford family's ownership, Miss Agnes Gibson rented the property.

She was born March 24, 1867, in Ayrshire, Scotland, to Richard Gibson and Margaret Brogan. A schoolteacher by trade, she came to Canada in 1870 and lived in Nanaimo until about 1922. Then, she lived here until about 1934. Agnes, who never married, died in Victoria on November 2, 1946, and is buried at Ross Bay Cemetery.[360] Mrs. Annie Brown lived here for over twenty years but, for some reason, there is virtually no information on her life. The property remained in the hands of John Herbert Elford until his death March 13, 1970.[361]

It is still a fine building although the use has changed to offices, rather than residential.

1254 Fort Street

This is one of the residences that were built adjacent to the grounds of the original Victoria High School. That site is now the home of Central Middle School.

In early twentieth-century Victoria, this address was noted as 42 Cadboro Bay Road. This home was built about 1900 for Thomas L. Davies and his wife, Catherine. Thomas was born in Wales while his wife was an American. He immigrated in 1877 and lived in Nanaimo, where he operated a general store. The couple moved to Victoria and were living in this house in 1901.[362] Thomas's occupation was shown as a wholesaler. When Thomas died in 1911, Catherine, known as "Kate," moved to Vancouver where she worked as the matron of the Catholic Children's Aid Home. She died of a diabetic coma August 26, 1926, in Vancouver, and was buried in the Ocean View Burial Park.[363]

1254 Fort Street, 2022

Real estate and insurance agent Ronald Alexander Conway Grant was the next resident of the home. Born in Newport, Wales, September 6, 1875, to Higginson F. Grant and Lucy Jane James, he came to Canada in 1898. He divorced his first wife Valena and married Mildred Sarginson, at Victoria, June 21, 1916. Early in his career, he was an employee of the BC Electric Company.[364] He first had a partnership with Leon Uscana Conyers, a Victoria native. When that partnership dissolved, both took on new partners, Ronald working with Arthur Lineham.[365] He moved to 1045 Fernwood Road and lived at several addresses until his sudden death September 28, 1934, at Victoria.

The next resident was plumber John Noble Carruthers. He was born in Carp, Ontario, December 9, 1861, to Nobel Carruthers and Judith Moorehead. He married Emily Marion Fairbairn October 15, 1888, at Otter Lake, Ontario, and then moved to Minnesota. After some time in Michigan, they moved to Victoria, living at this address. In 1911, they were living in Nanaimo but moved back to Victoria a few years later. John was living at 880 Colville Road, Esquimalt, when he died August 23, 1921.[366] He is buried in St. Michaels and All Angels Cemetery.

By 1913, Robert Bartlett Berks was living here. He was born July 13, 1855 at Newcastle under Lyme, England, to George Berks and Elizabeth Bartlett. He married Rosina Oldfield August 5, 1877, at St. Pancras Parish Chapel, Sussex, England. She died June 4, 1896, leaving Robert with two children, Sidney and George. He married Ethel Jane Goering at Preston, Sussex, England, November 10, 1897, Shortly after that, Robert and Ethel moved to Canada, leaving the two children in England to live with an uncle.[367] After the birth of son Harold and daughter Eileen in Victoria, Ethel died February 12, 1926.[368] For many years, Robert was a commercial traveller in the wholesale goods firm of J. Piercy & Co., after which he became head traveller for Turner, Beeton Co., until his retirement. He died at Royal Jubilee Hospital May 26, 1936 and is buried at Ross Bay Cemetery.[369]

After short-term residencies by John R. Eldridge, foreman of Nag Paint Company; Norman P. Macdonald, a janitor at Boys' Central School; and Edward Hodges, a masseur; the house sat vacant for about three years. Charles McEachern moved into his new residence in 1928. Born March 21, 1873, in Holstein, Ontario, to Archibald McEachern and Isabella McInnis, he came to Victoria in about 1921 with his wife, Mabel Coulter. Charles worked for several years as a mechanic at Thomas Plimley Ltd. and then began a career as a machinist at Victoria Machinery Depot. He died at Victoria January 9, 1951 and is buried at Ross Bay Cemetery.[370]

George Cox and his family lived in this house for decades. Born in England, September 13, 1885, to John Cox and Anne Clark, he married Mary Martha Day in England and immigrated to Canada in 1912. George worked as an auto upholsterer for his entire 50-year career, owning George Cox Auto Tops, first located at the corner of View and Vancouver Streets and then moving half a block down View to relocate at 941 View Street. He retired in 1954 but resided at 1254 Fort Street until his death October 1, 1968. He is buried at Hatley Memorial Gardens. Martha remained in the home until her death on April 23, 1970, having been a resident for over 34 years.

Today, the house has been painted in bright colours and remains a local landmark. How it has survived is a miracle, but I'm glad it did.

1260 Fort Street

FORMERLY 42 CADBORO BAY ROAD

This is another of the residences that were built adjacent to the grounds of the original Victoria High School. That site is now the home of Central Middle School.

The original owner of this property was Helena Cook. Born Helena Lenz October 31, 1844, to Jacob Lenz and Iette (or Yetta) in Prussia, she came with her family to the United States in the 1850s, settling in Madison, Wisconsin. She married Emanuel Cook on March 21, 1871. The couple had three children born in Madison, two of whom died in infancy. Alexander, born in 1877, moved with his parents to Canada in 1890. Emanuel worked as a storekeeper for Simon Leiser, importer and wholesale grocer, with the family living at the corner of Cook and Yates Streets.[371] He died February 24, 1892, at age 58, leaving Helena with a family to raise.[372] She had this house built in 1895 and moved in soon after, living here until her death September 26, 1907. She was buried in Colma, California, next to her husband.[373]

1260 Fort Street, 2022

For the next nine years, various families lived at this address, including John Hibberson, prospector; John P. McLeod, inspector of legal offices; Donald McKay, a machinist for the CPR; John Feyler, a glazier; and Wilbert McArthur.

In 1921, Mary Eleanor Oliver purchased the property. She was the widow of a noted Victoria resident. William Edgar Oliver was born January 19, 1867, in Edinburgh, Scotland, to John Scott Oliver and Catherine McLaren. His mother died when he was two years old. He received his education at Edinburgh University, studying for the Scottish bar. He came to Victoria in 1895, where he formed a partnership with the Honourable Gordon Hunter (later Chief Justice) and Lyman P. Duff (later of the Supreme Court of Canada) as Hunter, Duff and Oliver. He eventually practiced by himself as his former partners left Victoria. On April 15, 1895, William married Mary Eleanor Ward, daughter of a Victoria pioneer family; her father was William Curtis Ward, a noted banker. Their daughter, Catherine, was born February 7, 1897. The family lived at 1159 Beach Drive in Oak Bay in a home designed by his friend, Francis Mawson Rattenbury. William was instrumental in the formation of Oak Bay municipality and was its first

Reeve in 1907. He was re-elected in 1908 and served as a councillor in 1909. In 1910 and 1911, he ran for the mayoralty of Victoria, being defeated by Mayor Morley. He was again elected to Oak Bay Council in 1912 and was returned as Reeve two years later, retiring in 1915.[374]

During World War I, he was appointed as a provisional Lieutenant (supernumerary) with the 88th Regiment (Victoria Fusiliers).[375] Mrs. Oliver maintained a detailed account book, and, from that, one can determine their lifestyle. The entries ceased on June 12, 1920, likely because the family was travelling to their summer residence at Cowichan Lake.[376] That would be their last trip as a family, as William died August 9, 1920. Oliver Street in Oak Bay is named for him.[377] Soon after purchasing the property, Mary Eleanor Oliver converted it to four suites. She apparently never lived there, but her daughter occupied one suite briefly before her marriage to local rugby star Erroll Pilkington Gillespie, June 22, 1921.[378] Mary Oliver died February 17, 1959, at 1368 Craigdarroch Road. She was survived by her daughter and three grandchildren. The funeral was held at Christ Church Cathedral with Archbishop Harold E. Sexton officiating.[379]

At some point in recent years, the building was covered in stucco that obliterated the original trim details and had vinyl windows installed. Still, it remains as four suites and provides a link to its early history.

1333 Fort Street

This is another of the houses that I discovered while walking on Fort Street. I decided to document them all because how long they will remain is unknown.

The history of this property begins in 1849, with a land grant to an unknown person. It was acquired by Joseph Despard Pemberton April 8, 1861, who sold it to Walker James Davidson on September 18, 1863. Robert Dunsmuir purchased the site February 21, 1882. On his death April 12, 1889, all his property passed to his widow, Joan. She died October 2, 1908, and this site was inherited by the Dunsmuir daughters: Mary Jean Croft, Jessie Sophie Musgrave, Emily Ellen Burroughs, Annie Euphemia Calthorpe, and Henrietta Maud Chaplin. They sold it to Henry Thomson August 17, 1911, and he then sold it to Henry Edwin Munday November 27, 1913.[380]

1333 Fort Street, 2022

Born February 22, 1863, in London, England, to Joseph Munday and Martha Greening, he immigrated to Canada in 1899. He entered the contracting business when he first arrived in Victoria and built part of the first BC Parliament Buildings. He later built Work Point Barracks. He married Nora Woodward at Victoria June 25, 1892. According to his obituary, "During the Klondyke gold rush, he packed food supplies for miners to Alaska."[381] In 1899, he opened his first boot and shoe store at 89 Government Street. Over the years, he and his family opened more stores, including the one on Douglas Street that bore his name. The last store closed in the 1990s.

Munday Shoes store on Douglas Street, c. 1948
M00888, COURTESY OF CITY OF VICTORIA ARCHIVES

This fourplex was built in 1927. The first family to live here was that of accountant Louis Sebastian Vancouver York in 1927. Born July 29, 1879, at Victoria, to Joseph York and Martha Dickens, he married Mary Alberta Lee at St. James Church September 28, 1910. The Yorks only lived in this building for four years and then moved to 1941 Ash Street.[382] Louis died August 14, 1952 and is buried at Royal Oak Burial Park. The building was given the name "York House" and retained that name for decades.

It is unknown why the building bore the name "York," as that family did not appear to have anything to do with the rentals or operations. That was done entirely by Henry Edwin Munday. Starting in the 1929 City Directory, the entries for this address show "York House Apartments (H.E. Munday), 1333 Fort Street."[383]

This property stayed in the hands of Henry Edwin Munday until February 12, 1940, when it was purchased by Rosamond Nora Shepherd. Thus, it was not included in the assets of his estate[384] when he died January 26, 1954.[385] It is still operated as a fourplex today.

1413–1415 Fort Street

This short article about the move appeared in the Winter 2002 issue of the *Hallmark Society Newsletter.* Curious about the site's history, I conducted detailed research early in 2022 and can now tell the story about the house and its residents.

It was a dark and stormy night. Well, actually, it wasn't that stormy, but it sure was dark. What was the event? It was another nighttime house move by Nickel Bros. House Moving on October 8, 2002.

This time it was a two-storey Italianate structure located at the corner of Carberry Gardens and Fort Street. In a classic win-win situation, the owner was sympathetic to the value of the heritage house, although it did not fit into his plans. He agreed to sell and have it moved. The new owners were excited about their "new" home and planned to restore it to its former glory. Those who passed the house over the previous months would have noticed several differences. All the stucco was removed, revealing the original wood siding beneath. Missing trim elements could be duplicated using the shadows left on the surface. There were several early examples of wallpapers in some of the rooms, and many of the later unsympathetic renovations could be reversed.

1413–1415 Fort Street during move, October 8, 2002

It was eerie to watch the house inch its way down Yates Street through the fog. The roof followed on its own flatbed truck. Moving a house is a complicated procedure. All the overhead wires had to be disconnected and then protected from the tires of the trucks. BC Hydro and Telus crews disconnected, then reconnected their wires. The care with which the moving crew worked was extraordinary. Nothing moved until they were sure it was safe. The police provided an escort and blocked streets. Neighbours along the route came to wonder at the event. For a few souls who had obviously just left their local watering hole, the sight of a house moving down the road was too hard to believe.

The house was moved to the waterfront, where it was loaded on a barge and transported to its new home on Gabriola Island.

In 1892, when this residence was built for James Lidstone Crimp, the address was 95 Cadboro Bay Road. Born in Kingsbridge, Devon, England, in 1833, to Nicholas Crimp and Jane Lidstone, he came to Victoria in 1862 from Oshawa,

Ontario, where he had been living for some time. He was manager of the Harper cattle ranch at Clinton, one of the largest such outfits in the province. He later went to Cassiar as assistant to the gold commissioner, Mr. Vowell, and became the government agent at Cassiar, where he remained until 1890, when he came to Victoria. He married Elizabeth Carne October 14, 1891, at Victoria; the couple had no children. The couple lived in this house until about 1913 when they moved to 1792 St. Ann Street in Oak Bay. For about four or five years in the mid-1890s, he was a much-valued director of the Royal Jubilee Hospital.[386] James died October 18, 1915,[387] and Elizabeth continued to live in Oak Bay until 1941, when she moved to 1002 Vancouver Street, where she was living when she died June 20, 1945.[388]

William Kay and his wife, Margaret, lived at this address from 1915–1918. He was born October 22, 1865, in Aberdeen, Scotland, to Thomas Kay and Martha Ludlum. He came to Victoria in 1908 and married Margaret Hooey here September 11, 1926. He worked as the Secretary for Producers' Sand & Gravel Co. Ltd. until his retirement, two weeks before his death. William died April 13, 1946 and was buried at Hatley Park Burial Park.

The structure that replaced 1413–1415 Fort Street on Carberry Gardens

The next residents were Charles J. Quinan and his wife, Minnie. He was born in Antigonish, Nova Scotia, January 29, 1863, to Frances Quinan and Agnes Millar. He came to BC in 1897, settling in the Kootenays. He married Minnie Best June 8, 1909, at Nelson. A druggist by trade, he worked for W. M. Ivel while he lived in this house. The family moved back to the Kootenay area, and he died in Cranbrook January 16, 1942.

William and Agnes Gregson moved into the house in 1923. He was born February 25, 1859, in Derby, Derbyshire, England, to William Gregson and Hannah Loughenbury. He came to Canada in the 1880s, and married Agnes Maude Commander, a Toronto native, in her hometown, May 5, 1886. After a short stay in Winnipeg, the family moved to Victoria, where William worked as a carpenter and contractor. He died March 7, 1932, shortly after the family moved into 1415 Fort Street. Agnes and their son Douglas, a bookkeeper at Spencer's Stores, lived here until the early 1940s when Douglas married Margaret, who also worked at Spencer's Stores. The three then moved to 1531 Hampshire Road, where Agnes died January 28, 1948.

The house sat vacant for a couple of years and was then divided into two suites. Francis Basil Hood and his wife, Catherine, resided at this address for three years. He was born in Esquimalt September 5, 1905, to Colonel Francis George Hood and Helen Kendall Mouncey Prior. The family moved to Ireland and then to London, England, returning to Canada October 23, 1927. Francis married Catherine Anne McBride at Victoria December 1, 1934. He worked as a clerk at Hickman Tye Hardware for years and died at Sidney June 3, 1986.

There was a steady stream of residents who stayed one year or two over the years. The house remained at its location on the corner of Fort Street and Carberry Gardens until it was moved to its new home. The building has now been replaced by townhouses.

1416 Fort Street

I discovered this little gem and its neighbour when researching the property across the street. I wanted to learn about them and how they had survived on such a busy street. Their story is part of the fabric of Victoria's history.

The house's original address was 98 Cadboro Bay Road, but that changed to 1416 Fort Street in 1907.

This house was built in 1897 for Thomas Neil Rolfe. He was born December 15, 1854, in London, England, to John Hanbrook Rolfe and Elizabeth McNaughton. He was educated at Boughton House Boarding School in Boughton, Kent, England and began a career as a lithographic printer. Thomas came to Canada on the SS *Hector*, leaving London May 1, 1872, and arriving in Quebéc June 11, 1872. He married Emma Elizabeth Stilwell September 1, 1880, in Newcastle, Ontario. They had five children: Flora Beatrice (1882), Elizabeth Eugenie (1884), and Victor McNaughton (1887) were all born in Newcastle, Durham County, Ontario. The family came to Victoria in 1893, and Lillian Margaret (1894) and Charles J. (1895) were born here.[389]

1416 Fort Street, 2022

Thomas worked as a painter and paperhanger for Melrose Co. until about 1920, when he joined his son Victor in Rolfe Electrical and Battery Limited. His wife Emma occasionally worked as a dressmaker.

His daughter Flora Beatrice, who worked as a stenographer, married Private Irving Archer, 2nd Canadian Mounted Rifles, April 21, 1909, at St. John the Divine Church, Victoria. The couple had a daughter, Elizabeth Violet Archer, born January 1910 and a son, Henry Irving Archer, born January 3, 1915. Victor Floran Archer was born January 4, 1917, and his mother died three days later; he died December 27, 1917. He was living with his aunt and uncle, Mr. and Mrs. Victor McNaughton Rolfe, 1215 Seaview Road at the time of his death.

Elizabeth Eugenie married Robert Charles Blackbourn June 1, 1905, in Victoria. The couple had three children: Joseph Ralph, born March 22, 1906; Muriel Lillian Blackbourn, born February 3, 1908, both in Kamloops, BC, and Doris Evelyn "Dorie," born February 1910. The family lived in the Cariboo by 1911.

Victor McNaughton Rolfe married Janetta Jeeves August 20, 1913, at St. John's Church. He and his wife had no children but, as noted above, raised Flora Archer's children after her death in 1917.

Lillian Margaret married Donald Manson McGregor July 14, 1923, in Victoria, BC. She was widowed May 13, 1937. She was a schoolteacher at Strawberry Vale School and had no children.

Thomas retired in 1931 and lived at the residence until his death March 24, 1944, at Royal Jubilee Hospital; he is buried in Ross Bay Cemetery in an unmarked grave.

The property was then sold to Leo J. Bauer and his wife, Helen. He worked at the Six Mile House public house, and she was a saleswoman at Mallek's, one of Victoria's finer clothing outlets. They converted the building into four suites, and it subsequently went through a series of owners.[390] It is still divided into four suites, and has had some minor modernization, but the basic structure, including architectural details in the gable ends, remains 125 years later. How this house and its neighbour survived the massive tear-down of heritage properties in the 1970s is a mystery, but I am glad it is still there as a tribute to early Victoria and the families who lived here then.

1419 Fort Street

This was another gem I discovered while walking on Fort Street.

When this stylish two-storey home was erected in 1903, the address was 97 Cadboro Bay Road. Built by Leon Uscona Conyers and his wife Mary Ann Skillen, it remained in the family for decades. Their son, named after his father, was born in Victoria December 13, 1898. Listed as a "canneryman" in the 1903 City Directory, the elder Leon worked in the real estate business. First, he partnered with Ronald Alexander Conway Grant, who lived at 1254 Fort Street, in a real estate and insurance firm. When that partnership dissolved, he formed a new one with Hubert W. Wilders, under the name L.U. Conyers & Co., with offices at 650 View Street. When the older Leon died, his namesake joined the real estate firm. Before that, he had worked for the Liquor Control Branch after completing his education at Central and Victoria High Schools.[391] The younger Leon married Mary Hart Orr October 12, 1929. They had two sons, one also named Leon Uscona Conyers, born July 7, 1931, and Alan. The third Leon began his working life as a clerk at the Royal Bank but eventually joined his father in real estate. The L.U. Conyers & Co. offices relocated to 1025 Douglas Street. Leon and Mary moved at the same time to Ross Street.

1419 Fort Street, 2022

His sister, Amy Young Conyers, moved into the house at 1419 Fort Street. After she died January 24, 1937, the building was converted to five suites and was known as the Carberry House Apartments. It was later changed to six suites and remains a multiple unit dwelling today. The second Leon died January 2, 1942.[392]

Remarkably, the home has retained many of the historic features of its architecture, including leaded glass windows, exterior finishes, and porch.

1420 Fort Street

I discovered this little gem and its neighbour when researching the property across the street. I wanted to learn about them and how they had survived on such a busy street. Their story is part of the fabric of Victoria's history.

The house's original address was 100 Cadboro Bay Road and was changed to 1420 Fort Street in 1907.

This house was built in 1895 for Dr. Robert Hamilton. He was born November 10, 1867 in Lanark, Scotland. He received his early education in the grammar school of Lanark and then entered the Royal College of Veterinary Surgeons in Glasgow, from which he graduated on May 24, 1888, with the degrees of M.R.C.V.S. and F.V.M.A. He left Scotland in the fall of 1888 and came to Canada, working in Balgonie, Saskatchewan until he returned to Scotland in July 1890. He married Janet Gibb Clark (born March 23, 1865, in Lanark to Archibald Clark and Agnes Prosser) in Lanark, October 1, 1890, and the couple left for Canada, settling in Victoria, where he set up his practice.[393] The

Hamiltons had two sons: Archibald Prosser Clark, born April 15, 1892 and Robert William Stanford, born March 6, 1896. Both sons entered medical school, but Archibald died August 30, 1915 of a compound fracture of his leg. Robert completed his studies at the University of British Columbia and interned at Montreal General Hospital until July 1925. He then moved to Port Angeles, Washington where he established his practice. He died there November 11, 1959.[394]

1420 Fort Street: the house (upper) and garage (lower), 2022

Robert was a member of the Royal College of Veterinary Surgeons and a fellow of the American College of Veterinary Surgeons. He served as president of the British Columbia Veterinary Association in 1908 and 1909.[395] During World War I, he served as a member of the War headquarters staff for Military District 11, as chief veterinary officer with the rank of Captain.[396] He had previously served with the Lanarkshire Yeomanry of Scotland.

The family lived in this house until 1928 when they moved to 911 Richmond Road. Janet died December 12, 1942 and was buried in Ross Bay Cemetery. Robert died April 22, 1946, living at the Pacific Club at that time.

The next owners of the residence were Robert McDowall and his wife, Florence. Robert was born October 13, 1883 in Edinburgh, Scotland, to Robert McDowall and Harriet Emily Chambers.[397] He married Florence Ethel Burgess (born January 27, 1885 in London to William Burgess and his wife Eliza) in July 1907 in London. Their daughter Ivy Gladys was born there March 8, 1911. The family came to Canada in May 1912, arriving at Québec and then making their way across the country via the Canadian Pacific Railway.[398] Their son Eric Robert was born on March 23, 1914 in Victoria.

Robert was a foreman at Jamieson Motors and his daughter Ivy was a hairdresser who eventually set up her own business, Ivy's Beauty Nook, at 714 View Street. Eric married Marie Vintner in Victoria February 23, 1940 and worked as a manager of Auto Mart Limited. He enlisted in the RCAF October 1, 1946. The couple had two children, Carol Linda and Eric Bruce. Eric rose to the rank of Squadron Leader and was tragically killed in the crash of his CT-128 Expeditor 111 (#1420) aircraft at Trenton, Ontario. Flight Lieutenant Edward Arthur Elson also died in this accident.[399]

The family lived at 1420 Fort Street until 1950. Robert McDowall died in Victoria January 23, 1953, and Marie lived in Victoria until her death October 1, 2005.[400]

After two short-term owners, the house was purchased by Albert W. Ferriday who converted it into four suites.[401] It is still divided into four suites and has remained remarkably intact over the years. It still retains the cresting on the roof and the intricate detail in the gable ends. How this house and its neighbour survived the massive tear down of heritage properties in the 1970s is a mystery, but I am glad it is still there as a tribute to early Victoria and the families who lived here then.

1438 Fort Street

This was another gem I discovered while walking on Fort Street.

This elegant two-storey residence was built in 1905 for William Benjamin Sylvester and his wife, Emily Elizabeth Brooker. Born in Victoria January 1, 1874 to Frank Sylvester and Cecelia Davies, he was educated at Central School. In 1891, with his brother, Clarence, he established the Sylvester Feed Company at the city market. He married Emily June 27, 1905. They had three children: Cecelia Burdette, born January 20, 1905; William Beresford, born February 1, 1911; and Hubert Hope, born June 23, 1914. In 1907, the feed business moved to larger premises on Yates Street.[402] In 1929, William moved to the Sylvester Farm at Shawnigan Lake; he died there suddenly on September 27, 1931.

1438 Fort Street, 2022

Emily lived in the house for one year, and then it was vacant for a year. Watchmaker Milton D. White lived here with his wife, Hilda, for a couple of years. He was born to James White and Elizabeth Widdess April 25, 1868, at Orono, Ontario. He learned the jewellery business in Brantford and moved to Grand Forks, BC, in 1897, operating a store there until he moved to Victoria in 1914. While in Grand Forks, he was an alderman in 1898 and 1899 and mayor in 1901.[403] Milton married Hilda Pearl Broughton in Ferry, Washington, January 1, 1900;[404] their son Albert was born in 1902 and Winfield in 1908, both in Grand Forks. By 1911, the family was living in New Westminster.[405] Milton died in Victoria December 12, 1940.

Mrs. Isabell S. Friesen was a tenant in the house for eight years. There are no records of her in Victoria other than in City Directories. Harry Wilson Flett and his wife Rosalie rented 1438 Fort Street in 1946. He was born October 8, 1915, in Edmonton to Fred Flett and Violet Cloney. He married Rosalie 'Rose' Blischok Bliss in Edmonton in 1937.[406] They moved to Vancouver, where their daughter, Carolyn, was born a year later. When they lived in Victoria, Harry worked as a salesman. They moved back to Vancouver in 1949, where Carolyn died on November 8, 1956. Harry died there May 17, 1972. After they left the residence, it was divided into two suites.

William Sylvester's estate was finally settled in 1936, and this property was passed to his widow, Emily Elizabeth, and his unmarried sister, Louise Miriam Sylvester, a schoolteacher. After Louise died February 14, 1955, the property was sold to Rachel Valentine Campbell and Ruby Florence McCrae.[407] In 1965, it was sold in a tax sale.

This is still a striking building, although the lower portion has been coated with stucco.

1472–1474 Fort Street

This home is another survivor on Fort Street, where apartment blocks are prevalent.

It was built in 1891 by Edgar Marvin, an early merchant in Victoria. Born in Syracuse, New York, in 1824, he married Elizabeth Ashley on June 23, 1853. Their son Edgar was born February 24, 1856. The family arrived in California in 1858 and were in Victoria by 1862. Edgar purchased a hardware store from James Bell, operating at the corner of Fort and Langley Streets.[408] In 1866, he moved his very successful store to 67–69 Wharf Street (now 1129 Wharf Street).[409] This move meant he was operating from the heart of the business district. His second son, William Thatcher, was born on February 28, 1868.[410]

By 1879, Edgar Marvin was an agent for the California Powder Works, and an ad in the newspaper advised that "a full supply of these powders [is] kept constantly on hand."[411] In 1884, Edgar formed a partnership with Edward Gibson Tilton, who had been picked to build the railroad through the Fraser Canyon.

Once that was completed, he retired from railroading and moved to Victoria. The new firm advertised farming implements available from their store catering to farmers. They served the home improvement trade in the city as well as dealing in mining and lumbering equipment. At some point, Mr. Marvin was named American vice-consul, a title he held until his death.

1472–1474 Fort Street, 2022

In the meantime, William Thatcher had moved to California and had married Maye Belle Kewen on April 29, 1891, at Menlo Park, California. According to a newspaper account of the wedding, the couple planned to leave for Victoria, BC on May 10, where his father had built an elegant new home in readiness for their arrival. The new house was described in detail in the *Daily Colonist* as "a two-story house with hipped roof and stone casements. On the first floor, there will be two large parlors, dining room and a reception hall, 10 ft. 6 in. by 16 ft., with kitchen, bathroom and pantry. On the second floor there will be a library, three bedrooms and three servants' bedrooms. The principal rooms will have polished oak mantels and the dining room, a polished oak sideboard. This house will be of ornate design with a two-story bay window at the front and side and two particles. The front entrance will have double doors and the upper panels will be fitted with figured glass."[412] The address of the home at this time was 138 Cadboro Bay Road.

Edgar Martin died on July 15, 1891, and his obituary notes that his wife had predeceased him. However, there is no record of her death in local records. His funeral took place at Christ Church Cathedral with internment at Ross Bay Cemetery. Among the pallbearers were the United States Consul Myers and the Hon. J. H. Turner, M.P.P. Edward Tilton purchased the late Mr. Martin's share of the business but retained the name as it had been.[413]

Edgar Marvin Jr. left Victoria after his father's death and moved to London, England. William Thatcher Marvin only lived in the house for a couple of years, continuing to work at the firm and then moved to California.

The next owner of the property was Bernhard Casimir Moss. He was born in Stoke Newington, England, on March 26, 1860, and married Florence Bramell on July 6, 1892; and their first child Elsie Florence was born in England on

April 28, 1893. The family moved to Canada in 1894 and settled in Victoria. Bernhard worked at Findlay, Durham and Brodie, who were agents for several companies, including the BC Canning Company. He and his wife added three more children to their family: Eva Beatrice born February 28, 1895, Percy Bernard, born September 20, 1896, and Charles Bertram, born on May 7, 1899. The family lived in the house until Bernhard's death on June 30, 1925, with the children starting work and eventually leaving home. Florence then moved to 319 Vancouver Street.

Over the next decade, residents were generally short-term, with nobody living at the address for more than two years. In 1939, Charles Ozard, a schoolteacher with the Saanich district, moved in. He lived there for about three years. He continued to teach for decades and, at one point, was the conductor of the junior choir at St. John the Divine Anglican Church. Another teacher Hubert Cumberbirch, who taught in the city, lived in the home for six years with his wife, Kate.

The building was coated with stucco, at some point, but the original form is still evident. It has been duplexed but still represents the early residents of the area.

1489 Fort Street

This was another gem I discovered while walking on Fort Street.

This charming little cottage was built around 1907 for James Murray Whitney. He was born November 13, 1868, at Seaforth, Ontario, to Edmund Whitney and Frances Ann Mortimer, and married Anna May McCulloch January 18, 1898 at Woodstock, Ontario. Their two sons, Charles and Jack, were born in Ontario. They moved to Victoria in 1907, where their daughter, Anna, was born the following year. Unfortunately, tragedy struck the family when Jack, aged eight, died February 12, 1913. The family moved to 1345 Victoria Avenue in Oak Bay a year later. James worked as a jeweller for his entire career, operating James M. Whitney Co. from a location at 631 Yates Street. Anna died December 24, 1939,[414] and James followed her November 25, 1944.

1489 Fort Street, date unknown
M02964, COURTESY CITY OF VICTORIA ARCHIVES

The next long-term resident was Walter Stanley Byrd. Born September 19, 1869, to Thomas Byrd and Sarah Ann Bostock at Penkridge, Staffordshire, England, he came to Canada in 1879.[415] On June 4, 1886, he married Nina Clarke at Carleton, Ontario[416]; their two daughters were born in that province. In 1911, the family moved to the Revelstoke, where Walter worked as a master mechanic for the Canadian Pacific Railway. They moved to Victoria a few years later, where Walter joined the Esquimalt and Nanaimo Railway, living at 1489 Fort Street until 1924, when they relocated to 2311 Quadra Street. Nina died at that residence August 4, 1924.[417] Walter married Catherine Jamieson Steel January 2, 1926. He died December 1, 1930, after a lingering illness.[418]

After a series of short-term residents, Mrs. Jennie Boyd Hudson moved into this home in the late 1930s. She was the widow of Albert Charles Hudson, who was born about 1889 in Devon, England, to Albert Charles Hudson and Ellen Ralph. He came to Canada in 1909 and married Jennie Boyd Watson December 25, 1914, at Victoria. The couple had two children. Albert worked as a butcher at various outlets and died in Victoria in 1937. Jennie continued to live at 1489 Fort Street, until 1945. She died September 20, 1972, at age 83.

1489 Fort Street, 2022

Marie Claire Turgeon lived in the house for six years, but little is known about her. Her husband Marcel appears in the 1945 Victoria City Directory, shown as "on active service," but there are no records of him after that. Marie is listed as a clerk at Eddy's, the clothing outlet "on, over and under" Douglas at Fisgard Streets. In 1952, she hosted a going away party for her friends, James Gerald and Dorothy Atherley, on the occasion of the marriage of their daughter.[419] Ironically, that couple's son, William, moved into 1489 Fort Street with his wife, Aimée Fortier, who had previously lived next door at 1495 Fort Street.

William Francis Atherley was born December 10, 1922, in Winnipeg, Manitoba. Around 1949, he married Aimée, who was born January 11, 1926, at Lisieux, Saskatchewan. He worked as a driver for Shepherd's Dairy, and she was a registered nurse who graduated in 1951 under her married name.[420] The couple moved to Kelowna, where William worked in TV electronics. He died there April 30, 1980, and she followed him May 1, 2008.[421]

This residence, now known as "Humberside," has remained virtually unchanged over the years, except for the installation of modern windows. It still has decorative gable ends with quatrefoil cut-outs, half-timbering on the upper storey, and decorative posts on the open verandah.

1495 Fort Street

This is another gem I discovered while walking on Fort Street.

This corner location was built in 1909 for George Arthur Fraser. Born May 17, 1867, in Woodstock, Ontario, to George Fraser and Jane Burgess, he married Agnes Farrell October 30, 1889, in Oxford, Ontario. The couple then moved to Stewart, BC. George became active in politics and represented the electoral district of Grand Forks in the BC Legislature from 1903–1907.[422] The 1903 election, the tenth in BC history, was the first in British Columbia history to have a party system. Before this election, British Columbia elected individuals. From this time on, candidates for office were members of a political party and represented the view of that party in the legislature. George ran for the Conservative party, and his party formed the government with a slim majority of seats, 22–17. Richard McBride, as the leader of the Conservative party, became premier of the province.[423]

1495 Fort Street, 1959
M03983, COURTESY OF CITY OF VICTORIA ARCHIVES

The Fraser family moved to Victoria in December 1905. George purchased a drug store at 30–32 Government Street, the BC Land & Investment Building, from John L. White and opened for business. He called his new company the Empress Drug Hall. The announcement of the new owner noted that "Mr. Fraser is no stranger to Victoria, having for several years been a frequent visitor in connection with his duties as a member of the legislature."[424] Over the next few years, the business advertised new products, including French perfumes, soaps,[425] hot water bottles, and chest protectors.[426] On December 5, 1908, each customer would receive a free calendar, a ploy designed to bring in trade.[427] As was common in that era, patent remedies were popular and local druggists placed group ads to retail items such as Mothersill's Sea and Train Sick Remedy, an alleged cure for travel sickness.[428] George died in Victoria March 2, 1930, and Agnes followed him November 13, 1938.[429]

Over the next fifteen years, various people lived at this address, but none for more than two years. Finally, in 1937, the house was divided into two suites, and Miss Annie Lyssol Ethel James moved into one of them. Born in Hay, Wales, October 30, 1883, to Thomas James and Mary Joseph,[430] she came to Canada in September 1913, settling in Winnipeg. She then made her way to Victoria, where she worked as a music teacher for years. While living here, she made frequent trips to England and Wales to visit relatives. She died March 28, 1977, at 93 years of age, at Mount St. Mary Hospital at 999 Burdett Avenue.

Philip Fortier moved into one suite in the late 1940s with his wife, Marie; his son, Paul, a student; and his daughter, Aimée, a student nurse at St. Joseph's Hospital. Interestingly, Aimée married the "boy next door," William Atherley, who lived at 1489 Fort Street.

1495 Fort Street, 2022

In the early 1950s, John A. Franklin and his wife Mabel converted the building into rooms to rent. He was born to Ansel Franklin and Ruth Ester February 15, 1892, at Woodstock, New Brunswick.[431] John and Mabel married March 6, 1918, at Hawkshaw, New Brunswick. [432] He worked for years as a car mechanic. The couple came to Victoria around 1948 and, shortly thereafter, began to manage this building. John died March 11, 1969, living at 1190 Fort Street.

1501 Fort Street

This article appeared in the Winter 2009 issue of the *Rockland Neighbourhood Association newsletter*.

The Amethyst Inn at Regent's Park is one of Victoria's most recognized heritage buildings. Built as Regent's Park in 1885 for David William Higgins, a prominent Victoria newspaperman, the house was designed as a country retreat set in a ten-acre estate on land that was once part of the J.D. Pemberton estate. Born November 30, 1834, in Halifax, Nova Scotia, to William Burd Higgins Sr. and Mary Anne Williams, he went to California in 1852, where he founded the *Morning Call* newspaper. In 1858, he came to Victoria aboard the *Sierra Nevada* with a shipload of gold seekers. Within a year, he was a reporter for Amor De Cosmos's *British Colonist*. In 1862, Higgins established the *Victoria Daily Chronicle*. Four years later, he took over the *Colonist* newspaper, merging it with his earlier enterprise. Under Higgins' ownership, *The British Colonist* became the area's first daily newspaper. David married Mary Jane Pidwell March 12, 1864; the couple had seven children.

During the late 1860s, he strongly supported the admission of British Columbia into Confederation. However, he openly opposed any form of union which did not give assurance of responsible government. When he travelled to Ottawa in 1868 to meet with Sir John A. Macdonald, he was assured that proper attention would be paid to British Columbia. He strongly opposed the idea of annexation of Vancouver Island by the United States, and after he attacked the ideas in the newspaper, that idea soon vanished. On October 16, 1886, after editing the *Colonist* for 25 years, he sold it to Ellis. Higgins was very active politically, serving as a Victoria councillor in 1886–1887, and was elected as a Liberal-Conservative MLA for Esquimalt in 1886. From 1890–1897, he was Speaker of the Legislative Assembly.

1501 Fort Street, 1959
M05875, COURTESY OF CITY OF VICTORIA ARCHIVES

He also wrote two books portraying colonial life in the early days of Victoria: "The Mystic Spring" and "The Passing of a Race." He was the first president of the National Electric Tram & Light Company, whose line coincidentally ran right past his home. He died November 30, 1917, his 83rd birthday.[433] His obituary was one of the largest ever printed and gave a detailed outline of his remarkable life.[434] The home is a rare survivor, providing a glimpse into high society life in early Victoria.

Between 1904 and 1926, the property was acquired by Dr. Ernest Amos Hall and his wife, Mary Louisa. Born about 1862 in Esquesing, Ontario, to Robert Skirrow Hall and Jane Greenwood, he married Mary Louisa Fox on January 15, 1885. By 1901, they were living in Victoria, where their sons, Victor and Frederick, and daughter, Grace, were born. The building was operated as the Restholme Sanitarium for about three years and later as a home for nurses. Known to have a gruff exterior, Dr. Hall was enthusiastic about medical discoveries and performed many acts of philanthropy during his long career.[435] He died December 8, 1932, after a long illness.[436]

Between 1927 and 1963, the house was owned by the Evans family. David Evans was a nurse and later an orderly at St. Joseph's Hospital. He lived here with his wife Ida Madeline and their children until Ida and her premature baby died March 27, 1930. David continued his residency until his death, after which his son, David P., lived here.

In 1963, David P. Evans sold the property to Carl Rudolph. Carl was born in Victoria April 12, 1916, to Robert Andrew Rudolph and Mary Hannah Tennant. He attended Central School, quitting after Grade 8 when he apprenticed at wood-turning and cabinet making with Charlie Whitfield on Johnson Street. After his father had an accident and started a furniture shop, Carl and his brother Tom built the furniture, with their father doing the upholstery. After trying his hand at boatbuilding, he and Tom went to Vancouver, where they bought up mortgages and houses. He returned to Victoria in 1949 and worked as a shipwright at the Esquimalt Naval Base for 30 years but kept buying old houses and fixing them up. Eventually, he rescued 1501 Fort Street from demolition. Over the next twenty-three years, he worked to bring Regent's Park back to its former grandeur. He scoured demolition sites for artifacts and building materials that he incorporated into the house. 1501 Fort Street was the first privately owned residence in Victoria and BC to be designated heritage. In 1975, Heritage Canada presented Carl Rudolph with an Award of Honour for his tireless efforts. However, as the years passed, he became unable to maintain the building. Carl Rudolph died on September 24, 1997. An open house at his former residence drew crowds of curious Victorians.[437]

1501 Fort Street, interior staircase

The subsequent owners were Karl and Grace Sands, who undertook the task of completing the restoration work while turning the building into an economically viable enterprise. They proposed to accommodate 13 guest rooms in the 8,500-square-foot main house and three in a coach house at the rear of the property. An examination of archival photographs showed the building as essentially intact on the exterior, with the most significant alterations occurring in the area of the front porch and entry stair. The project was complicated by the desire to retain the original interior finishes that in particular were extant on the main floor. Along the way, a continuous re-evaluation of the additions made to the decor by Carl Rudolph was necessary. Although much was removed, particularly of the "donnaconna board edged with rope" variety, much of his contribution remains, and is now an integral part of the history of the building.

The design concept was based on the retention of the main and second floor rooms as restored to the maximum practical extent, while completing additional rooms on the basement and top floor levels in a period style, sympathetic to the remainder of the house. Seismic upgrading and the resolution of several structural issues were required, and a sprinkler system was installed to establish acceptable levels of protection for the building and occupants. The Sands wished to provide bathrooms for each guest room. Incorporating these upgrades while retaining the interior and exterior finishes was a complicated process, requiring a high degree of cooperation among the consultant team, the owners, and the project manager.

1501 Fort Street, 2022

Exiting proved to be a difficult problem. The house had an existing metal fire stair at the rear, and it was eventually decided to rebuild this stair as the least intrusive solution available. This stair, combined with the sprinkler system, permitted the opening up and restoration of the original grand staircase. Changes to the exterior were clearly directed toward restoration as based on archival photographs. The house initially had a conservatory on the south side; this was replicated as a bedroom for one of the guest suites. The exit stair and railing are based on archival photographs. The front verandah, stairs, and handrails were rebuilt, based on one of the two available options, using archival photographs, while the window in the attic dormer was replaced to match the original. The finished project provides an exceptional blend of comfort and ambiance and allows the Higgins house to remain a key component of the Fort Street/Rockland heritage area.

Although the Sands have sold and moved on, the mansion remains as a quiet testament to over a century of Rockland life – and, due to the efforts of both Carl Rudolph and the Sands, will last far into the future. As the Amethyst Inn, it welcomes guests from all over the world who enjoy its old-world charm.

Endnotes

1 https://www.sidewalkingvictoria.com/blog/2019/5/11/goodbye-westholme-hotel
2 *The Daily Colonist*, May 6, 1913, page 18.
3 *The Daily Colonist*, June 26, 1913, page 2.
4 "Prizes Awarded for Masquerade," *The Daily Colonist*, March 21, 1914, page 12.
5 This is the date that is shown on the 1901 Canadian census as Jeremiah's birth date. A search of Scottish records notes his baptism in Glasgow on March 19, 1837. Scottish archival officials advise that often citizens did not know their birthdates as, until 1855, the only records were kept in parish churches. It was not until the requirement for national registration of births that documents could be considered accurate.
6 Record of the 1871 census for Scotland as accessed via http://scotlandspeople.gov.uk.
7 OPR Births and Baptisms accessed via http://scotlandspeople.gov.uk.
8 The origin of his surname dates back to William Le Chievre, who accompanied William the Conqueror to England in 1066. The name evolved to different forms, including Chevre, Chevyr, Chever, Chevers, Cheevers, and Chivers. The original name was anglicized on arrival in the British Isles and appeared in different forms in diverse regions of England, Scotland and Ireland. The Irish branch is best known for its manufacture of jams, jellies, and preserves; an enterprise that continues today.
9 The earliest "Jeremiah Chivers" that can be found so far in Scotland was Jeremiah's grandfather born in 1777; there are several generations of "Jeremiahs" in England and Ireland.
10 Jeremiah Chivers' great great grandnieces in New Brunswick are currently cataloguing the family records and have been the source for much of the content of this article.
11 "Nonagenarian Pioneer Dead," *The Daily Colonist*, November 9, 1927, p. 17.
12 For more information on Frederick Dally and his work in British Columbia check the Canadian Encyclopedia at http://www.thecanadianencyclopedia.com.
13 "The Log of the China Clipper built Tea-Ship *Cyclone* from London May 5th, 1862, to Sep 18th, 1862 to Victoria, Vancouver Island" found in British Columbia Archives MS-2443.
14 Confirmation of the family's passage was found in the manifest of the *Ethiopia* as located at Ancestry.com.
15 Margaret Shaw Walter, *Early Days among the Gulf Islands*, p. 44–45.
16 All information on land acquisitions was obtained from the British Columbia Archives.
17 The 1901 Scottish census, the last to be made publicly available, lists many Chivers descendants and has been a valuable source of information.
18 Wallace Island was initially named Narrow Island by Captain Wallace Houston, RN, who surveyed it, naming Trincomali Channel after his ship, HMS Trincomalee (the name was changed slightly over the years). In a later survey in 1905, Captain John Parry changed the name to Wallace Island to recognize Captain Houston's connection with the island.
19 "Wallace Island Reported Sold," *The Daily Colonist, January 23, 1936.*
20 "Leaves Wife Here," *Victoria Times*, October 10, 1929, p. 10.
21 Ken Coates and Bill Morrison, *The Sinking of the Princess Sophia: Taking the North Down With Her*, (Don Mills, ON: Oxford University Press Canada, 1990).
22 David Conover, *Finding Marilyn:*

A Romance by David Conover, The Photographer Who Discovered Marilyn Monroe, (New York: Grosset & Dunlap, 1981).
23 David Conover, *Once Upon an Island*, (Vancouver: publisher unknown, 1967).
24 Pat Burkette, "An island in history," *Times Colonist*, March 14, 2004, page D12.
25 *The British Colonist*, February 28, 1861, page 2.
26 *The British Colonist*, September 9, 1864, page 3.
27 *The British Colonist*, September 6, 1864, page 5.
28 *The British Colonist*, September 8, 1864, page 2.
29 https://www.britannica.com/art/quadrille-dance
30 *The British Colonist*, July 4 1865, page 1.
31 *The British Colonist*, May 19, 1866, page 2.
32 *The British Colonist*, June 28, 1866, page 2.
33 *The British Colonist*, November 13, 1868, page 3.
34 *The British Colonist*, September 24, 1869, page 3.
35 *The British Colonist*, June 29, 1869, page 3.
36 *The British Colonist*, November 29, 1870, page 1.
37 *The British Colonist*, May 31, 1871, page 3.
38 *Daily British Colonist*, February 9, 1873, page 3.
39 *Daily British Colonist*, January 19, 1875, page 3.
40 *Daily British Colonist*, January 30, 1875, page 2.
41 *Daily British Colonist*, April 2, 1878, page 4.
42 *Daily British Colonist*, April 26, 1879, page 2.
43 *Daily British Colonist*, June 13, 1879, page 2.
44 *Daily British Colonist*, May 9, 1891, page 2.
45 *Victoria Daily Colonist*, January 31, 1891, page 5.
46 *The Daily Colonist*, May 14, 1892, page 3.
47 *Victoria Daily Colonist*, June 14, 1893, page 5.
48 https://boxrec.com/media/index.php/Denver_Ed_Smith.
49 Canada census, 1901.
50 Victoria City Archives, Ross Bay Cemetery search.
51 https://victoria.citified.ca/condos/200-douglas/
52 "Hotels That Flourished in the Past," James K. Nesbitt, *The Daily Colonist*, February 13, 1949, Section 3, page 6.
53 *The Daily Colonist*, October 18, 1895, page 1.
54 Rhone census 1836–1911, accessed through ancestry.ca.
55 Canada census, 1901.
56 *Victoria Daily Times*, September 20, 1909, page 5.
57 *Victoria Daily Times*, August 21, 1906, page 5.
58 "Tilikum's famous captain died 70 years ago today," *Times Colonist*, February 27, 1992, page 39.
59 *Victoria Daily Times*, April 15, 1935, page 13.
60 Canada, World War I CEF Personnel Files, 1914–1918.
61 *Victoria Daily Times*, April 27, 1932, page 15.
62 https://www.timescolonist.com/local-news/steward-of-city-hall-news-is-shutting-shop-that-began-in-1915-4611091#sthash.jrk57zE0.dpuf
63 *Times Colonist*, online edition.
64 *Daily Colonist*, August 31, 1955, page 4.
65 *Daily Colonist*, November 4, 1955, page 9.
66 *Daily Colonist*, January 20, 1957, page 21.
67 *Times Colonist*, February 14, 2015.
68 "Pioneer Passes Away," *Victoria Daily Times*, February 26, 1914, page 11.
69 *Victoria Daily Times*, November 16, 1896, page 5.
70 *Victoria Daily Times*, May 26, 1911, page 18.
71 *Victoria Daily Times*, September 4, 1969, page 8.
72 *Victoria Daily Colonist*, July 9, 1890, page 5.
73 *Seattle Post-Intelligencer*, September 18, 1892, page 12.

74 "John Cochrane, Early Druggist, Dies in Hospital in 82nd Year," *Victoria Daily Times,* August 1, 1949, page 3.
75 Gwen Cash, "An Aging Duchess in Dirty Diamonds" *Victorian* (Victoria, B.C.), February 16, 1972, 15.
76 Dorothy M. Powell, "Louis the Parrot" *Westworld* (Vancouver, B.C.), May/June 1969, 19–22.
77 Last Will and Testament, Elizabeth Jane Wilson.
78 *Victoria Daily Times,* July 25, 1922, page 2.
79 "Tony Zarelli Dies. Lived Here 52 Years," *Victoria Daily Times,* January 6 1943, page 8.
80 "S. J. Pitts, City Pioneer, Dies," *Victoria Daily Times,* August 1, 1942, page 16.
81 The Victoria Native Friendship Centre (VNFC) opened its doors in April 1970 as a one-room facility, run by an Executive Director on a small grant from the provincial First Citizen's Fund. The Centre quickly became a progressive hub for Indigenous peoples in Victoria but, unfortunately, financial concerns forced its closure. However, the Board of Directors remained active, and in September 1972, a new facility was opened on the corner of Fernwood and Gladstone Streets where it flourished with stable funding in place. It now occupies more than 38,000 square feet of a former elementary school under a 99-year lease. The Centre has become a vital resource for urban Indigenous individuals and families and is strategically positioned to play a significant role in the development and implementation of urban Indigenous governance on southern Vancouver Island. Their goal is to "stitch the fabric of Indigenous traditions into everything the VNFC does, and to greet each other and the natural world in a good way every day." https://vnfc.ca
82 https://www.timescolonist.com/local-news/after-159-years-wj-wilson-leaves-downtown-will-focus-on-sidney-and-oak-bay-stores-4689627.
83 https://www.saanichnews.com/business/birks-departure-from-victoria-marks-shift-of-downtown-makeup-business-association/
84 *Victoria Daily Times,* April 28, 1910, page 9.
85 *Times-Colonist,* May 5, 2002, page 51.
86 *The Daily Colonist,* June 2, 1909, page 13.
87 "Noted Photographer Wilfric Gibson Dies," *Daily Colonist,* January 7, 1968, page 37.
88 *Victoria Daily Colonist,* August 11, 1912, page 10.
89 *Victoria Daily Colonist,* May 10, 1918, page 12.
90 "New Victoria Homes," *Victoria Daily Times,* July 5, 1912, page 5.
91 "Arthur Lineham Passes in South," *Victoria Daily Times,* December 7, 1923, page 16.
92 "Mass for Last of Well-known Madigan Clan," *Victoria Daily Times,* June 24, 1952, page 11.
93 Washington, U.S., Marriage Records, 1854–2012 accessed through ancestry.ca.
94 https://shawniganlakemuseum.com/pages/shawnigan-lake-lumber-company.
95 *Victoria Daily Times,* September 9, 1922, page 9.
96 *Surrey Leader,* January 6, 1972, page 6.
97 *Surrey Leader,* April 13, 1072, page 6.
98 *Victoria Daily Times,* August 4 1966, page 2.
99 *The Province,* August 25, 1934, page 11.
100 *The Province,* May 13, 1937, page 13.
101 Family tree accessed at ancestry.ca
102 *The Province,* December 4, 1969, page 36.
103 Washington, U.S., County Marriages, 1855–2008 accessed through ancestry.ca.
104 Ontario, Canada Births, 1832–1916 accessed through ancestry.ca.
105 Alberta, Canada, Marriages Index, 1898–1944 accessed through ancestry.ca.
106 *Nanaimo Daily News,* January 9, 1953, page 1.
107 Manitoba, Saskatchewan, and Alberta, Canada, Homestead Grant Registers, 1872–1930 accessed through ancestry.ca.

108 Scotland, National Probate Index (Calendar of Confirmations and Inventories), 1876–1936 accessed through ancestry.ca.
109 1870 United States Federal Census.
110 California, Voter Registers, 1866–1898.
111 California, U.S., Wills and Probate Records, 1850–1953 at Ancestry.ca.
112 1880 United States Federal census.
113 Eve Lazarus, *Sensational Victoria: Brights Lights, Red Lights, Murders, Ghosts & Gardens*, University of Toronto Press, 2012.
114 https://www.findagrave.com/memorial/138370730/christina-louise-haas
115 *Victoria Daily Times,* October 9, 1909, page 12.
116 "Owners Ask Big Sum From City For Land," *Victoria Daily Times,* February 3, 1911, page 1.
117 "Asks Big Sum From the City," *Victoria Daily Times,* March 23, 1911, page 1.
118 *Victoria Daily Times,* March 30, 1911.
119 "Capt. W. H. Logan Famous Salvage Operator Passes," *Victoria Daily Times,* March 4, 1927, page 1.
120 "Funeral To-day of Late Capt. Logan," *Victoria Daily Times,* March 7, 1927, page 9.
121 UK, University of London Student Records, 1836–1945 accessed at ancestry.ca.
122 *Victoria Daily Times,* November 9, 1970, page 23.
123 *Victoria Daily Times,* May 5, 1979, page 72.
124 *The Gazette*, May 23, 1955, page 17.
125 https://lop.parl.ca/sites/ParlInfo/default/en_CA/People/Profile?personId=182.
126 *Victoria Daily Times,* June 30, 1911, page 15.
127 *Victoria Daily Times,* January 25, 1929, page 13.
128 *Vancouver Daily World*, September 2, 1919, page 6.
129 JewishGen Online Worldwide Burial Registry accessed through ancestry.ca.
130 *The Province*, April 27, 1923, page 24.
131 *Victoria Daily Times,* April 28, 1923, page 26.
132 *Victoria Daily Colonist,* December 12, 1978 page 38.
133 https://www.showcase.com/617-vancouver-st-victoria-bc-v8v-3t9/22013735/
134 *The Daily Times,* March 19, 1885, page 3.
135 *Victoria Daily Times,* March 12, 1920, page 7.
136 https://www.nationalarchives.gov.uk/
137 *Victoria Daily Times,* March 8, 1943, page 12.
138 Attestation Paper, Canadian Over-seas Expeditionary Force, accessed through ancestry.ca.
139 *Victoria Daily Times,* November 3, 1923, page 2.
140 *Victoria Daily Times,* May 22, 1950, page 15.
141 *Victoria Daily Times,* August 9, 1955, page 14.
142 Washington, US Marriage Records, 1854–2013.
143 *Victoria Daily Times,* February 1, 1958, page 23.
144 Oxford University Alumni, 1500–1886, accessed through ancestry.ca.
145 *Victoria Daily Times,* August 9, 1894, page 5.
146 "Librarian of the Province is Dead," *The Chilliwack Progress,* January 1, 1921, page 1.
147 *Victoria Daily Colonist*, May 6, 1896, page 8.
148 *The Province,* July 12, 1939, page 15.
149 "Well-Known Nurse Died Early To-day," *Victoria Daily Times,* August 9, 1922, page 6.
150 "Wm. A. Lorimer, Well-known City Official, Dead," *Victoria Daily Times,* March 9, 1929, page 15.
151 *The Vancouver Sun,* August 12, 1946, page 13.
152 *Victoria Daily Times,* September 3, 1929, page 15.
153 *Victoria Daily Times,* December 27, 1961, page 17.
154 *Victoria Daily Times,* February 11, 1950, page 17.
155 1910 United States Federal Census.
156 "B.C. Justice Robertson Dies," *The Vancouver Sun,* June 8, 1961, page 26.

157 Washington, US, Death Index, 1940–2017, accessed through ancestry.ca
158 *Victoria Daily Times,* March 8, 1943, page 11.
159 Edward Ernest Greenshaw story accessed on ancestry.ca.
160 *Victoria Daily Times,* February 21, 1968, page 33.
161 *Victoria Daily Times,* April 17, 1946, page 16.
162 *Victoria Daily Times,* April 10, 1925, page 5.
163 "Death Summons Fred H. Worlock," *Victoria Daily Times,* July 31, 1926, page 2.
164 "An Easter Wedding," *Victoria Daily Times,* April 12, 1898, page 5.
165 "Late Asa B. Steele," *Victoria Daily Times,* January 14, 1918, page 15.
166 https://www.wikitree.com/wiki/Steele-7311
167 *Victoria Daily Times,* April 19, 1965, page 21.
168 *Victoria Daily Times,* January 16, 1928, page 7.
169 "Retired chemist Called to Rest," *Victoria Daily Times,* May 17, 1932, page 13.
170 *Victoria Daily Times,* July 5, 1928, page 8.
171 *Victoria Daily Times,* October 15, 1935, page 13.
172 *Victoria Daily Times,* May 1, 1936, page 13.
173 "Funeral Tuesday for Newspaperman," *Victoria Daily Times,* July 21, 1958, page 22.
174 *Times Colonist,* May 31, 1982, page 33.
175 *Victoria Daily Times,* June 12, 1975, page 33.
176 "Another Pioneer Dies This Morning," *Victoria Daily Times,* December 13, 1909, page 13.
177 https://nauticpedia.ca.
178 *The Daily Colonist,* August 1, 1882, page 3.
179 *Victoria Daily Times,* July 11, 1945, page 12.
180 *Times Colonist,* March 8, 1985, page 38.
181 *Victoria Daily Times,* October 19, 1946, page 7.
182 *Times Colonist,* October 26, 2010.
183 "Tributes to Capt. Gosse," *Victoria Daily Times,* August 4, 1903, page 8.
184 *Victoria Daily Times,* July 14, 1903, page 8.
185 *Victoria Daily Times,* January 31, 1920, page 27.
186 *The Ottawa Citizen,* July 25, 1989, page 30.
187 Ontario, Canada, Marriages, 1826–1938 accessed at ancestry.ca.
188 *Vancouver Daily World,* October 24, 1901, page 1.
189 *Victoria Daily Times,* August 24, 1935, page 11.
190 *Victoria Daily Times,* April 15, 1939, page 18.
191 *Victoria Daily Times,* February 17, 1939, page 3.
192 Ontario, Canada, Marriages, 1826–1938, accessed through ancestry.ca.
193 "City Mourns E. C. Heywood," *The Daily Colonist,* February 15, 1933, pages 1 and 2.
194 *Victoria Daily Times,* February 15, 1933, page 11.
195 *Victoria Daily Times,* August 12, 1946, page 14.
196 *Victoria Daily Times,* November 20, 1902, page 2.
197 "Soldier-Surveyor Dead Here at 95," *Victoria Daily Times,* April 12, 1961, page 20.
198 https://sites.rootsweb.com/~bcvancou/ships/nmor53.htm.
199 https://www.findagrave.com/memorial/75941344/john-stevenson.
200 *Victoria Daily Times,* July 24, 1924, page 9.
201 Ontario, Canada, Roman Catholic Baptisms, Marriages and Burials, 1760–1923, accessed through ancestry.ca.
202 *Victoria Daily Times,* January 6, 1936, page 11.
203 "Miss Wigley Passes Away," *Victoria Daily Times,* January 3, 1936, page 3.
204 *The Daily Colonist,* May 18, 1936, page 18.
205 *Victoria Daily Times,* September 10, 1936, page 6.
206 *Victoria Daily Times,* November 2, 1922, page 2.

207 "Douglas Grandson Dies at 84," *Victoria Daily Times,* February 10, 1967, page 32.
208 *Victoria Daily Times,* February 11, 1967, page 4.
209 *Victoria Daily Times,* March 19, 1962, page 18.
210 https://mavrikoscollective.com/5828-2/.
211 https://westendvancouver.wordpress.com/biographies-a-m/biographies-i/johnson-stanley-mainwaring-1880-1926/
212 https://paperspast.natlib.govt.nz/newspapers/TS18751004.2.11?end_date=31-12-1875&itemspage=10&page=3&query=e+mainwaring+johnson&snippet=true&start_date=01-01-1875
213 *Daily Colonist,* November 28, 1880, page 1.
214 *Victoria Daily Colonist,* February 20, 1920, page 7.
215 *Victoria Times,* June 24, 1919, page 6.
216 *Nanaimo Daily News, September* 16, 1944, page 1.
217 *Victoria Daily Times*, March 9, 1963, page 3.
218 Canada, Imperial War Service Gratuities, 1919–1921, accessed through ancestry.ca.
219 Canada, World War II Records and Service Files of War Dead, 1939–1947, accessed through ancestry.ca.
220 *Victoria Daily Times,* November 1, 1975, page 42.
221 1911 Census of Canada.
222 Canada, World War I CEF Personnel Files, 1914–1918, accessed through ancestry.ca.
223 https://findagrave.com/memorial/178125694.
224 *Victoria Daily Times,* July 10, 1928, page 15.
225 *Victoria Daily Times,* July 1, 1952, page 14.
226 *Victoria Daily Times,* July 21, 1964, page 24.
227 Ontario, Canada Births, 1832–1916, accessed through ancestry.ca.
228 *Victoria Daily Times,* November 19, 1925, page 8.
229 *Victoria Daily Times,* July 13, 1938, page 12.
230 *Victoria Daily Times,* December 27, 1916, page 7.
231 "City Will Lose Able Official," *Victoria Daily Times,* October 12, 1916, page 15.
232 "Death Claims A. E. Foreman," *The Vancouver Daily Province,* February 19, 1944, page 2.
233 "Pioneers at Funeral of Alvah E Foreman," *The Vancouver Sun,* February 22, 1944, page 7.
234 *Victoria Daily Times,* August 1, 1961, page 13.
235 "A Pretty New Home," *The Colonist,* May 2, 1890, page 1.
236 England and Wales Birth Registration Index, 1837–2008, accessed through ancestry.ca.
237 *The Province*, July 14, 1894, page 8.
238 "T. S. Futcher Died Sunday," *Victoria Daily Times,* November 19, 1928, page 15.
239 *Victoria Daily Times,* May 15, 1928, page 13.
240 Manitoba Marriage Index.
241 Canada, Immigrants Approved in Orders in Council, 1929–1960, accessed through ancestry.ca.
242 *Victoria Daily Times,* March 27, 1906, page 5.
243 *Victoria Daily Times,* August 21, 1911, page 16.
244 *Victoria Daily Times,* October 11, 1955, page 24.
245 "Veteran Sealer Called by Death," *Victoria Daily Times,* December 27, 1938, page 11.
246 "Aged Resident Passed Away," *Victoria Daily Times,* May 11, 1936, page 13.
247 "Rites for Former Librarian," *Times Colonist,* April 21, 1982.
248 "New Hospital Formally Opens," *Victoria Daily Times,* October 5, 1908, page 16.
249 http://dictionaryofarchitectsincanada.org/node/1125.
250 "City Architect Dies After Long Illness," *Victoria Daily Times,* July 30, 1062, page 13.
251 "C. M. Forrest Dies Suddenly," *Victoria Daily Times,* February 28, 1941, page 16.

252 A. I. Grierson, "Adventuring in Apartment Building," *The Sunday Province,* December 9, 1928, page 45.
253 *Victoria Daily Times,* May 10, 1952, page 16.
254 *The Province,* October 24, 1938, page 11.
255 *Victoria Daily Times,* June 22, 1935, page 7.
256 https://www.familysearch.org/tree/person/details/LXHD-GCD.
257 *Victoria Daily Times,* September 19, 1998, page 61.
258 *Victoria Daily Times,* July 25, 1953, page 18.
259 *Victoria Daily Times,* February 26, 1968, page 21.
260 "T. 'Duff' Pattullo, Former Premier Dies," *The Vancouver Sun,* March 31, 1956, page 3.
261 Wikipedia.com.
262 *The Daily Colonist,* September 21, 1932, page 15.
263 "Was Employee of City for Many Years," *Victoria Daily Times,* September 20, 1932, page 11.
264 "Holiday calamity," *Times Colonist Islander, May 26, 1996, page 29.*
265 "Victoria Officers Wounded Overseas," *Victoria Daily Times,* May 5, 1945, page 11.
266 "Walter Engelhardt Dies in City Home," *Daily Colonist,* July 14, 1962, page 25.
267 "Funeral Friday for Saanich Horse Breeder," *Victoria Daily Times,* September 15, 1954, page 17.
268 *Victoria Daily Times,* March 12, 1920, page 7.
269 *Victoria Daily Times,* February 10, 1921, page 9.
270 Family tree accessed at familysearch.ca.
271 Family tree accessed through ancestry.ca.
272 *The Gazette,* April 8, 1957, page 41 and *Victoria Daily Times,* April 9, 1957, page 16.
273 https://victoriaheritagefoundation.ca/HReg/Fairfield/Collinson907.html.
274 *Victoria Daily Times,* November 18, 1935, page 15.
275 https://www.findagrave.com/memorial/147753466/ethel-may-wood.
276 *Victoria Daily Times,* March 17, 1944, page 12.
277 UK Royal Navy Registers of Seamen's Services, 1848–1939, accessed through ancestry.ca.
278 Canada, Ocean Arrivals (Form 30A), 1919–1924, accessed through ancestry.ca.
279 London, England, Church of England marriages and Banns, 1754–1938, accessed through ancestry.ca.
280 *The Vancouver Sun,* July 20, 1937, page 3.
281 *Victoria Daily Times,* July 20, 1937, page 12.
282 1921 Canada census.
283 *The Vancouver Sun,* August 19, 1957, page 30.
284 "Fred G. Gorse, City Musician, Dies Aged 69," *The Vancouver Sun,* January 13, 1949, page 10.
285 *Victoria Daily Times,* March 8, 1983, page 36.
286 *Times Colonist,* June 21, 2006, page B11.
287 *The Victoria Daily Times,* September 5, 1912, page 19.
288 California, U.S., Arriving Passenger and Crew Lists, 1882–1959 accessed through ancestry.ca.
289 *Victoria Daily Times,* November 30, 1925, page 9.
290 Washington, US, Marriage Records, 1854–1903, accessed through ancestry.ca.
291 1916 Canada census of Manitoba, Saskatchewan, and Alberta, accessed through ancestry.ca.
292 US, World War II Draft Registration Cards, 1942, accessed through ancestry.ca.
293 Washington, US, Death Records, 1883–1960, accessed through ancestry.ca.
294 "DND Chauffeur Succumbs at Home," *Victoria Daily Times,* October 6, 1956, page 17.
295 *Victoria Daily Times,* June 29, 1976, page 39.

296 *The Province,* June 13, 1964, page 27.
297 *Nanaimo Daily News,* March 6, 1958, page 5.
298 Washington, U.S., Marriage Records, 1854–2013, accessed through ancestry.ca.
299 United States, Naturalization Records, 1795–1972, accessed through ancestry.ca.
300 Washington Death Index, 1940–1996, accessed through ancestry.ca.
301 *Victoria Daily Times,* November 29, 1917, page 7.
302 Canada, World War I CEF Personnel Files, 1914–1918, accessed through ancestry.ca.
303 *Victoria Daily Times,* March 31, 1916, page 15.
304 Family tree accessed through ancestry.ca.
305 *Victoria Daily Times,* January 5, 1939, page 12.
306 Family tree accessed through ancestry.ca.
307 Obituary posted to findagrave.ca.
308 *Victoria Daily Times,* April 19, 1962, page 20.
309 *Times Colonist,* online obituary.
310 England, The National Roll of the Great War, 1914–1918 accessed through ancestry.ca.
311 *Victoria Daily Times,* November 14, 1966, page 28.
312 *Victoria Daily Times,* May 17, 1976, page 36.
313 "H H Woolison Passes Away," *Victoria Daily Times,* May 29, 1936, page 15.
314 Familysearch.org.
315 *Victoria Daily Times,* August 29, 1936, page 16.
316 *The Cheltenham Looker-on,* December 11, 1897, page 20.
317 *Victoria Daily Times,* January 5, 1938, page 14.
318 US, Border Crossings from Canada to US, 1895–1960, accessed through ancestry.ca
319 California, County Birth and Death Records, 1800–1994, accessed through familysearch.org.
320 "Mona Rickaby Dies at Age 75," *Victoria Daily Times,* July 22, 1968, page 17.
321 1911 Census of Canada.
322 *Times-Colonist,* January 7, 1981, page 43.
323 *Victoria Daily Times,* February 12, 1944, page 12.
324 *Victoria Daily Times,* November 5, 1960, page 22.
325 *Victoria Daily Times,* January 31, 1922, page 2.
326 "Victoria Resident Died at Auckland," *Victoria Daily Times,* May 23, 1922, page 9.
327 New Zealand, Cemetery Records, 1800–2007, accessed through ancestry.ca.
328 *Victoria Daily Times,* April 5, 1921, page 14.
329 "Had Resided Here Thirty-eight Years," *Victoria Daily Times,* April 7, 1928, page 15.
330 *Victoria Daily Times,* October 28, 1971, page 36.
331 "George P. Kelly, Old-timer Here, Died To-day," *Victoria Daily Times,* August 6, 1930, page 15.
332 *Victoria Daily Times,* February 17, 1928, page 13.
333 *Daily Colonist,* January 23, 1969, page 26.
334 *Victoria Daily Times,* March 27, 1911, page 2.
335 *Victoria Daily Times,* September 3, 1958, page 22.
336 "Pioneer Pharmacist Died Friday at 79," *Victoria Daily Times,* September 21, 1968, page 23.
337 https://victoriaheritagefoundation.ca/HReg/Fairfield/Meares949.html.
338 *Victoria Daily Times,* January 5, 1935, page 13.
339 1921 Census of Canada.
340 *The Province,* March 26, 1946, page 13.
341 Commonwealth War Graves Commission records.
342 "Geo. C. Grant Passes Away," *Victoria Daily Times,* September 15, 1937, page 1.
343 *Daily Colonist,* August 1883, page 2.
344 *Daily Colonist,* August 12, 1883, page 2.
345 *The Victoria Daily Colonist,* February 6, 1892, page 5.
346 *Victoria Daily Colonist,* June 3, 1892, page 6.

347 *Victoria Daily Colonist,* October 12, 1906, pages 5 and 7.
348 Biographical history from the City of Victoria Archives.
349 "Dean of Local Dentistry Buried Today," *Victoria Daily Times,* January 23, 1924, page 5.
350 *Victoria Daily Times*, January 22, 1924, page 14.
351 "Man Electrocuted When Transmission Line Fouls Wiring," *Victoria Daily Times,* January 7, 1924, page 1.
352 Ibid.
353 Norman Gidney, "Trebatha Transformed," *Times Colonist Homes,* May 17, 1992, page 16.
354 Hallmark Heritage Society Archives.
355 "Death of a Well Known Resident," *Victoria Daily Times,* February 18, 1908. page 5.
356 "Dentist Shows Old Time Instruments," *Victoria Daily Times,* June 17, 1947, page 2.
357 *Victoria Daily Times*, September 15, 1952, page 1.
358 Information from BC Land Titles.
359 "Pioneer Contractor Dies," *Victoria Daily Times,* June 18, 1917, page 12.
360 *Victoria Daily Times,* November 2, 1946, page 15.
361 *Daily Colonist*, March 14, 1970, page 26.
362 1901 Canada census.
363 *The Province,* August 7, 1926, page 2.
364 *Victoria Daily Times,* October 1, 1934, page 13.
365 Arthur Lineham was the first owner of 1 Cook Street.
366 *Victoria Daily Times,* August 243, 1921, page 9.
367 Family tree accessed on ancestry.ca.
368 *Victoria Daily Times,* February 12, 1926, page 9.
369 *Victoria Daily Times,* May 27, 1936, page 13.
370 *Victoria Daily Times,* January 10, 1951, page 18.
371 1891 Victoria City Directory.
372 *Victoria Daily Times*, February 25, 1892, page 8.
373 *Victoria Daily Times*, September 27, 1907, page 12.
374 *Victoria Daily Times,* August 20, 1920, page 9.
375 *Victoria Daily Times,* March 25, 1916, page 7.
376 Charles Lillard, "Mrs. Oliver spared no expenses," *Times Colonist,* May 6, 1990, page C1.
377 "Oliver Street in Oak Bay," *Times Colonist,* July 25, 1980, page 63.
378 *Victoria Daily Times*, June 23, 1921, page 6.
379 *Victoria Daily Times*, February 19, 1959, page 3.
380 All information on land transactions obtained from BC Land Titles.
381 *Victoria Daily Times,* January 28, 1954, page 13.
382 *The Daily Colonist,* October 3, 1931, page 8.
383 1929 Victoria City Directory.
384 GR-3016; British Columbia. Supreme Court (Victoria). Probate/estate file 200/1954.
385 *Victoria Daily Times,* January 28, 1954, page 13.
386 *Victoria Daily Times,* October 18, 1915, page 11.
387 *Victoria Daily Times,* October 19, 1915, page 9.
388 *Victoria Daily Times,* June 22, 1945, page 12.
389 Information obtained from ancestry.ca and familysearch.org.
390 Information obtained from Victoria City Directories available at https://bccd.vpl.ca/index.php/browse/index
391 "L. U. Conyers Dies Suddenly," *Victoria Daily Times,* January 3, 1942, page 11.
392 Family tree accessed on ancestry.ca.
393 Scholefield, Ethelbert Olaf Stuart and Howay, Frederic William, *British Columbia from the Earliest Times to the Present*, Vancouver; Portland; San Francisco; Chicago: The S.J. Clarke Publishing Company, 1914, Volume IV, pages 1156 and 1157.
394 United States Directory of Deceased Physicians.
395 Scholefield, page 1157.
396 https://www.veterans.gc.ca/eng/remembrance/memorials/books/units-orders-ranks-decorative-pages/ww1_units03
397 https://www.scotlandspeople.gov.uk/

398 Canada, Incoming Passenger Lists accessed at ancestry.ca.
399 https://www.findagrave.com/memorial/140970702/eric-robert-mcdowall.
400 *Times Colonist,* October 4, 2005, page 30.
401 Information obtained from Victoria City Directories available at https://bccd.vpl.ca/index.php/browse/index.
402 "W.B. Sylvester Died Suddenly," *Victoria Daily Times,* September 28, 1931, pages 1 and 2.
403 "Pioneer Mayor Dies at Victoria," *Vancouver Province,* December 12, 1940, page 19.
404 Washington, U.S., Marriage Records, 1854–2013 accessed at ancestry.ca.
405 Canada 1911 census.
406 Alberta marriages.
407 Information on land details obtained from a BC Land Title search.
408 *The British Colonist*, March 28, 1862, page 2.
409 *The Daily British Colonist,* March 15, 1866, page 2.
410 *The Daily Colonist,* August 27, 1930, page 5.
411 *Daily British Colonist*, November 30, 1879, page 1.
412 *Daily Colonist*, May 9, 1884, page 2.
413 *The Colonist*, March 9, 1982, page 2.
414 *Vancouver Daily Province,* December 28, 1939, page 15.
415 1921 Census of Canada.
416 Ontario, Canada, Marriages, 1826–1938, accessed through ancestry.ca
417 *Victoria Daily Times*, August 5, 1924, page 12.
418 *Victoria Daily Times,* December 1, 1930, page 15.
419 *Daily Colonist*, November 5, 1952, page 16.
420 *Victoria Daily Times*, March 17, 1951, page 2.
421 Family tree accessed on ancestry.ca.
422 Wikipedia, George Arthur Fraser.
423 https://elections.bc.ca/voting/outreach-and-education/electoral-history-of-bc/
424 *Victoria Daily Times,* December 19, 1906, page 6.
425 *Victoria Daily Times*, November 20, 1907, page 2.
426 *Victoria Daily Times*, February 1, 1908, page 2.
427 *Victoria Daily Times*, December 8, 1908, page 9.
428 *Victoria Daily Times*, May 17, 1909, page 8.
429 *The Daily Colonist,* November 15, 1928, page 15.
430 England and Wales, Civil Registration Births Index, 1837–1915 accessed at ancestry.ca.
431 New Brunswick, Canada, Births and Late Registrations, 1810–1906
432 NB, Canada, Marriages, 1789–1950 accessed at ancestry.ca.
433 "S.F. 'Morning Call' Founder is Dead," *The San Francisco Examiner,* December 1, 1917, page 5.
434 "D. W. Higgins Pioneer of Coast Newspapermen and Ex-speaker, Passes Away," *Victoria Daily Times,* November 30, 1917, page 1.
435 *The Daily Colonist,* December 10, 1932, page 4.
436 *Calgary Herald,* December 10, 1932, page 7.
437 "Heritage restorer had heart attack and no one stopped," *Times Colonist, November 2, 1997, page 2.*

Sources

NEWSPAPERS AND MAGAZINES

The British Colonist and its successors
Calgary Herald
The Cheltenham Looker-on
The Chilliwack Progress
The Gazette
Nanaimo Daily News
The San Francisco Examiner
Seattle Post-Intelligencer
Surrey Leader
Vancouver Daily World
The Vancouver Province
The Vancouver Sun
The Victoria Daily Times
Victoria Times Colonist
Victoria News Group
Westworld, Vancouver, BC

ONLINE SOURCES

https://www.sidewalkingvictoria.com/blog/2019/5/11/goodbye-westholme-hotel
http://scotlandspeople.gov.uk
http://www.thecanadianencyclopedia.com
https://bccd.vpl.ca/
https://www.ancestry.ca/
https://www.britannica.com/art/quadrille-dance
https://boxrec.com/media/index.php/Denver_Ed_Smith
http://www.automatedgenealogy.com/
https://victoria.citified.ca/condos/200-douglas/
https://shawniganlakemuseum.com/pages/shawnigan-lake-lumber-company
https://www.showcase.com/617-vancouver-st-victoria-bc-v8v-3t9/22013735/
https://www.wikitree.com/wiki/Steele-7311
https://sites.rootsweb.com/~bcvancou/ships/nmor53.htm
https://www.findagrave.com
https://westendvancouver.wordpress.com/biographies-a-m/biographies-i/johnson-stanley-mainwaring- 1880-1926/
https://paperspast.natlib.govt.nz/newspapers
http://dictionaryofarchitectsincanada.org
https://www.familysearch.org
https://victoriaheritagefoundation.ca/
https://www.cwgc.org/
https://www.veterans.gc.ca/
https://elections.bc.ca/
https://en.wikipedia.org/wiki/Main_Page

BOOKS

Ken Coates and Bill Morrison, *The Sinking of the Princess Sophia: Taking the North Down With Her,* (Don Mills, ON: Oxford University Press Canada, 1990).

David Conover, *Finding Marilyn: A Romance by David Conover, The Photographer Who Discovered Marilyn Monroe,* (New York: Grosset & Dunlap, 1981).

David Conover, *Once Upon an Island,* (Vancouver: publisher unknown, 1967).

Eve Lazarus, *Sensational Victoria: Brights Lights, Red Lights, Murders, Ghosts & Gardens,* (University of Toronto Press, 2012).

Scholefield, Ethelbert Olaf Stuart and Howay, Frederic William, *British Columbia from the Earliest Times to the Present,* (Vancouver; Portland; San Francisco; Chicago: The S.J. Clarke Publishing Company, 1914, Volume IV, pages 1156 and 1157).

ARCHIVES AND OTHER REPOSITORIES

British Columbia Archives
British Columbia Land Titles
City of Victoria Archives
Hallmark Heritage Society Archives
UK National Archives
Victoria Heritage Foundation

Index

C

D

Volume Two: Watch for it!

Volume Two of *The Heritage Detective* will be published in late May 2023. Watch for it at your favourite bookstore.

Learn about the heritage buildings of the Victoria area and discover the amazing lives of the ordinary people who lived and worked in them.

Softcover copies are also available from the author at heritagelady@gmail.com with free delivery for local purchasers. Digital and softcover copies will also be available from Amazon.

Here's an excerpt from a story from Volume Two.

1178 View Street

I decided to research this building as I knew the owner, the daughter of the builder, when I was a child, and I was curious about the story behind its construction.

This building, next door to the home my grandparents would eventually own, was built in March 1908 by William Donald McKillican. He was born May 16, 1836, in Vanleek Hill, Ontario, one of five children of Donald McKillican and Margaret Robertson, Scottish immigrants. He made his way to Victoria, arriving in 1871 after stops in Minnesota, Montana, Iowa, Colorado, Missouri, and the Kootenays of British Columbia, where he worked as a builder and miner. He married Nehalennia Jane Burges February 23, 1875, in a ceremony performed by Reverend Edward Cridge, minister of the Reformed Episcopal Church.

I wonder if he had any idea of the family history of his bride. She was born to William and Margaret Burges in Sydney, Australia, April 19, 1853. Her father, William Burgess, had been transported to Van Diemen's Land (Tasmania) on the *Joseph Somes,* leaving England December 18, 1845, and landing at his destination May 18, 1845, one of 250 convicts on that voyage. He had been sentenced at the Chester Assizes to 7 years of hard labour for larceny. This was his second offence, and the article he stole was a tablecloth. He was somewhat luckier than previous transportees as the system had changed to a probation system where the convicts now served a period of "on probation" with stages of punishment. Convicts were imprisoned at a penal settlement, worked in gangs, or were sent to probation stations. Depending on their behaviour, they passed through stages, with restrictions reduced as they moved towards "Ticket of Leave" status. From the record of his incarceration, we learn that William committed several minor offences, such as smoking, returning too late to the facility, and not taking the work seriously. However, he was released early in the day, August 9, 1852. It is interesting to note that over 75,000 convicts served time in Van Diemen's Land. The *Calcutta* carried the first convicts from New South Wales in 1803, and the *St. Vincent* disembarked the final convicts to Hobart in 1853. The *Indefatigable* had brought the first transported convicts directly from England in 1811. Over 20% of current Australians can trace their family back to a transported convict, and it has been as high as 74% in Tasmania.

CONTEST:
Now it's your turn!

Do you have a building that you would like to see researched and featured in a future volume of* The Heritage Detective*?

Please let me know at heritagelady@gmail.com giving me what information you have.

I will conduct research on all buildings suggested and will write a short article on each.

One person who submits a suggestion will be chosen at random to write the introduction to the article on their building.

It's your chance to contribute to a social history of Victoria!

Rockland Avenue, gateway to Volume Two of The Heritage Detective